D1302556

Praise for *Coached to Lead*

"*Coached to Lead* is a flight plan for high-altitude success. Battley distills her years as a trusted CEO adviser into performance-boosting strategies and solutions. Whether you are a top executive, a rising star, or a coach yourself, don't take off without this book."
                    —Howard Putnam, former CEO, Southwest Airlines

"I was impressed with many aspects, including the case studies, leader interviews, and easy writing style. *Coached to Lead* will no doubt capture a wide readership of end-users of coaching and executive coaches."
          —Manuel London, professor of management and director, Center for Human Resource Studies, Stony Brook University

"This is an excellent resource for business leaders and technical professionals who want to maximize their effectiveness in today's global marketplace. Read it to get the most from working with an executive coach."
          —Nido Qubein, chairman, Great Harvest Bread Company

"This book has a high 'reality quotient' in terms of practical application and business impact. Battley brings a refreshing genuineness to explaining how leaders think and act. Insightful and results-oriented."
                    —Brendan J. O'Halloran, vice-chair and regional head USA, TD Securities

"Highly recommended to executives at the front end of a coaching engagement, to coaches, and to HR procurers and generalists. In quite a few places I found myself saying, 'That's a good idea' or 'That's a good checklist for a client or a coach to go through.' This book will be a big hit in the marketplace. I wish I'd written it!"
                    —Randall P. White, Ph.D., The Executive Development Group and Duke University

COACHED
TO LEAD

COACHED TO LEAD

How to Achieve Extraordinary Results with an Executive Coach

Susan Battley

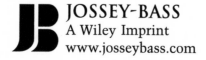

JOSSEY-BASS
A Wiley Imprint
www.josseybass.com

Published by Jossey-Bass
A Wiley Imprint
989 Market Street, San Francisco, CA 94103-1741   www.josseybass.com

Jossey-Bass books and products are available through most bookstores. To contact Jossey-Bass directly call our Customer Care Department within the U.S. at 800-956-7739, outside the U.S. at 317-572-3986, or fax 317-572-4002.

Jossey-Bass also publishes its books in a variety of electronic formats. Some content that appears in print may not be available in electronic books.

Library of Congress Cataloging-in-Publication Data

Battley, Susan, date.
  Coached to lead: how to achieve extraordinary results with an executive coach/Susan Battley.
      p. cm.
  Includes bibliographical references and index.
  ISBN-13: 978-0-7879-8144-0 (cloth: alk. paper)
  ISBN-10: 0-7879-8144-3 (cloth: alk. paper)
  1. Executive coaching.   2. Executives—Training of.   3. Executives—Attitudes.   4. Executive ability.   5. Leadership—Study and teaching.   I. Title.
  HF5385.B39 2006
  658.4'092—dc22   2006004534

Printed in the United States of America
FIRST EDITION
HB Printing   10 9 8 7 6 5 4 3 2 1

CONTENTS

To Ted,
husband extraordinaire

Preface

*Our chief want is someone who will inspire us to be what
we know we could be.*
RALPH WALDO EMERSON

This book is the first consumer's guide to executive coaching. It is
intended to help leaders and those aspiring to leadership positions
make smart decisions about how to work with an executive or business coach.

The purpose of executive coaching is to produce better leaders faster. My purpose in writing *Coached to Lead* is to provide you
with actionable, evidence-based advice to capitalize fully from executive coaching while avoiding costly mistakes. This book will give
you and other results-driven professionals powerful yet simple
methods and tools to stack the success deck in your favor. You will
discover how executive coaching can deliver bottom-line solutions
to today's urgent leadership and management challenges. You will
learn precisely how the right executive coach can demonstrably
raise your performance for maximum impact. Grounded in business pragmatics and behavioral science, this book will help you
confidently and profitably distinguish quality executive coaching—
and coaches—from all the rest:

- If you are a high achiever in the business or professional
  world, constantly striving to elevate your game, *Coached
  to Lead* will expand your options for rapid, sustainable
  improvement.
- If you are considering executive coaching services for
  yourself or someone else, this book will help you obtain

results that substantially enhance your on-the-job effectiveness and career scalability.

- If you are already working with a coach, you will learn how to optimize your partnership and outcomes.
- Collateral and support professionals, such as human resource and organization development specialists, executive recruiters, career and outplacement counselors, attorneys, accountants, and management consultants, will find field-tested advice here that can inform their own recommendations to clients and customers.
- Executive and business coaches can use my client-centered approach to benchmark their own quality and service delivery methods.

The executive coaching field is a relatively new and evolving discipline. The marketplace includes practitioners with many different credentials and backgrounds. Navigating this maze is not easy. Hire the right coach, and you can raise your performance to drive business results and your career. Hire the wrong coach, and not only do you waste time and money, but you can send an organization down an aimless, unproductive path.

The inspiration for this book arose from countless interactions with clients, business groups, and the news media. For more than twenty years, I have been a consultant and executive coach to world-class organizations such as Olympus, JP Morgan Chase, Brookhaven National Laboratory, Marsh & McLennan Companies, Jones Apparel Group, Chase Manhattan, and Bookspan. I have advised Fortune 500 CEOs, university presidents, public officials, technical and health care professionals, sales and marketing executives, nonprofit officers, entrepreneurs, and business owners. I have helped leaders and their organizations succeed, individually and collectively, at postmerger integration, business turnaround, executive transition and assimilation, top team optimization, strategic planning and implementation, and succession management.

In other words, I'm accustomed to hearing skepticism from potential coaching clients.

Responsible managers are correct to question what they don't understand and therefore cannot evaluate with confidence. Invariably when the subject of executive coaching would come up for the first time with my clients, I'd find myself facing a barrage of questions, some based on the bottom line, others on hearsay. Because of its newcomer status and short track record, executive coaching was terra incognita to these veteran decision makers. I was routinely asked:

- Why should I hire a coach? How will I be better off?
- When should I hire a coach?
- How do I pick the right one? Shouldn't I just let Human Resources handle this?
- How much does it cost? How long will it take?
- Who's a good candidate for coaching?

Responding to their questions, born of curiosity and legitimate concern, I often needed to correct misconceptions as well as fill in information gaps.

When speaking to business and professional groups, journalists and television anchors, and graduate students in both the United States and abroad, I encountered the same interest, the same reservations and misconceptions, the same knowledge void.

I was on vacation in Barbados, pondering nothing in particular in my customary palm-shaded spot, when the obvious hit me with the figurative force of a falling coconut. No wonder decision makers and organizations that could otherwise benefit from executive coaching were staying away, or those that had invested the time and money were often experiencing subpar results.

What was desperately needed was glaringly missing: a client's guide to executive coaching, a consumer-focused resource.

Coached to Lead is the result. (I define "extraordinary coaching results" as those that demonstrably add value as measured by on-the-job performance, business impact, and return on investment.)

In writing this book, I've held nothing back. To the contrary, I have packed it with proven, step-by-step information about executive coaching so that you—the coaching client, candidate, or sponsor—can make winning decisions quickly and confidently. *Coached to Lead* covers all the issues typically raised, plus some you might not think to ask. You will find frequently asked questions, insider tips, handy decision tools and checklists, and sample documents. I share cases and success stories drawn from my twenty-plus years of advising elite leaders worldwide. You will also read exclusive interviews based on my conversations with an international array of CEOs and public leaders. Throughout this book, illustrative quotations link today's peak performance challenges with the timeless wisdom of past thought leaders. I've kept the tone conversational, similar to the "me-to-you" style of an actual consultation or coaching session.

This powerful knowledge arsenal is sure to transform you into a savvy consumer of executive coaching services. Consequently, you will be able to get the most from your program and scale to even loftier heights.

THE RISE OF THE PLUG-AND-PLAY MANAGER

I strongly believe in two aspects of executive coaching. First, I believe that executive coaching has staying power as a value-added service. It should not be dismissed as a management fad that's here today and gone tomorrow. Second, I expect the demand for quality coaching—whether it's called "executive," "leadership," or "business" coaching—will increase significantly in the coming years.

In the first instance, I'll let history support my position. Indeed, in many ways, executive coaching is old wine in new bottles. Since time immemorial, leaders and other high achievers have relied on counselors to help unleash their full potential. Alexander the Great had Aristotle; Susan B. Anthony had Elizabeth Cady Stanton; Werner Heisenberg had Niels Bohr; Katherine Graham Post had Warren Buffett. The terminology and designators and real-world applications may have morphed, but the value of one-on-one advice and feedback is indisputable.

Does the current executive coaching scene reflect a hype-inflated bubble? Probably. But over time, I think this state of affairs will self-correct. When it does, I believe the residual value proposition will prove impressive. The real executive coaching headline is quality, not faddishness. *Coached to Lead* will keep you on the quality path.

The concepts of value and quality bring me to my second point. I predict that the demand for executive coaching services will rise sharply in the coming years. For starters, globalization, industry consolidation, geopolitical uncertainty, and 24/7 information flow have converged to produce a radically new performance model: the "plug-and-play" manager. This new breed of manager must be able to learn rapidly and execute nimbly. The so-called soft leadership skills have come to be recognized for what they really are: advanced leadership skills. Today, effective communication, influencing, and team-building capabilities have become make-or-break differentiators in attracting and retaining key stakeholders. These pressures will likely intensify as 60 million baby boomers, many of them highly knowledgeable professionals, retire over the next fifteen years in the United States alone.

Another reason that I expect the demand for coaching to rise involves an emerging trend that has yet to hit the mainstream literature. In the twentieth century, vast sectors of professional talent and economic productivity were able to operate and compete successfully without extensive use of leadership and management development services. Professional service firms, public agencies, cultural institutions, hospitals and health care facilities, universities, research institutions, and nonprofit organizations all fall into this category. However, the global trends I've described are now sweeping over their worlds too, forcing them to upgrade their non-technical, interpersonal skills in order to stay vital and competitive. The secretary general emeritus of the International Council for Science, Maurits La Rivière, emphasized this point when he told me, "Today's scientific leaders need to be good, charismatic communicators—in speaking and writing—who can convey a clear vision of common goals and cultivate an esprit de corps."

Whether you are a chief executive, college president, investment banker, marketing executive, board director, theoretical physicist, military or public safety official, museum director, business owner, or the head of a government agency, there can be times when working with the right executive coach on the right goals will make sense.

How to Use This Book

You can read this book from cover to cover for a complete soup-to-nuts education, or you can turn to chapters selectively based on your interest or immediate needs.

Chapter One is a general overview that debunks ten common myths and misconceptions about executive coaching. I set the record straight about what executive coaching is and how today's leaders and managers can benefit from it.

Chapter Two helps you to decide if executive coaching is right for you. I do this by taking you through a set of ten screening questions that I've determined are key predictors of extraordinary coaching results. I also provide a decision checklist that summarizes these success dimensions. Case in Point stories drawn from actual client engagements introduce real-world situations and applications.

Chapters Three and Four deal with the all-important preliminaries of choosing your Perfect Coach and contracting for services. In Chapter Three, you will learn about the traits and qualifications that distinguish the most effective coaches from the rest. I will equip you with complete step-by-step strategies, exercises, and screening tools. I explain the relative merits of employer-funded versus private-pay arrangements and external versus internal coaches. I point out the selection activities you can delegate and those you should not. You will be able to pick your perfect coach quickly and with confidence.

Chapter Four delves deep into the terms of engagement, that is, the ground rules that will supercharge your coaching program from the start. I pay particular attention to confidentiality and the respective responsibilities of coach and client, emphasizing why it's important to take the time at the start to review these points together. Case in Point selections bring these issues to life and drive home the importance of "beginning the way you want to continue." I've also included several sample agreements to inform and guide your contracting process.

Chapter Five introduces the powerful yet simple Five-Step Coaching Model, a science-based approach to executive coaching that delivers proven results. I illustrate this model's usefulness with detailed client vignettes of brief, extended, and retainer-based programs. You will come away with a winning methodology to keep your coaching on track and on target.

Chapters Six, Seven, and Eight take you through the phase-specific activities you're likely to encounter or want in your coaching program. These chapters include exclusive leader spotlights, plus insider tips and tools, vivid client stories, and illustrative quotations. You will learn about the exciting behavioral science behind the coaching chemistry. In Chapter Six I take the mystery and anxiety out of personal assessment. I introduce the concept of a 360-degree data mirror and explain the benefits of robust diagnostics in ensuring that your coaching goals are of highest value and accurately set. You will also become familiar with the different types of assessment tools, methods, and materials commonly used.

Chapter Seven unveils an insider's secret weapon: the Powerhouse Plan. You will learn why this detailed road map is an essential tool, along with step-by-step instructions on how to create one along with your coach. In Chapter Eight, we dive directly into the heart of action coaching to discover what really goes on behind closed doors. I will arm you with little-known troubleshooting pointers that can make a big difference. Chapter Nine shows you how to review your program and your coach. I explain how to determine if your goals have been met and how to differentiate between tangible and intangible coaching results. Decision tools and lists will make this process painless and crystal clear. You (and others) will be able to recognize extraordinary results when you see them!

In Chapters Ten and Eleven I discuss executive coaching in terms of today's complex workplace realities. Both chapters set out frequently asked questions complemented by case studies. Chapter Ten takes a closer look at sensitive questions that a coaching client or candidate may have but not ask. Chapter Eleven addresses concerns and issues that sponsors of coaching services, such as supervisors, human resource professionals, and mentors, often raise. I share my in-the-trenches experience and expertise as an executive coach and leadership psychologist by way of guidance.

I have two final points to call to your attention. First, I have modified all client source material to protect individual client confidentiality. Pseudonyms are used in all Case in Point stories and in the extended case vignettes in Chapter Five. For the same reason, I have subtly altered other identifying aspects while preserving the overall flavor and substance of these scenarios.

Finally, although this book should significantly increase your knowledge about executive coaching and executive coaches, at no time should you rely solely on it for advice or to resolve a problem.

It does not offer legal advice. To get help with your unique needs and objectives, you should consult a competent professional.

Stony Brook, New York   SUSAN BATTLEY
February 2006

ACKNOWLEDGMENTS

Coached to Lead is the result of the extraordinary experiences and interactions I have had over the years with clients, professional colleagues, and the many leaders in business, science and education, and public life who contributed to my research. My thanks to these exceptionally talented and dedicated people, one and all.

I owe a particular debt of thanks to the leaders who generously shared their time and experiences with me and whose insights appear in this book. Their participation in the project was invaluable.

A number of other people helped make this work a reality. Special recognition and thanks go to Lawrence Bassett, friend and mentor, who provided sound advice, critical input, and constant support. Many colleagues and professionals gave earlier drafts of the manuscript the benefit of their expertise. They included Randy White, Linda Byars Swindling, Siegward Strüb, Manny London, Nido Qubein, Martha E. Sherman, George Morrisey, Maurits La Rivière, and Ellen Singer. My agent, John Willig, of Literary Services, was an encouraging advocate and results-oriented guide.

I would also like to thank Arthur Schmutz, Lynn Najman, Lorri Allen, David Hahn, Jeff Keller, Chantale La Casse, Rob Bailey, Callie Oettinger, Marilyn Haig, and Patricia Brady Danzig. They all helped advance this project by a variety of behind-the-scenes contributions.

At Jossey-Bass, my editor, Neal Maillet, deserves recognition for his enthusiastic support and diligent oversight from acquisition to publication. Xenia Lisanevich was a skilled production editor. My thanks go as well to Matt Kaye, Jessie Mandle, and Beverly Miller.

My family and friends were a steady source of encouragement and interest. It is a pleasure to acknowledge their essential support.

My husband, Ted, who now knows more about executive coaching than any other microbiologist on the planet, endured my months of writing with his customary patience and good cheer.

—*S. B.*

COACHED
TO LEAD

CHAPTER ONE

TEN MYTHS ABOUT EXECUTIVE COACHING

> *myth* n. *A fiction or half-truth, esp. one that forms part of an ideology.*
> AMERICAN HERITAGE DICTIONARY (4TH ED.)

You're talented, focused, and deliver outstanding results. You're up-to-date on trends in your industry or profession; perhaps you're in a senior leadership position now. You regularly see references to executive coaching in leading newspapers and business magazines.

WHAT IS EXECUTIVE COACHING?

Executive coaching is a confidential, one-on-one partnership between a management-level client and a qualified coach with relevant performance enhancement expertise. It is also popularly known as leadership or business coaching.

Possibly you've encountered an executive coach at a conference or industry meeting and heard other people describe their experiences with coaching and coaches. These points of information and contact may have raised your awareness but have yet to produce a clear and meaningful picture of executive coaching in your mind. You might even be confused or dubious and wondering whether coaching is the latest management fad du jour, a fix-it service, or a form of therapy for leaders.

You're not alone in your uncertainty. Executive coaching is a relatively new service compared to traditional training or executive education programs. Like anything else new, it runs the risk of being misunderstood, regarded with skepticism, or undervalued. (Consider that back in 1943, IBM chairman Thomas Watson Sr. said, "I think there is a world market for maybe five computers.")

As an international CEO coach, I hear people voice misinformation and invalid assumptions about executive coaching all the time. This confusion is not their fault. The marketplace for business coaching services is nothing if not confusing and inconsistent. In addition, we all have a tendency to generalize on the basis of our current knowledge, as well as on past experiences and first impressions. This often leaves us vulnerable to misjudging.

Just as clearing your closet of outdated clothing makes it easier to install a new and more functional wardrobe, eliminating misconceptions about executive coaching at the start will prepare you for fresh perspectives and interpretations. This chapter will help you do this. As a quick and ready way to distinguish fallacy from fact, I've compiled ten common myths about executive coaching. Don't be surprised if some of these reflect your own beliefs or opinions. Here's an opportunity for you to test and adjust those assumptions.

MYTH 1: THE MYTH OF THE INDIVIDUAL

Successful People Don't Need Coaches

Those who subscribe to the Myth of the Individual believe that people succeed or fail solely on the basis of their own talents and efforts. Given that superstars ranging from Olympic athletes to opera greats to elite business leaders use coaches to elevate their performance, this mind-set flies in the face of reality and common sense. The fact is that coaching helps the best get better. At championship levels, even small incremental gains in performance can have a profound effect on the result, often being the difference between winner and runner-up, between capturing the gold medal or the bronze.

For years Tiger Woods, arguably the world's greatest golfer, relied on swing coach Butch Harmon to elevate and optimize his game. When talking about the legendary coach Vince Lombardi, football player Jerry Kramer said, "He made us all better than we thought we could be."

In the corporate world, chief executives at eBay, Charles Schwab, Pfizer, Maytag, Ford Motors, and Silicon Graphics have all turned to executive coaches to improve their effectiveness. eBay CEO Meg Whitman began working with a coach in 1998 in preparation for the company's initial public offering. David S. Pottruck, co-CEO of Charles Schwab, sought help in correcting his abrasive leadership style. In the public sector, Treasury Secretary Paul H. O'Neill engaged a coach to help him galvanize a stodgy government department. As these high-profile examples show, the right coach can help you discover underused strengths, acquire new skills, maintain focus, eliminate blind spots, and master new challenges.

The value proposition for coaching has never been more compelling than it is now: customized, targeted expertise that addresses your needs and challenges. A 2001 study by Manchester Consulting of executives who received coaching, for example, showed an average return on investment (ROI) of 5.7 times the initial investment. (We'll discuss coaching ROI more fully elsewhere in this chapter.)

In today's hypercompetitive world, the chasm continues to grow between what people are being asked to do, what they have been prepared to do, or what they may have natural ability to do. With business and product cycles often measured in months, not years, wins and losses are quickly determined and visible for all to see. If your performance in Act One is not a success, you're unlikely to make it to the second act, let alone an encore. Put another way, no matter who you are—Fortune 500 executive, entrepreneur, public sector administrator, middle manager, or project director—the greater your success, ambition, and responsibility are, the greater are the risks associated with subpar decision making and execution. Coaching is a proven way of reducing your downside risk while maximizing your upside potential.

When you work with an executive coach, you demonstrate a strong commitment to excellence, continuous improvement, and being as effective as possible on a day-to-day basis. When your employer is underwriting coaching services, you have a powerful indicator of your real and perceived value to the enterprise.

I often smile when I hear about "coaching envy," since people are starting to view an executive coach as a standard perk among those who are already at the pinnacle of success.

Myth Buster: Professionals have coaches; amateurs do not.

MYTH 2: THE JADED MYTH

I Get All the Feedback I Can Possibly Use Now

Feedback comes in all shapes and sizes: 360-degree reports, organization climate studies, customer satisfaction surveys, annual performance reviews, quarterly business scorecards, operational safety reviews. At times we seem to be drowning in opinion data and expert advice.

Notwithstanding this state of affairs, I have observed a few things about organizational behavior over the course of two decades as a coach and an adviser to senior management teams. The first is that certain types of information, particularly tough, sensitive, or contradictory messages, do not always get voiced, let alone acted on. This can happen for a variety of reasons. Employees may be afraid to criticize or confront their superiors. Executives may protect their leaders from unflattering feedback. Managers may minimize behaviors and situations they do not know how to change.

Consequently, despite all the feedback mechanisms and performance systems to be found in the twenty-first-century workplace, leaders and high achievers can have difficulty getting an accurate data mirror to judge how they are doing.

For top executives, directors, business owners, and public officials, feeling isolated—"lonely at the top," the expression goes—is a common phenomenon, since it can be difficult to find people who will challenge them or stretch their thinking. Entrepreneurs and small business owners in particular may be accountable to no one but themselves, with few opportunities to benchmark their performance or learn how to translate feedback into a viable change program.

Technical professionals such as physicians, attorneys, and scientists may not be able to rely on their peers for the kind of performance feedback they need to succeed in certain management positions. As the head of a professional services firm once described his partner colleagues to me with great pride, "They're absolutely brilliant, but when it comes to people issues, they don't know what they don't know."

Ironically, as your span of authority and responsibility grows, the harder it can be to get unfiltered, unbiased information from colleagues, subordinates, and bosses too.

Assuming that your performance feedback is an accurate re-flection of how you are doing, there is still the matter of how to use it to best advantage. For example, if development issues or prob-lem behaviors are mentioned, are these symptoms or root causes? If you get mixed reviews, such as rave reviews from key customers but lukewarm ones from your colleagues, are your strengths also creating situational weaknesses?

If you win kudos all around, there may be no clear indication of what you should do to be even more successful. Consensus can lull you into a false sense of complacency, reaffirming what you are doing well now but giving no indication of how you can continue to raise the bar for yourself.

MYTH BUSTER: Coaching can help you maximize the benefits of the feedback you have and identify what feedback you might need but not have.

MYTH 3: THE "SHRINK" MYTH

Executive Coaching Is the Same as Psychotherapy or Counseling

Although executive coaching shares some methods with psycho-therapy, it is a mistake to equate one with the other. Yet for those unfamiliar with coaching (and coaching professionals), the simi-larities can be more striking than the differences. Hence the exis-tence of the "Shrink" Myth.

Let's set the record straight. First and foremost, executive coaching focuses on work and career-related goals. It is action oriented, looking to current and future performance, with your coach keeping the process on track and moving forward. It does not delve deeply into your past or personal relationships, and it does not try to determine how you came to be the person you are now.

A primary aim of executive coaching is to produce or facilitate desired business results. Of course, what constitutes business results varies from situation to situation. For people in profit-driven orga-nizations, such as companies and professional service firms, this translates into having a bigger impact on top- and bottom-line out-puts. For those in public sector and mission-based enterprises, such as government agencies and universities, this means increasing success at delivering key projects or services.

Coaching can help you:

- Improve your current job effectiveness.
- Prepare for higher levels of responsibility.
- Manage work-related stress better.
- Clarify or modify career goals.

Coaching typically occurs at the point where your skills, talents, interests, and motivation intersect with job demands, career goals, and marketplace drivers. Certain types of work-life issues also fall legitimately within the scope of executive coaching.

Why then is coaching so frequently confused with therapy?

One reason is that both involve confidential, one-on-one relationships with a helping professional. They also share a number of methods, such as behavioral assessment, discussion, introspection, and action experiments. Both seek to promote positive client change. Finally, many executive coaches hold credentials in fields traditionally associated with psychotherapy, such as counseling, psychology, and social work. Yet despite these similarities, it is important to recognize the substantial differences in goals and focus between these two services.

MYTH BUSTER: A therapist's role is frequently that of a healer. A coach's role is that of a supercharger.

MYTH 4: THE DEPENDENCY MYTH

Coaching Fosters an Unhealthy Dependency on Others

Whenever someone brings up the Dependency Myth, I reply with my Joe Torre test: Would you fire the manager of the New York Yankees? After all, the Yankees are repeat World Series champions. Does their continuing reliance on Torre's expertise indicate a weakness, or does it reflect their awareness that expert advice is critical to sustainable success?

Put this way, most people see my point. Yet it's amazing how often I hear the Dependency Myth, and from very smart people no less.

Let me repeat: the more successful you are, the more you need input from people who can support your ongoing success. There is always another game to win, another challenge to master, either against the competition or your personal best.

Consider too that research shows that as people progress within organizations, they are more likely to overrate their performance compared to how others rate them. In other words, the more successful you become, the greater the potential discrepancy is between how well you think you're doing and how well others think you're doing.

The truth is that we all need others—friends, teachers, spouses, bosses, customers—for our physical, emotional, intellectual, and economic well-being. Dependency is neither bad nor unhealthy; it's a fact of life.

Executive coaches are no different from other experts you rely on to maximize results. Very likely you regard your accountant, financial planner, or personal trainer as valued contributors to your welfare. You establish goals with them, set up a strategy together, and then monitor progress against plan. You work jointly to achieve the best outcome. They improve your condition.

The same value proposition applies when you work with the right executive coach. (Of course, by "right," I mean right for you.) Coaches are hardly twenty-first-century Svengalis out to enthrall you or impose their will. Not only does coaching *not* foster dependency, but a coach is likely to push you to think and behave in new ways that increase your self-confidence and expand your horizons.

Often those who subscribe to the Dependency Myth are self-made people who have achieved a certain level of success based on raw talent, intuition, hard work, and sometimes some lucky breaks. Over time, they have come to see themselves as the sole architects of their success. Consequently they may reject anything that smacks of outside interference (like coaching) as unnecessary or a sign of weakness or failure.

In real life, it's often the lone wolves or free agents who run a greater risk of derailing or hitting a career plateau, since they rarely seek (and get) feedback and advice about how they are really doing. Or they may fall victim to overconfidence or egotism. No matter how it's done, they unwittingly lower the ceiling on their prospects.

To be sure, people are also shaped by broad cultural and generational values. Asking for help, especially around one's public life and stature, can be downright contrary to how some people were raised. This is not to say that old attitudes cannot be jettisoned or new attitudes embraced with the arrival of new norms and tools.

Benjamin Franklin observed, "Learn of the skillful; he that teaches himself hath a fool for a master." Enduring winners are aggressive, lifelong learners. Executive coaches accelerate learning and unleash performance potential.

MYTH BUSTER: At heart, coaching is a tool for individual growth and empowerment, not dependency.

MYTH 5: THE CRUTCH MYTH

Coaching Should Be Only Short Term

The Crutch Myth is a variation of the Dependency Myth. It says that a little coaching is okay, but more is not.

Imagine going to the gym only twice a month because you don't want to overrely on a personal trainer to stay fit, or taking only half of a prep course for professional licensure so you don't depend too much on an instructor. Faulty logic? Self-limiting behavior? Absolutely.

Budget considerations aside, desired results should determine the format and duration of your coaching program. Much as an architect designs a building based on its intended purpose and user needs, the specifics of your coaching program, including duration and contact frequency, should be determined according to what you want or need to achieve. Rome wasn't built in a day. Neither are careers, projects, and track records.

We're an impatient society, looking for results yesterday. An executive coach can accelerate your progress and identify legitimate shortcuts. But there is no getting away from the fact that learning new skills and behaviors, or applying existing ones to new situations, takes time and practice. (Unlearning habits and ingrained attitudes also takes time.)

When the scope of coaching is targeted and narrowly defined, such as interpreting a 360-degree feedback report or crafting an individual development plan, a few sessions or weeks may suffice. If the scope is broader, such as guiding, monitoring, and refining these same development goals, then coaching might properly continue for months rather than weeks.

Extended coaching is no more a crutch to personal excellence than a tune-up is for a Ferrari. To the contrary, both make peak performance possible and ongoing. Big challenges and goals are not accomplished overnight; they take time and focused effort to execute and consolidate. They usually involve incremental steps and multiple phases.

Leading a business through a merger, scaling up from an individual contributor role to a supervisory post, or moving into a job in a different industry are all complex, high-stakes cases. In such circumstances, working with a coach for six months, a year, or even longer can yield substantial benefits. For example, you might have regularly scheduled sessions, or periodic check-ins, or you might touch base on an as-needed basis. (The fact that coaching is so customizable is part of its appeal.)

To debunk the Crutch Myth, we have only to look at how corporate America actually uses executive coaching services. A survey conducted by Linkage, an executive education firm, found that the average duration of coaching increases—and increases substantially—with seniority. The average duration for top-level executives was more than twelve months, compared to an average of six months or more for those at lower levels. (Morgan, Harkins, and Goldsmith, 2004). In other words, leaders used coaching more than their subordinates do, rather than less.

The Crutch Myth can have serious unintended consequences, really wreaking havoc with people's success. When coaching goals are overambitious for the time period allowed, those being coached can unwittingly be set up to fail, or feel as though they have failed against the expectations they or others have of them. Their performance and morale can subsequently suffer. They may be less likely to stretch themselves or take calculated risks in the future. This is an unfortunate outcome for all concerned.

MYTH BUSTER: Winners welcome long-term partnerships with the right coach.

MYTH 6: THE EMERGENCY ROOM MYTH

Executive Coaching Should Be Reserved
as a Last-Ditch Effort to Fix Problems

Those who believe the Emergency Room Myth (the ER Myth, for short) regard executive coaching basically as a crisis intervention tool, an option of last resort. They view coaches as emergency technicians whose job is to save those in dire straits. Consequently, decisions to bring in an executive coach are reactive in nature and often occur only after conditions have become critical.

Of course, the ER Myth does not stand up to scrutiny. Studies such as the one conducted by human resource consulting firm Drake Beam Morin clearly indicate that the key drivers for coaching are performance enhancement and grooming those with high potential. Let's not forget that prominent leaders and senior executives are the heaviest users of executive coaching. Furthermore, coaching is being increasingly used to prepare preexecutives and middle managers for higher leadership positions.

What is really happening in the marketplace—and in executive suites worldwide—is about as far as possible from a "damaged goods" view of coaching that one can imagine. As a Fortune 100 human resource executive reported in a 2004 Corporate Leadership Council Survey, "We . . . tend to invest in the up-and-coming executives rather than the low-performing executives."

Despite its gross inaccuracy, the ER Myth continues to hold sway for a number of reasons. First, in companies and institutions that do not yet have an established coaching program or culture, a coach might first appear on the scene to help "salvage" a valued but struggling performer. When this happens, executive coaching falls victim to the perception that it is a last intervention before showing someone the door. Consequently, even if that person's coaching outcome is extremely positive, a generalized view of coaching as triage gets established that is subsequently hard to dispel.

The ER Myth can also be perpetuated when a coach is called in to help someone with an acute skills gap. Of course, people's competency gaps can widen for a variety of reasons, many through no fault of their own and even as a result of positive change, such as a sudden promotion or reassignment. However, when this happens, the individual may flounder in silence for fear of appearing incompetent. Or he or she may not even be aware of how serious the gap is until matters reach a crisis.

Situations like these can occur when a technical professional, such as an attorney, accountant, physician, or academic, assumes broader administrative and people management responsibilities. In such cases, their individual expertise and accomplishments may not prepare them adequately for their new post, which becomes apparent only after the fact.

Entrepreneurs and business owners can find themselves in similar situations of suddenly feeling deskilled. This is most likely to occur when their companies undergo rapid expansion, and they or their executives suddenly need to oversee more complexity. Consequently, their attitudes toward coaching may be colored and limited by their own experiences during difficult transition points.

In cases like these, when the focus tends to be narrowly on what is not working, or missing, or otherwise very troublesome, the urgency of the help needed can overshadow any recognition that coaching is actually an improvement tool.

You should be aware that the ER Myth can create expensive and unnecessary barriers to both individual and organizational success. Just as with one's physical health, routine checkups optimize performance far better than treating acute conditions. By the time a person's performance or issues reach the "911" stage, it may be too late to bring in a coach, or results may be less robust than they might otherwise have been.

MYTH BUSTER: Executive coaching may be less—not more— successful when a person's needs and issues have reached critical condition.

MYTH 7: THE MENTOR MYTH

An Executive Coach Is the Same as a Mentor

The terms *coaching* and *mentoring* often are used in the same sentence, or interchangeably, to describe popular career-building activities. People often naturally assume the two words are synonyms, referring to the same activities and relationships. In truth, there are similarities, and even some overlap. However, there are significant differences as well that you should be aware of.

Mentoring and executive coaching both involve a one-on-one helping relationship. In Greek mythology, Mentor was the trusted adviser of Odysseus. In the twenty-first century, a mentor is still someone who imparts wisdom or can facilitate events that have a positive effect on your fortunes.

Mentors are usually more senior and experienced people in the same profession or business as the mentee. In the traditional sense, a mentor is someone who can pass along occupation-based knowledge and possibly open doors for you that might otherwise not be accessible. For example, a current or past boss or a former professor might serve in a mentoring capacity, advising you on any number of matters, ranging from broad career strategy to specific workplace tactics. In fact, having a dual relationship with a mentor is not all that uncommon, since he or she might also be your supervisor or your supervisor's supervisor. Often a mentoring relationship evolves over time out of a different preexisting relationship.

Mentoring is usually done informally—and on an unpaid, voluntary basis. There may not be any set agenda with your mentor, let alone the expectation on either side that specific outputs will occur within specific time frameworks.

Mentors usually take a personal interest in your progress and success. You can even have multiple mentors, each providing something special in terms of their experience and perspective. Mentoring relationships tend to be open-ended and can last for many years. You and your mentor might be in touch frequently or on an as-needed basis. The two of you might not even be located in the same city or region.

Now let's compare mentoring to executive coaching. Unlike a mentor, your coach may or may not possess an occupational background and work experiences similar to yours. He or she may be older than you, or not. Even if your coach is an internal coach, that is, an employee of your organization, it is unlikely that you will have a dual relationship with this person, such as boss-subordinate.

There are additional fundamental differences. A mentoring relationship is usually informal and open-ended; a coaching relationship typically has clearly defined goals, activities, time limits, and mutual accountabilities. It is a structured fee-for-service arrangement, whether you personally pay your coach or your employer assumes the cost. Also, although you might interact with multiple mentors, you would ordinarily work with only one executive coach at a time.

It's possible for an executive coach to be an informal mentor, especially if you have an extended working relationship with the person. However, it is less the case that a mentor will get "down in the weeds" with you to acquire new skills or change certain behaviors. He or she is likely to suggest other resources to you at this point, including possibly working with a coach.

MYTH BUSTER: The terms *mentor* and *coach* refer to roles that have similarities but also significant differences.

MYTH 8: THE WALK-IN-MY-SHOES MYTH

An Executive Coach Should Have a Background and Experience Similar to Mine

The Walk-in-My-Shoes Myth is expressed fairly frequently. It maintains that in order to be effective, a coach must possess a résumé that closely mirrors your own industry and job title experiences. According to this thinking, if you lead an Inc. 1000 company, then your coach should have experience leading a comparable enterprise. If you are a senior marketing executive, your coach should have an equivalent track record in this field. If you are a practice head in a professional service firm, your coach should have similar formal training or certifications. And so forth.

This myth is flawed at its core because it assumes that the best coach for helping you take your game to the next level is *always* someone very much like yourself in terms of work experience and professional accomplishments. It mistakenly assumes that in order to be capable and effective, your coach must be able to say, "I've been there and done what you're doing myself."

Just because someone is a peak performer does not necessarily mean that he or she can help you achieve equivalent levels of success. This is why the Walk-in-My-Shoes Myth is such a fallacy, albeit a popular one. Put another way, knowing how to be a winner yourself does not automatically mean you know how to help others become winners, even when they have the talent and motivation to do so. What works for you in terms of an approach or system may not work for someone else.

To be effective, a coach needs to understand what constitutes success in your particular job and industry. He or she should be familiar with trends, norms, and key drivers in your field or be able to acquire a working knowledge of these quickly. Put another way, a coach need not have an accounting background to be able to supercharge a chief financial officer's performance.

Indeed, much executive coaching occurs around soft skills associated with leadership and managerial effectiveness rather than acquiring more technical know-how. What you likely need in an executive coach, therefore, is someone with complementary types of expertise—someone who is a skilled catalyst or change agent who can teach you how to do things, not just tell you how he or she does things.

It's certainly possible to find such people within your company or industry. The important point here, though, is not to assume that their track record of success equates automatically to an ability to coach others. For example, action-oriented achievers may not have patience for the trial-and-error learning that coaching others can require. Moreover, a coach who closely mirrors your own background may also share your same attitudes and biases, with the result that certain behaviors and issues can persist as undetected blind spots.

Many of the world's greatest coaches have never been superstars themselves and are certainly not household names. After all, everyone knows tennis champion Pete Sampras, but who recognizes the name of his coach, Pete Fischer? Luciano Pavarotti is an international opera legend, but the same cannot be said of his vocal coach, Gildo Di Nunzio.

MYTH BUSTER: To coach an Olympic athlete to victory, you do not need to have competed in the Olympics yourself.

MYTH 9: THE UNIVERSALITY MYTH

Everyone Is Coachable

The Universality Myth takes a rose-colored view of coaching that simply does not reflect the complexities of the real world, even if it is guided by good intentions. It needs to be dispelled because of the potential disappointment and frustration it can cause.

People are coachable to a greater or lesser degree based on a combination of factors. Some pertain to their unique internal attributes and some to external, or situational, conditions. Internal attributes include innate talent, personal motivation and ambition, and personality traits. External factors are variables such as job characteristics, company compensation and promotion policies, relationships with colleagues and supervisors, and organizational culture.

For example, if you worked in a hypercompetitive business like mergers and acquisitions (M&A), you might have no interest in being coached on improving your teamwork skills. Being more collaborative might not be important to your day-to-day activities, or it could dilute the credit you personally receive for a deal. In other words, you might well have the innate capacity to improve in this area, but you have little actual motivation to do so.

In the context of executive coaching, your coachability takes into account how much you can change, plus how much you want to change in a particular area. The first part refers to your innate potential, the second part to your motivation level. You also need to have sufficient opportunity to try out new behaviors and activities.

In reality, everyone is coachable to the extent that they have untapped potential, are motivated to change, and operate in a work environment that supports new learning.

Working with an executive coach will not motivate you, let alone promote performance change, unless you see a clear benefit. A coach can point out benefits that might not be obvious to you, thus triggering or strengthening your motivation, but this is not a substitute for your own inner drive. (I discuss motivation and benefits further in Chapter Two.)

The Universality Myth can be problematic, not just false, because people may not be coachable for a number of reasons. In addition to the earlier example involving team building, here are some scenarios where coachability could be low:

- When a person is not open to feedback or different points of view
- When a person is very set in his or her ways
- When a person is on probation or under threat of separation

- When the organization's culture does not view coaching favorably

Each of these instances touches on an internal, personal variable or an external workplace one. If, for example, you were someone with a change-averse nature, you would likely not regard coaching in a very positive light at all.

The view that everyone is coachable can leave a person feeling considerable pressure either to comply or be seen as oppositional. It also perpetuates unrealistic expectations of what coaching or an executive coach can accomplish. For both reasons, this myth does a disservice to all concerned and needs to be debunked.

MYTH BUSTER: Most people are coachable some of the time, but all people are not coachable all of the time.

MYTH 10: THE FUZZY RESULTS MYTH

There's No Way to Measure Outcomes from Executive Coaching

A common complaint I hear is that dollars spent on executive coaching disappear into a black hole, with no hard and fast way to assess results or the return on investment (ROI). Does executive coaching really pay off, or do you just pay? Enter the Fuzzy Results Myth.

There are many robust ways to determine the value-added benefits of coaching. When coaching goals involve current improvement, comparing before and after performance is a straightforward way to assess ROI. Simply put, does the person who was coached see improvement? Were specific performance targets actually achieved? Do others who interact with this person notice a positive change? These are legitimate criteria for establishing investment return, always assuming that coaching goals were high value in the first place.

Other ways to assess coaching ROI include metrics that even the most hard-nosed numbers professional should respect:

- Increased profitability
- Higher customer satisfaction

- Accelerated promotion rates
- Successful project or deal execution
- Improved talent retention
- Lower recruitment and replacement costs

If we move from evaluating individual coaching to looking at larger organizational and industry studies, the evidence becomes even more persuasive that coaching can be a cost-effective way to enhance performance and productivity.

The Manchester Consulting Group study (McGovern and others, 2001) I cited earlier in the chapter was a survey of Fortune 100 executives that found that coaching provided an average ROI of almost six times the cost of the coaching, or more than $100,000. Other outcome studies include the following:

- A study of a Fortune 500 telecommunications company done by MetrixGlobal (Anderson, 2001) found that executive coaching resulted in a return on investment of 529 percent. Moreover, when the financial benefits from increased retention were factored in, the overall ROI of coaching rose to 788 percent.
- Metropolitan Life Insurance Company put part of its retail sales force through an intensive coaching program and subsequently found that productivity among those salespeople increased by an average of 35 percent, with 50 percent of them identifying new markets to develop. Even more important, MetLife retained all of the salespeople who had the coaching, a significant savings given that at the time, industry replacement costs for a representative with three years of experience amounted to $140,000 per person. The program, which cost MetLife about $620,000, delivered $3.2 million in measurable gains, as reported by Anne Fisher in *Fortune* magazine.
- An International Personnel Management Association survey on training and development (Olivero, Bane, and Kopelman, 1997) found that when training was combined with coaching, productivity increased an average of 88 percent compared to 22 percent with training alone.
- In their coaching work with more than one hundred managers at Agilent Technologies, the Alliance for Strategic Leadership

found that over 78 percent of participants improved their leadership effectiveness as measured by stakeholder surveys (Carter, Ulrich, and Goldsmith, 2004).

These results show that coaching ROI not only *can* be calculated, but that it *has been* calculated and continues to be monitored.

Myth Buster: Research shows that executive coaching can deliver an impressively high return on investment.

Final Analysis

Executive coaching has been with us for a relatively short time. As both its real and perceived value continue to skyrocket, it's important to distinguish valid information from invalid assumptions and misconceptions.

Here are the ten myths about coaching stated as positives:

Fact 1: Successful people routinely use executive coaching to extend and elevate their game.

Fact 2: An executive coach can help you use existing feedback for maximum results and optimize feedback loops going forward.

Fact 3: Executive coaching focuses primarily on your current and future performance in the workplace.

Fact 4: Executive coaching is growth oriented, expanding your awareness, capabilities, and prospects.

Fact 5: The purpose of your coaching program should determine its duration and format.

Fact 6: Top performers and high-potential candidates are the primary users of executive coaching services.

Fact 7: There are important basic differences between the roles of executive coach and mentor.

Fact 8: Many highly effective executive coaches possess backgrounds and credentials that are different from your own.

Fact 9: A person's readiness for coaching depends on both individual personal traits and external circumstances.

Fact 10: There are proven ways to calculate tangible cost-benefit data for executive coaching services.

On the basis of what you've learned in this chapter, you can now speak more knowledgeably about executive coaching than most of your colleagues and counterparts. Next, we'll ascertain how—and if—you can benefit from coaching.

CHAPTER TWO

IS EXECUTIVE COACHING
RIGHT FOR YOU?

A client I will call Ralph came straight to the point. "Executive coaching wasn't around twenty years ago when I started out," he told me. "Frankly, I'm wondering if this old dog can learn new tricks." A confident, methodical person with a solid track record in the consumer products industry, he continued, "Look, I need to be satisfied that I'm making the right decision for me. How do I do this?"

Whether he knew it or not (and I think he did), Ralph had just asked the $64,000 question. Was executive coaching right for him? Would it pay off for him individually?

Although he had no previous experience with coaching, Ralph was a savvy consumer of consulting services. His question launched us into a broad discussion of some of the key variables to consider. By the time we finished, he had the answers he needed to make an informed decision.

If you pride yourself on making top-quality decisions, especially when key resources such as time and money are involved, then the coaching readiness questions and checklist I've prepared here will enable you to do so. If you already know you will be working with a coach, reflecting on these issues will supercharge your program from the start.

If you're not a candidate for coaching yourself but instead are sponsoring or supervising someone who is, the information here will help you gain insight into the personal qualities and situational factors that are predictive of successful coaching outcomes.

Ready for Coaching:
Ten Questions to Ask Yourself

Insider's Tip: If you substitute the word *you* for *I* in these ten questions, you will be thinking like an executive coach. A skilled coach will want to find out where you stand on all these points, the better to know how—and if—he or she can help you.

1. Do I Have Ready Funding, or
Can It Be Easily Secured?

Executive coaching, like tuition of any other kind, can be a substantial monetary investment, especially if a change program has an extended duration, such as six or twelve months. Coaching rates currently range from one hundred to six hundred dollars an hour. Extended programs with top-flight coaches have corresponding investment fees. As of this writing, the top coaches in large metropolitan areas charge in the low- to mid-five-figure range for six months. Celebrity coaches, such as high-profile CEOs and academic gurus, can command per-client fees upward of $100,000 annually.

For comparative purposes, consider that a five-day group executive education program at a premier academic institution is likely to cost $6,000 to $10,000 for tuition alone. When you factor in travel, lodging, and job downtime while you are away, the investment fee for a customized one-on-one coaching program takes on a different light. Consider also that registration fees for executive-level conferences and seminars generally run upward of $1,000 per day, before travel, lodging, and lost work time are added to the total expenditure.

Whether you're paying for coaching out of personal or business funds or your employer is underwriting the costs, it makes sense to start off by confirming that the investment fee associated with coaching is readily available. If you're the economic buyer (that is, the person who can authorize payment), then the decision is yours to make. If you've already gotten approval to proceed, you're also in good shape.

If there has been no firm commitment yet or just a conditional one, you might want to begin clarifying who has ultimate approval power, such as your supervisor or human resource manager, and determine what information the decision maker will want before authorizing coaching services. In other words, what will you need to do or provide to make the strongest case for funding?

It can be a good idea as well to identify everyone at work whose support can bolster your case for funding—or whose dissent might derail your request. Likely people include bosses, mentors, human resource professionals, past bosses, clients, colleagues, and even those you supervise.

ASK YOURSELF: Is there money or a budget available for coaching? If someone else must authorize the expenditure, who is this person? If I plan to pay for coaching myself, can I afford the investment?

Case in Point: Power in Numbers

The senior vice president sounded positively jubilant on the phone. "Are you sitting down, because you won't believe this!" he said. "I got the go-ahead for coaching."

I was just as surprised as he was. His boss, the executive vice president, was an inveterate bean counter, a former marine who saw his job as a constant battle to control costs. His philosophy of management development was well known throughout the company: on-the-job and on-your-own.

"What happened?" I asked.

He chuckled. "When I met with him last week, things didn't go very well. I had lots of hard data, including a detailed cost-benefit analysis. He wasn't convinced. Then today, as our weekly project review meeting was wrapping up, he made a reference to my coaching request that a number of people overheard. I think he expected I would back down. But before I could say a word, several of my group spoke up in favor of the idea. Some spoke very positively about working with coaches at other companies. Even the folks conferencing in on the telephone got into the act." He paused. "In the end, I had overwhelming force on my side—my own people," he said with pride.

2. DO I HAVE A STRONG DESIRE TO IMPROVE NOW?

Success has a physics all its own. "Nothing happens until something moves," Einstein observed. In today's 24/7 world, success itself has become a rapidly shifting target. Competition is no longer a contest between the tortoise and the hare but between two equally fast and focused hares. If you're not pressing forward, you're traveling in reverse.

If someone were to describe your accomplishments to date, which of these three words would they be more likely to use: *satisfactory, stellar,* or *unmatched?*

How would you like your career to be described one, five, ten years from now? If you possess the inner fire to attain, or retain, the highest levels of achievement, then you are intrinsically motivated. You approach work goals spurred on by innate curiosity and the desire to best your own track record. Perhaps your incentive to achieve greater success is driven by the lure of a bonus, the appreciation you get from your team, the recognition that a promotion brings. You are driven by extrinsic or outside sources.

More likely, your motivation is an amalgam of both intrinsic and extrinsic factors, inner ambition and external reward each playing vital roles in your quest for peak performance. Some people consciously search for self-improvement; others set goals on demand. Entrepreneurs, for instance, often acquire skills on an as-needed basis to move their businesses forward. (If landing a major contract depends on Internet savvy, a computer-challenged accountant will quickly become a search-engine wizard.)

If you're motivated to gain a more competitive edge, you may find great value in executive coaching. If you're at or near the top of your field, you may believe that you've maxed out on your ability to improve, that your current performance is as good as it gets. Many technical experts such as doctors, attorneys, and academics fall into this trap ("I'm already an expert. What more can I learn?") But if their worldview of improvement could be expanded to include acquiring complementary skills, such as people management and other soft skills, they too could learn how profoundly results are affected by even small incremental gains.

When do you want to improve: now, or at some distant, undefined point on the horizon? Successful coaching requires that your motivation be grounded in reality, not wishful thinking. You can't wish for a winning tennis serve. You have to be willing to do the work that produces a consistent, masterful stroke. Similarly, your circumstances and personal motivation must be genuine, not theoretical. And you can have a strong desire to change now even if your work conditions don't demand imminent improvement. Many people value coaching as a way to groom for future positions and opportunities. In other words, they are coached for development purposes rather than immediate performance.

Factors outside work can affect your motivation and coaching readiness too. Family and personal issues, discussed more fully in question 9, need to be considered but are unlikely to impede your success in a training program.

ASK YOURSELF: Am I motivated to improve? Do I want to improve now? If you answer yes to both questions, then executive coaching can help you hit the ball out of the park.

3. DO I HAVE SOME IDEA OF MY COACHING GOALS?

Motivation doesn't occur in a vacuum. It's results oriented. You need to have a vision of what success will look like so you will know it when you see it.

If your personal trainer asked you to describe your fitness goals, would you say you wanted to lose weight, improve your flexibility, or look better than anyone else at your class reunion? If a financial planner asked you to define your objectives, would you say you wanted to retire in ten years, save for your children's college education, or shelter your assets from taxation?

Coaching agendas give change programs a purpose, a set of measurable goals. To attain the most value from executive coaching, think about desired results.

These aims needn't be highly specific or prioritized at this point, but it will be helpful to begin giving some thought about what you would like to accomplish. Coaching goals commonly fall into one or more of these broad categories:

- *Increase or enhance current competencies.* Do you want to assert your influence with greater ease or diplomacy, become better organized, develop stronger presentation skills?
- *Link existing competencies to a new career or business situation.* The vice president of a Fortune 100 financial corporation might have an opportunity to become CEO of a smaller accounting firm and wonder how and if he could make the transition.

- *Acquire a new skill or capability.* A salesperson poised for promotion into the managerial ranks might need to learn how to achieve results through others rather than directly.
- *Troubleshoot issues.* Many executives seek an outsider's fresh perspective as a ready sounding board to discuss emergent issues, options, and tactics.

Even if the genesis of your coaching agenda is not self-initiated (perhaps goals were set by your boss or are part of a formal management or leadership program), it will be productive for you to consider what *you* want to gain from coaching.

Most of your time with a coach will be one-on-one, so think about your personal goals, not just those assigned to you by a superior or designated for all executives by your company's human resource or leadership development department.

Your goals and your company's agenda may mesh perfectly. For example, the CEO wants to prepare you to head an overseas office and you want the position. Or your desire for stronger management skills might be more far reaching: you want to move not just across the ocean but eventually into the CEO's office yourself. Can you envision how executive coaching can meet your company's immediate goals and your own loftier aspirations?

Setting agendas, even broad-based ones, take thought. If you're not certain where to start, try completing one or both of these statements:

"I want to improve my ability to . . . "

"I want to acquire skills to . . . "

ASK YOURSELF: What would I say to an executive coach who sat down in my office and asked, "What do you want to achieve in coaching?"

Case in Point: What the Doctor Ordered

The new director of clinical services had never before managed a large full-function department. This would be her first time overseeing operations and facilities staff, not just health care professionals. The hospital's human resource director had suggested to her that coaching might help support her success in this new role. However, the director, a medical doctor and noted authority in her field, wasn't at all sure.

"Look, I only took this job because it's a rotating position, and it was my turn," she told me. "I have no ambitions whatsoever of becoming a full-time administrator. I really just want to get back to my patients and research. So what's the point of working on management skills?"

A legitimate question. Behind it, I suspected, was a host of objections just waiting to be aired.

I asked her, "What if you were able to manage the department not just effectively but efficiently, so you could devote as much time as possible to your primary interests?"

The director's demeanor changed abruptly. She leaned forward. "Now that's something I'd love to learn how to do. When can we start?"

4. HOW CAN I BENEFIT BY ACHIEVING MY GOALS?

"The world makes way for the man who knows where he is going," Ralph Waldo Emerson observed. If, in answering the previous question, you thought about some goals you'd like to meet through executive coaching, your next step is to identify likely benefits to achieving them. Consider the goals identified in the previous section:

- Increase or enhance current competencies.
- Link existing competencies to a new situation.
- Acquire a new skill or capability.
- Troubleshoot issues.

Now expand your thinking to include assessing the value of reaching these goals. Will improving my performance advance my career? If I learn to apply my skills across the business unit, will it result in increased profitability? Could the company as a whole become more productive and innovative if I became a more strategic leader?

Sometimes when focusing on a pressing business need or skills gap, people confuse coaching *goals* with actual *benefits*. Back in the 1980s, when executives acquired computers and lost secretaries, many were advised to take up typing. And the first time a manager had to hunt and peck his way through a memo draft, the idea of signing up for a word processing class at work or adult education might have held appeal.

But suppose the manager had sat back and considered, "If it takes five hundred dollars and fifty hours of my time to learn how to type, how will I realize a return on my investment?" Unless the manager were a true visionary who foresaw the impact of the Internet before its invention, the value-conscious executive might have decided that acquiring typing skills was a goal without benefit.

The value proposition for executive coaching really stands out when you consider carefully the *benefits* of the *goals* you would like to reach.

Look again at the two sentences you were given to complete earlier:

"I want to improve my ability to . . ."
"I want to acquire skills to . . ."

In assessing the benefits of reaching your goals, expand your thinking (and the statements) to include bottom-line benefits:

"I want to improve my ability to . . . so I can . . ."
"I want to acquire skills to . . . in order to . . ."

Your completed statements might look something like these:

"I want to improve my ability to *manage my time better* so I can *increase my sales prospecting activities.*"
"I want to *acquire skills to hire more effectively* in order to *increase employee retention, build a stable, winning team, and reduce recruitment costs.*"

It makes sense to improve your time management capabilities if an important benefit such as increased sales prospecting is the result. But if you perceive no value in learning how to better manage your time (you avoid sales prospecting activities because you don't enjoy them, not because your schedule is too crowded), you will realize little benefit in a coaching program targeted at time management. Similarly, if there's no payoff for acquiring hiring skills (the company is planning a major layoff), the goal would be without short-term benefit. (Of course, it might still be a valuable addition to your managerial repertoire in the long term.)

Executive coaching can be costly and should be subjected to the same bottom-line tests as other significant investments. Don't be shy about calculating or projecting an expected yield or return on investment. For example, what's the impact likely to be when results are annualized? What's the upside potential to your career prospects and earning power?

ASK YOURSELF: If I set goals and accomplish them with the help of an executive coach, what immediate or long-term benefits can I expect?

5. AM I OPEN TO NEW WAYS OF THINKING AND BEHAVING?

Change is like a remote control device. Everything is fine as long as you're the one doing the channel surfing, but it becomes frustrating and annoying when someone else is clicking away at will.

People unfamiliar with executive coaching sometimes fear that they will be forced to change too much. If you're worried that you will be converted from an analytical to an intuitive thinker or from a handshake to a group-hug kind of person, you can exhale and relax. Coaching doesn't demand (or anticipate) your willingness to undergo a personality transplant or to uproot your entire system of behavior. You don't have to throw away your spreadsheets or learn a mantra.

Rather, coaching leverages two key characteristics that all peak performers possess: creativity and problem solving. No matter the field or discipline—business, science, law, sports, or entertainment—those who are the best, or aspiring to be the best, tend to be aggressive lifelong learners. When something they do yields a subpar result, they try something else. When they have a new insight, they test it out in a variety of situations. They constantly renew and reinvent themselves.

One great advantage of working with an executive coach is the opportunity to accelerate your learning curve. So, yes, you need to be open to new ideas and to revising existing opinions and attitudes. In evaluating your willingness to change, ask yourself these questions:

- *When was the last time I learned something new?* Yesterday? Six months ago? Still making long-distance calls manually rather than using the speed-dial feature? Learning agility is a valuable attribute and a key to ongoing success in general.
- *Do I modify my behavior when demands and circumstances change?* In your personal life, you probably do this all the time, often without conscious thought. We learn to avoid controversial topics when we don't want to get into arguments with friends and change our wardrobe when certain styles are no longer appropriate. Consider, then, your willingness to revise your thinking about cause and effect, change your management style, or adopt a radically different new strategy.
- *What do other people say about my adaptability?* If you're not sure how to assess your response to new ideas and behavior patterns, ask people who will give you straightforward, honest answers, such as a trusted colleague or your spouse. Accelerating your rate of improvement involves both learning the new and unlearning the old.

No one is, or should be, asking you to change for the sake of change. Your willingness to learn does not mean you must embrace every new concept to hit the market or lecture circuit, just to consider alternate ways of thinking and behaving.

ASK YOURSELF: Do I enjoy having my thinking stretched? Does the prospect of learning new information and techniques appeal to me?

Case in Point: Caught in the Undertow

"I'm burning out fast," the president of a biotech startup told me. In his late thirties, married, with two young children, this founder-entrepreneur knew he was in trouble. "Our revenues are up 40 percent over last year, but work just isn't fun anymore. My blood pressure is too high. My family complains that they never see me. My staff complain that I micromanage. I'm even growling at our bankers."

What I was hearing was a classic case of drowning in success. Having grown his business from scratch, this newbie chief executive was having a hard time relinquishing control and responsibility. Intellectually, he knew what he should be doing, but something was getting in the way—and adding to his frustration and stress levels.

"I need to get a grip on what's blocking me," he said. "I really want—I need—to grow beyond where I am now. I can't just manage anymore. I have to know how to lead."

6. CAN I BE HONEST WITH MYSELF?

The ability to see the world and ourselves accurately is vital to ongoing success. A general must know the capabilities of his own army and that of the enemy. The lyric soprano can sing Mozart, but Wagnerian roles, no matter how tantalizing, will shred her voice. An investor has to determine when to cut losses and move on.

If it's just you, a room, and a mirror, do you stop to look at your reflection, or do you avert your eyes so you don't have to get an up-close look at your graying hair? Maybe it makes sense *not* to stare into the mirror and obsess about the size of your nose or the tilt of your chin, issues you can't solve before the 10:00 A.M. project meeting. But what if you missed some leftover toothpaste on your face, something you could have removed easily if you'd taken just a few seconds to examine your appearance?

While you certainly don't have to be a philosopher or deeply introspective, executive coaching does involve self-inspection. In private moments, when no one is looking or listening, could you:

- List your weaknesses relative to your strengths? Are you better at organization than implementation? Are you better at motivating others than completing tasks yourself? Do you sometimes get too wrapped up in minutia and fail to see the bigger picture?
- Identify situations where you performed less well than you would have liked or made decisions that might not have been

optimal? Can you remember a time when you were so eager to close a deal that you missed an opportunity to expand the project and its profit potential? Have you treated an employee in a manner you regret? Have you ever made a decision that you would have liked to change, and could have changed, but you didn't because you feared losing credibility?

If you can identify performance areas you'd like to improve or expand, the next step is to ask yourself if you could share these concerns with someone else. You need to be able to be honest *with* yourself so you can be candid *about* yourself with a coach. An executive coach might ask you these questions, for example:

"What happened when you tried a new approach?"

"Are there things you've consciously avoided doing, to your detriment?"

"Are you able to acknowledge your responsibility in a sticky situation?"

"Are you able to admit you don't know when you don't?"

The point of this self-assessment is not to turn you against yourself. There's absolutely no need to become hypercritical. However, if you think you're already perfect, coaching is probably not for you!

ASK YOURSELF: Can I discuss my strengths, relative weaknesses, ambitions, and concerns honestly with someone who wants to help me achieve valuable improvements?

7. AM I OPEN TO FEEDBACK, EVEN WHEN IT IS MIXED OR NEGATIVE?

It is one of life's paradoxes that we often need to hear most what we want to hear least. A key hurdle that high achievers need to overcome early and often in their careers involves feedback. Indeed, we would all do well to emulate former New York City mayor Ed Koch, whose signature phrase, "How am I doing?" became part of the Big Apple's vocabulary.

Imagine that you are learning how to fly an airplane. Would you want your flight instructor to offer feedback:

(a) Often, if it's positive?

(b) Frequently, no matter what?

(c) Only at the end of a lesson?

(d) Never, unless the plane is about to crash?

If you want to earn your pilot's license as quickly as possible, *b* is the sensible choice. It's tempting to choose feel-good answer *a*, but this choice limits your access to valuable, less laudatory information. You may never get to *c* if you make a serious mistake before returning to the hangar, and good luck getting anyone to fly with you under the conditions in *d*.

An executive coach is like a pilot instructor, ready to share expertise in ways that will help you soar. One of my clients, a retired air force officer working in the public sector, described coaching this way: "No matter how good we are, having someone say, 'You're a little off center; move a tad to the left,' can make a big difference to the mission."

If you want to derive the maximum benefit from executive coaching, you need to be able to hear what others think about your performance. This starts with your coach; depending on your circumstances, it could include others, such as your boss, business partners, customers, employees, or coworkers. Are you eager to know what others think about how you're doing? If you think their points are valid, do you modify your behavior as a result?

It's natural to dislike criticism, particularly when we've worked hard and tried our best, and defensiveness is a common reaction to news that differs substantially from our own self-image. But in the privacy of a one-on-one helping relationship, can you move beyond any sensitivity if the feedback is valid? It's not necessary to agree with everything suggested by a coach or someone else similarly invested in your success. But it is crucial that you be able to heed input without shutting down or overly rationalizing your behavior. In fact, today more than ever before, it's critical to know how others perceive you.

Coaching involves receiving feedback from the coach, from others with whom you interact, and from yourself. In evaluating the weight of each source of feedback, can you accept that although no one knows you better than you know yourself, others may sometimes see you more clearly?

If you've spent much of your career working for large corporations, you might be a veteran of performance reviews, executive assessments, 360-degree surveys, and industry rankings. If, however, you're an entrepreneur or technical professional or you work in the public or nonprofit sector, this could be the first time your performance really gets scrutinized.

Of course, feedback is the "breakfast of champions" in all endeavors: sports, the performing arts, education, and business. And winners are typically review-rich. They might not always like their feedback "Wheaties," but like my ex-military client, they want to know sooner rather than later if they are on course or need to adjust. Given the speed with which information travels and reputations can be made or lost, knowing how you're doing and how other people think you're doing gives you a competitive edge.

ASK YOURSELF: Do I accept feedback well, even when it is not totally positive? Do I welcome opportunities to compare my own perceptions about myself with those of others?

Case in Point: Eyes on the Prize

A managing director at a global brokerage house was the lead candidate for a newly created position in Europe. The job, a significant step up in responsibility and status, would involve building a multinational team and penetrating a highly competitive market.

"She's absolutely the best when it comes to industry knowledge and expertise, and she's completely dedicated to the business," her boss told me. "Everyone agrees that she's earned this promotion. But her hard-charging style can backfire on her at times, with both clients and her own colleagues. Whoever ultimately gets the job will need to have strong partnership skills to assemble the team quickly and hit the ground running."

In person, the managing director seemed to fit her boss's description: razor-sharp, ambitious, an articulate, rapid-fire communicator. She knew she was the frontrunner and that the assignment was, in her words, "hers to lose."

She sighed when I mentioned the issue of her abrasive style.

"I've been hearing this for a couple of years," she said. "Frankly, I don't see it myself. But if I've learned anything in life, perception is reality. I really want this assignment, so anything I do that could possibly hold me back has got to change."

8. Can I Be Patient When I Know the Payoff Is Worth It?

We tend to forget that many apparent overnight successes are actually years in the making. Before penning her first Harry Potter novel, author J. K. Rowling wrote two books, neither of them ever published: "You have to resign yourself to wasting lots of trees before you write anything really good. It's like learning an instrument. You've got to be prepared for hitting wrong notes occasionally, or quite a lot" (Richards, 2000). For Rowling, the payoff for patience has been phenomenal: she's the world's first billionaire author.

Excellence is often a matter of dogged determination. The bigger or more complex the goal is, the more that patience becomes a differentiating factor among talented people. Often those accustomed to quick results or instant gratification find that they've reached a plateau.

Some years ago, the head of a multinational accounting firm hired an executive coach at his own expense and amid great secrecy. He didn't want anyone to know about the chink in his corporate armor, particularly when the adviser told him that their work could take awhile.

"What do you mean by 'awhile'?" the executive asked. "A couple of weeks?"

The coach smiled.

"A month?" The executive now looked agitated.

The coach said nothing.

"What are you saying? That it's going to take months, years? I don't have time. I can't wait forever!"

And he paced the room, darting angry glances at the still-silent coach.

About thirty seconds later, the coach spoke: "What was the skill you said you most needed to work on?"

"Patience!" the executive shouted.

"And how long do you think it will take you to learn how to be more patient?"

The executive sighed. "Awhile."

Of course, even before the Internet created an on-demand global economy, executives were seldom noted for their patience. Corporate leaders don't reach the upper echelons with sit-back-and-wait attitudes. It's the do-it-now (or sooner) mentality that helped them gain their corner offices, so it can take a bit of a mental adjustment for them to accept that coaching takes time and that the results will be worth the wait.

Can you cope with a practicing phase and not get discouraged? Can you stay the course in achieving your goals and not lose interest and motivation? People may avoid learning new things because they don't like becoming novices again. They don't have the patience for the interim frustration, or they expect too much of themselves and become discouraged when they don't master a new skill overnight. Those who have already achieved a high level of expertise as leaders in their fields are sometimes more challenged in this area than more junior counterparts. They've grown accustomed to quick results.

Remember the impatient CEO? He is no less fond of quick results than he was a decade ago. But he's much better at waiting for solutions that can't be rushed and has discovered that patience often pays big dividends.

ASK YOURSELF: If patience is the bridge between goals and results, am I willing to undertake the journey?

9. DO I HAVE TIME—OR CAN I MAKE TIME— IN MY SCHEDULE FOR COACHING?

Executive coaching requires two resources on your part: money and time. However, unlike money, time is a nonrenewable resource. Once it's gone, you can't get it back. Smart people invest and leverage their time; they don't just spend it.

You may not have enough information yet to know how much of a time investment coaching is likely to involve. Much depends on how targeted or ambitious your goals are, and you may still be formulating these at this stage. But here are some components for guidance purposes:

Direct contact. Coaching usually involves contact through face-to-face meetings, telephone conversations, and e-mail correspondence. Could you add this commitment to your current schedule?

Assignments. You may need time to complete assignments, take assessments, and review materials provided by your coach. Assignments can involve real-life experiments, talking or following up with others, and preparing and reviewing materials.

Travel. If you are planning a three-month tour of your company's overseas offices beginning next week, this is probably not an auspicious time to initiate a coaching program. Travel generally does not hinder successful coaching once a program has gotten under way. However, if you are often away from the office, this is something to discuss during coach selection or with your manager or human resource liaison.

Current obligations. Are there likely to be extended periods when you will not be able to work or follow through with a coach because of a big project, seasonal high activity, or budget reviews? How susceptible is your schedule to last-minute changes? These are important considerations for many business people, where breaking news, client demands, or market developments need to be addressed immediately.

Personal commitments. Are family demands—young children, an ailing parent, buying a house—impeding your regular work schedule? Does the thought of taking on another commitment overwhelm you? Consider personal commitments before embarking on a coaching program, although if you are having time management problems, you might want to consider a limited-focus program to deal with this issue.

Coaching is a partnership. An executive coach is a facilitator and a catalyst; he or she is not going to do the work for you. Execution is up to you. Some coaching programs are tightly targeted, in which case your work schedule or other commitments may not be an issue. Also keep in mind that pressing performance needs are often the best reason to work with a coach. A looming time crunch should not automatically rule out coaching. In fact, it can be another reason for moving forward sooner rather than later.

ASK YOURSELF: Do I normally make time for things I consider important? Would I consider coaching a valuable investment of my time?

Case in Point: Where There's a Will . . .

The regional sales director for a large retail chain wanted to take stock of his midlife career path and options. He was getting tired of the road warrior aspect of his job and was not at all certain that he wanted to spend the next decade of his life making the numbers and motivating sales representatives.

He intended to pay for coaching himself. However, a potential problem was finding time for face-to-face coaching sessions. His aggressive travel schedule (he logged over fifty thousand flight miles in the past six months) appeared to limit his availability. In fact, we were having this exploratory discussion by telephone while he was at an out-of-town airport, waiting for a connecting flight.

I pointed this out to him.

"It's kind of a catch-22, I know," he said, "but I've thought about doing this for myself for a long time. Since I make my own schedule, I can definitely consolidate my travel for a couple of months. I could also have my reps come to see me more often—they love visiting headquarters. What do you think?"

His solution made sense and spoke volumes about his motivation.

10. DO I TYPICALLY FOLLOW THROUGH ON COMMITMENTS AND ASSIGNMENTS?

When you're traveling in the fast lane, success does not follow the Woody Allen formula of just showing up. Rather, it's all about execution. Warren Buffett underscored this point in a *Fortune* magazine interview: "A lot of people start out with 400-horsepower motors but only get a hundred horsepower of output. It's way better to have a 200-horsepower motor and get it all into output" (Schlender, 1998).

You've agreed to be patient with the process and with yourself. You've agreed to devote the necessary time to a coaching program. *Isn't this commitment enough?* To answer this question, think of it this way: if a person accepts a charity board position but never attends meetings or events, is that person committed to the organization? If someone joins a gym but never works out, how committed is he or she to real self-improvement?

Commitment happens when the rubber meets the road. It's about staying on track even when no one is looking. Can you stay focused on your goals and engaged in the process of achieving them?

It's not uncommon for executives to have short attention spans, to begin a project enthusiastically and then want to move on to the "next big thing." This tendency is not all bad—companies need visionaries—and does not automatically preclude you from a coaching program. But if you make a commitment, large or tiny, do you follow through?

A coaching program usually includes an action plan and timetable jointly agreed to by you and your coach. It will have taken into account your known obligations (travel, meetings, project deadlines) and left room for unknown contingencies. Once you've settled on a schedule, though, will you approach it with the same attitude and passion that you apply to your other professional activities? Winners don't give up. They also don't overpromise or overcommit.

ASK YOURSELF: Do I typically hold myself accountable once I make a commitment?

FINAL ANALYSIS

Let's take a final look at the core variables associated with coaching readiness. They can be summarized as an equation consisting of three elements. Align all three and you have a winning formula:

Coaching Readiness = Personal Motivation + Time + Funds

We've also identified key traits associated with those who are good candidates for coaching:

- Open-minded; a flexible thinker
- Curious; an agile learner
- Persistent, goal oriented
- Feedback seeking

Congratulations! you're in an excellent position to assess your own candidacy for coaching. The ten screening questions are presented as a checklist in Exhibit 2.1. The more "Yes" responses you give, the stronger are your readiness indicators. If the majority of your answers are "No," coaching may not be the right approach for you, or this may not be the optimal time. Where you respond

EXHIBIT 2.1. COACHING READINESS CHECKLIST.

Decision Statement	Yes	No	Uncertain
1. Funding for coaching is readily available or can be easily obtained.			
2. I have a strong desire to improve now.			
3. I have some idea of my coaching goals.			
4. I can identify benefits to achieving these goals.			
5. I am open to new ways of thinking and behaving.			
6. I can be honest with myself.			
7. I am open to feedback, even when it is mixed or negative.			
8. I can be patient when I know the payoff is worth it.			
9. I have time—or can make time—in my schedule for coaching.			
10. I typically follow through on commitments and assignments.			

"Uncertain," you might want to get more information or consider your circumstances further.

If you're not a candidate yourself but rather a sponsor or supervisor, this checklist provides a handy decision tool that you can use to assist others. Just substitute *you* for *I* in each item.

Is executive coaching right for you? Now you can decide, and proceed, with confidence.

┌─────────────────────┐
│   CHAPTER THREE   │
└─────────────────────┘

HOW TO PICK YOUR PERFECT COACH

After speaking at a senior leadership conference, I had contrasting conversations with two attendees that highlight the importance of choosing your coach wisely. The first involved the executive director of a national trade association; I'll call her Charmaine. The second was with a senior university administrator whom I'll call Bill.

A Tale of Two Executives

"I had a terrible experience with a coach," Charmaine announced in a voice clearly intended to be overheard. "It was a *total* waste of time and money. Boy, did I get burned."

"What made it terrible?" I asked.

"He was a well-known management professor. Turned out he was all theory and no application. His answer to everything was, 'Let me think about it.' He had nothing useful to share. In fact, I think he learned more from me than the other way around."

"How did you find this person?"

"Well, our association's accountant suggested him. They went to college together."

"How many other referrals did you get?"

"None." Charmaine paused. "I just assumed he was good."

A little while later, another conference attendee came over to chat. He too was eager to talk about his personal experience with coach hunting.

"I had a really tough time picking a coach," Bill told me.

"How so?" I asked, wondering if I was in for another tale of woe.

"I had to choose between two people, both really qualified. I liked both of them too."

Curious, I asked Bill what made them qualified in his eyes.

"Oh, I knew what I was looking for: someone who could help me with my communication skills. I was getting a lot of flack from the president about being verbose and putting people to sleep instead of inspiring them. So I drafted a job description as if I were hiring someone. Then I asked around, got a couple of names, and met with three coaches. Two of them were really fantastic. In the end, I wound up flipping a coin, it was that close."

Whether in our professional or our personal lives, finding the right person can make a profound difference. Smart choices make rewarding, and even transforming, relationships. As my story shows, this is certainly the case with executive coaching. The partnership first has to click before it can hum on all cylinders. Trust needs to be present. Of course, finding the right person to meet our needs can also be a challenge. Consider how difficult it can be to hire for a "whole person fit" or choose a truly compatible mate or life partner.

There's no need to panic. I'll show you all you need to know to find and pick your Perfect Coach. *Perfect Coach?* you may be asking. *This sounds more like a quest for the holy grail than a service provider.* Relax. As you'll see, there are many professional coaches who can meet your needs and can become your Perfect Coach. And I'll give you an easy step-by-step system and tools for fast, winning results. Even if you have someone on staff to do the initial screening and prequalifying, such as a human resource or organization development manager, the final choice—and responsibility—is yours. Let's make it *perfect*.

IT'S ALL ABOUT COMPATIBILITY

Selecting a coach is nothing more than a compatibility exercise. Winning coach selections are high-compatibility choices. There are many highly qualified and potentially perfect coaches for you. Distilled to basics, there are two key elements to high compatibility:

- Your particular coaching needs and preferences
- The coach's capabilities and qualifications to address your needs and objectives

Configured as an equation, these same elements comprise the Perfect Coach formula:

Perfect Coach = Your Needs and Preferences + Coach Capabilities and Qualities

SIX STEPS TO SELECTION PERFECTION

You may be thinking, *Fine and well, but how do I go about transforming a generic formula or equation into an actionable plan?* I've broken the process down into six steps that we'll review in detail:

Step 1: Identify your coaching needs and goals.

Step 2: Identify your personal preferences.

Step 3: Build your Perfect Coach profile.

Step 4: Identify coach candidates.

Step 5: Evaluate coach candidates.

Step 6: Choose your coach.

Use this powerful, data-based approach and you will expedite your Perfect Coach search for sure.

STEP 1: IDENTIFY YOUR COACHING NEEDS AND GOALS

In Chapter Two, one of the key questions you asked yourself was, *Do I have an important goal or set of goals?* Whether this is general or specific, it should form the basis of building your coach's profile.

Complete one or both of these statements:

"I want to improve my ability to . . . so I can . . ."

"I want to learn how to . . . so I can . . ."

At this point, don't hesitate to talk to others as you identify or clarify your coaching goals. The more specifically and comprehensively you can describe your needs and goals, the easier it will be to identify what you will be seeking in terms of your coach's capabilities and personal attributes. Colleagues, supervisors, spouses, or anyone else who knows you well and can offer constructive advice can make a valuable contribution.

When you have answered these questions, you have identified a preliminary goal or set of goals. Now transpose what you have written:

"I need a coach who can help me . . ."

Here are some examples:

"I need a coach who can help me . . . :

- Improve my strategic focus and ability to delegate.
- Form a team out of people who used to be business rivals.
- Learn to pitch my start-up successfully to venture capitalists.
- Close more deals at higher margins.
- Be more effective communicating with my board.
- Interpret my performance feedback and create a targeted development plan.
- Acquire more adaptive ways to manage work stress."

What if you can identify your problem areas or symptoms (or someone else can) but are uncertain how to convert them into coaching goals? No problem. You're still in good shape at this early stage. Often, clarifying and finalizing your goals occurs only after you and your coach get under way. Nothing is written in stone at this point.

KEY POINT: Even if your coaching program will follow a prescribed format and process, as is the case with many company-based programs today, do not skip this step. Similarly, never abdicate or delegate identification of *your* goals to someone else, such as a manager, business partner, or human resource professional.

Step 2: Identify Your Personal Preferences

Step 1 dealt with your objective needs and goals. Step 2 focuses on your subjective preferences. Specifically, do you have strong feelings about working with a certain kind of person—feelings that range from a pronounced preference to a make-or-break level? Taking a few moments now to reflect on these variables will pay off handsomely when it comes to building your Perfect Coach profile:

Gender: Are your coaching issues or goals gender-specific? Can you talk candidly about yourself with someone of the opposite sex?

Age: Do you want a coach who is close to your own age? Older?

Ethnicity: Is it important that your coach come from a particular ethnic or cultural background?

As you can see, these are personal characteristics commonly associated with "diversity" distinctions. Coach characteristics associated with professional expertise and credentials will be addressed in the next step.

This exercise is intended to reveal any critical inclusion or exclusion criteria for the purpose of optimizing your coach selection. It is not intended to promote or reinforce prejudices or stereotypical thinking. The bottom line is that you will need to have a certain baseline level of comfort and trust to work well with your coach. Mutual commonalities and shared experience are factors not to be denied. Indeed, they can be the basis for highly productive coach-client relationships. However, they might figure prominently in coach selection for some individuals and very little or not at all for others.

An additional benefit to reviewing your preferences around coach attributes is a less obvious one. Whenever a strong preference or bias exists, it can be helpful to check out the underlying rationale. It could signal a possible avoidance strategy. For example, a male manager might reflexively resist the idea of working with a female coach, when in fact such an arrangement could improve his cross-gender communication or teambuilding skills.

Key Point: Keep an open mind, and do not exclude potential coaches prematurely on the basis of age, gender, race, or ethnicity. You might be pleasantly surprised if you cast your coach selection net wide at this point.

Not long ago I needed to buy a new mattress. It turned out that a lot had changed in mattress technology since my last purchase a decade or so ago. Now, besides innerspring products and water beds, the range of choices included memory foam, dial-a-number air beds, and latex models. And the choices didn't stop there. There were firm, plush firm, ultraplush, pillow-top, and Euro-top versions. I had no idea of the consumer's hornet's nest I had walked into.

Perhaps you're wondering what a mattress has to do with this question. In this case, it was easy to delegate the initial product research to someone else. The relative merits and special features of one type of construction over another did not need my personal attention. However, there came a point when only I could decide what felt comfortable for me. No one else could do this if I wanted the absolute best choice *for me*. Off to the showroom I went, confident that the investment of my time would pay rich dividends for years to come.

Similarly, when it comes to selecting your executive coach, you might delegate the initial activities to someone else. Many large organizations have in-house specialists who take care of sourcing logistics and referral requests. In the end, though, only you can decide which coach candidate truly meets your needs and preferences. Otherwise you're likely to be less than delighted with a proxy's choice.

♦ ♦ ♦

STEP 3: BUILD YOUR PERFECT COACH PROFILE

You listed your coaching needs and goals in step 1. Step 2 prompted you to consider certain distinguishing coach characteristics. Taken together, these steps complete one variable in the compatibility formula. You are now ready to tackle the second variable: identifying relevant coach expertise and capabilities. You are likely an expert on your own needs, opinions, goals, and personal tastes, but you may not feel so confident about completing this half of the equation. But you will.

What makes a great coach? The short answer is competency. But all-around competency encompasses a number of domains:

- Experience-based knowledge
- Formal education
- Coaching competency
- Ethics-based knowledge
- Personality and character

Your Perfect Coach is someone who brings a wide range of knowledge and interpersonal skills to the job. Let's take a closer look at each domain.

Experience-Based Knowledge

Effective coaches possess experience-based knowledge, the kind of real-world smarts that comes from business-based learning and keen observation over time. Of course, how you define *business* depends on your particular situation and work context: multinational corporation, trade association, small business, hospital, university or school, law firm, and so forth. This said, a key benefit to working with an executive coach is the opportunity to access his or her experiential knowledge and leverage this information into legitimate performance shortcuts that you can undertake. Many coaches are recognized authorities as authors of books and articles. International and cross-cultural experience can also be an asset.

Real-world smarts, especially in the areas of managerial, leadership, and career wisdom, involve deep contextual knowledge that cannot be acquired from a professional, graduate, or certificate program, whether the program is six years or six weeks long. After all, there is a reason that newly minted medical doctors have extended residencies before they become board-certified physicians.

How much business experience goes into acquiring real-world smarts? A person typically needs eight to ten years of progressive activities and challenges to acquire a rich and ready knowledge base. Back in the 1960s, the expression, "Never trust anyone over thirty," was common among youthful skeptics. Today a twist on this saying has its place when choosing a coach. As a general rule of thumb, look to work with someone well over the age of thirty. According to Benjamin Franklin, "At 20 years of age the will reigns, at 30 the wit, at 40 the judgment."

Formal Education

Should education and professional degrees, licenses, and certificates figure into the competency equation? It depends. A combination of real-world smarts with a solid technical education, such as a graduate degree in business administration, psychology, accounting, or social work, can be a powerful and highly effective combination. For example, coach practitioners with formal training in adult personality and learning often bring sophisticated diagnostic and behavioral change skills that can yield results faster. They can often differentiate between legitimate coaching issues and those that should be addressed in personal counseling.

Technical credentials and advanced degrees usually are salient when you are a technical professional yourself and seek a coach with a similar or complementary background. Indeed, in settings where credentials such as C.P.A, J.D., Ph.D., M.D., and M.B.A. are highly valued, such as professional service firms, universities, and research and medical centers, an advanced degree in some field is typically considered an essential credential. However, beware of falling victim to the Walk-in-My-Shoes Myth described in Chapter One.

Coaching Competency

Effective coaches are astute observers and diagnosticians. They can communicate information, including sensitive messages and data, tactfully and constructively. They have a repertoire of tools and strategies at their fingertips for facilitating insight and transferring knowledge and skills.

Coaching competency is different and distinct from both experience-based knowledge and formal education. For instance, many of us can recall a professor who was a world-renowned scholar but an ineffectual teacher. (Remember Charmaine's story at the beginning of the chapter?) Similarly, you have probably encountered industry veterans who could tell you in great detail how they did something but had no aptitude—or interest—in adapting their approach to your particular situation, talents, or style.

By contrast, effective coaches are able to achieve performance in other people. They take a positive, problem-solving approach. They can adapt quickly to new information and situations and can tolerate short-term ambiguity and uncertainty. As legendary basketball coach John Wooden noted, "Knowledge alone is not enough to get desired results. You must have the more elusive ability to teach and to motivate" (Wooden, 1997).

Whether through formal training programs, internships, continuing education, experiential learning, or some combination, qualified coaches possess these capabilities:

- Inspire rapport and trust quickly
- Listen actively and accurately
- Convey empathy
- Ask clarifying and insightful questions
- Have strong planning and goal-setting skills
- Deliver effective feedback
- Move between direct tutoring and guided inquiry modes
- Are results oriented
- Know how and when to be patient
- Know how and when to apply pressure
- Display cultural sensitivity
- Understand system and group dynamics

This last area, knowledge of systems and group dynamics, is critical because individual performance does not occur in a vacuum. Rather, it occurs in the context of broader imperatives, a distinct organizational culture, and numerous stakeholders.

Ethics-Based Knowledge

In the United States, many executive and business coaches come from the ranks of advanced-degree psychologists, attorneys, social workers, family counselors, and accountants. Those who hold state-issued licenses typically have a legal obligation to observe a professional practice and ethics code. If they violate that ethics code, they can be sued for malpractice, disbarred, or otherwise penalized. Other countries' policies may vary in this respect.

However, the vast majority of executive and business coaches do not fall into this category. Rather, as with management consultants, organizational trainers, and many other types of business advisers, they offer value in the marketplace as unregulated service providers. To be sure, many coaches belong to one or more national and international associations that require their members to subscribe to a published code of conduct. However, compliance is purely voluntary.

Ethical coaches are committed to principles of integrity and client welfare. They accurately convey their qualifications and expertise and undertake engagements only within their scope of competence. They tell the truth and do not overpromise, and they never engage in practices that are deceptive, manipulative, illegal, or likely to harm the client.

At the beginning of the engagement, if not earlier, ethical coaches clearly explain the bounds of confidentiality, including what information will be shared, when, and with whom. They review roles and responsibilities, fee and scheduling arrangements, and anything else that could have a substantive impact on the coaching relationship or program. They avoid conflicts of interest and dual relationships with clients who have the potential to exploit or harm them. They discuss up front with clients all relevant contracting issues and third-party arrangements or obligations. They enter barter-style agreements cautiously and only after ascertaining that the client is unlikely to be adversely affected.

Ethical coaches describe their conduct code and policy guidelines clearly. They also supply their guidelines in written format to their clients. In sum, they have a strong moral compass and put their clients' interests first.

Coach Personality and Style

Market researchers often speak in terms of "Q-scores," a measurement used to calculate a celebrity or public figure's overall likability. The more likable a person is rated, the higher is the corresponding Q-score.

It can be helpful to think of the coach personality and style domain as a type of expanded Q-score. As with all other valuable and rewarding relationships, you have to like and respect the coach you will be working with. True, your coach's personality and style may be less critical if you will be working with him or her only over a short period of time. But in general, this domain is vitally important to your Perfect Coach profile.

There's no single right coach personality to worry about here; effective coaches come in all shapes and sizes. Instead, consider these overarching personal attributes:

Professionalism: The coach is prepared, appropriate, respectful, and trustworthy.

Maturity: The coach is self-aware, authentic, confident, reliable, and consistent.

Likability: The coach is positive, considerate, and someone you would like to emulate.

Flexibility: The coach is adaptable, patient, and creative.

In order to discuss sensitive and private information, you need to have rapport and trust with your coach. Breaking this domain down into these subcomponents allows you to identify essential characteristics that otherwise can be overlooked when you are evaluating possible coaches.

Eminent Domains Summary

There we have it—the five domains of coach competency: experience-based knowledge, formal education, coaching competency, ethics knowledge, and personality and style. As to whether any of these domains are optional or less critical to building a Perfect Coach profile, I'd say that formal education might fall squarely into this category. Consider, for example, that Michael Dell, founder and chairman of Dell Computer, dropped out of college to start his PC business. His real-world smarts could probably trump those of many business school professors. (I say this as a lifelong proponent of higher education and the holder of five earned degrees, including two doctorates.) How you weight each domain is up to you and any funding sponsors.

Additional Considerations for Those in Large Corporations

If you work in a large corporation or public sector enterprise, you may have one or two additional coach selection choices to make. First, you may need to decide whether to opt for employer-funded or private-pay coaching. Second, you may have to choose between an internal coach and an external one.

Employer-Funded or Private-Pay Coaching.   The choice here focuses on who will underwrite the investment: your employer or yourself. Many companies have well-defined and extensive coaching programs or are willing to fund coaching on a case-by-case basis. One critical decision involves the intended scope and goals of your coaching (see Table 3.1). If your objectives are clearly aligned with your current job, day-to-day responsibilities, and advancement

TABLE 3.1. EMPLOYER-FUNDED AND PRIVATE-PAY COACHING:
A COMPARATIVE ANALYSIS.

Service Option	Advantages	Possible Drawbacks
Employer-funded service	No out-of-pocket expense. Coaches are typically prequalified. Coaching occurs during work hours as on-the-job effort. Coach may be familiar with the organization.	Coaching scope and duration may be limited. Employer has rights to certain information. Restricted pool of coaches. Coach may be familiar with the organization.
Private-pay services	Unrestricted coach selection. Unrestricted range of coaching goals and topics. Coaching relationship unaffected by employment changes. Highest degree of privacy and confidentiality.	Personal budget may limit coach selection and duration. Selection process may take more time and effort. Coach may be unfamiliar with situational context. Coaching occurs during personal time.

within the company, a strong case can be made for taking advantage of employer-provided services.

If you are interested in broader or sensitive issues, such as a major career assessment or a possible change of employment, then a private-pay arrangement unfettered by your employer's interests and sponsorship terms is likely the preferred—and proper—option. The same applies if you want your coaching to be completely private. Invariably, when coaching is employer funded, some people will know that you are working with a coach, and you should expect that some general information about goals, methods, and contact frequency will be shared.

External or Internal Coach. An *external coach* is a nonemployee who is engaged by your organization as an independent contractor or consultant. An *internal coach* is an employee of the organization

TABLE 3.2. EXTERNAL AND INTERNAL COACHES: PROS AND CONS.

Type	*Advantages*	*Possible Drawbacks*
External coach: *An independent contractor or consultant*	Independent, outsider perspective Strong credibility, especially at senior levels Greater confidentiality and privacy	Unfamiliar with the organization's culture, players, and politics Higher investment fee
Internal coach: *An employee of the organization who coaches other employees*	Organizational know-how and know-who Typically less costly than external coaches More opportunities to observe the client in action and give feedback Relationship can be long term	Possibility of a dual work relationship or potential conflict of interest Limited pool of coaches Coach may have limited time or perspective Coach may lack expertise or credibility at senior-most levels

who provides coaching services to other employees on a full- or part-time basis (see Table 3.2). Put another way, she or he may have additional job duties or responsibilities in addition to those as an internal coach.

Many organizations have added internal coaches to their leadership and management development programs as a way of extending the benefits of individual coaching throughout the organization. Today, internal coaches are most often found working with middle managers and up-and-coming talent. Since they are insiders themselves, they often possess valuable "know-who" as well as "know-how," both of which can yield tangible benefits for ambitious people at this stage of their careers.

External coaches may work exclusively as coaches, or they may provide coaching services as part of a broader range of professional services, such as management or human resource consulting. They can be sole proprietors, members of a boutique firm, or employees of an international executive search, management consulting, or outplacement company.

Top decision makers show a marked preference for working with external coaches. At the senior-most levels of an organization, executives are typically looking for a high degree of confidentiality, an independent sounding board, and top-tier credentials and expertise.

KEY POINT: If you will be working with an internal coach, be sure to ask about the matching process. Speak up early about any preferences or special issues you have. Otherwise you and your coach may be matched randomly or solely on the basis of mutual time availability.

BURNING QUESTION: IF I PAY FOR COACHING MYSELF, MUST I TELL MY EMPLOYER?

If you opt for a private-pay arrangement away from your place of employment, you typically have no obligation to advise your employer of the fact. However, here is one caveat: if you intend to discuss work-related issues or share work-related documents with your coach, be sure that doing so in no way compromises or violates your employer's interests. Just because you are personally paying and your coaching arrangement is private does not automatically release you from compliance with your employer's policies. A gray zone can exist, for example, when companies urge employees to seek outside coaching for job-related reasons but will not foot the bill. The wise course here is to discuss the situation with your coach or seek guidance from your employer or an expert third party, such as an attorney.

◆ ◆ ◆

STEP 4: IDENTIFY COACH CANDIDATES

You are now ready to begin your active coach search. Just as with many of your key service providers—physician, accountant, attorney, personal trainer, hair stylist—your best sources for referrals are people you know and trust. Moreover, firsthand endorsements serve the purpose of prescreening and prequalifying coaches. Since you now have a comprehensive Perfect Coach profile, you can explain in detail the kind of coach and coach qualifications you're seeking. So access your personal network first: colleagues, friends, supervisors, human resource professionals, mentors, past bosses, and business advisers. You may be surprised at how many prospective candidates you can quickly identify this way.

Regarding employer-funded coaching, a human resource or leadership development specialist may be a powerful ally in your coach search. Typically companies prescreen the coaches they hire as independent contractors to be sure they meet specified standards and best practices. You may be able to review individual coach profiles on the company intranet and build a short list of interview candidates directly from there.

Think about any speakers or presenters you might have heard at a conference, business meeting, or trade show and with whom you were impressed. Do any of them offer coaching services? Possible additional referral sources are business schools, university-based executive education programs, trade associations, professional coaching associations, small business development agencies, and alumni organizations. Exercise caution with business-referral associations, where the person making the recommendation gets a commission, because their interests and yours may not coincide. In fact, consider asking anyone you do not personally know if they receive commissions on referrals. You are better off knowing up front if they have a monetary interest in promoting a particular person or firm.

The Internet can be extremely helpful. You can often follow up leads by going online to do additional research. Do a Web search of any specific coach referrals. See if they have a Web site where you can check out their background, services, and clients. Perhaps they are published authors. Leading national and international coaching associations often have Web sites with searchable databases that you can sort by region and coaching specialty. But just because a coach does not have a Web site is no indication that he or she is to be avoided. Many successful coaches have clienteles built primarily on positive, word-of-mouth recommendations.

Use your Perfect Coach profile to craft what is essentially a position description. An easy way to do this is to complete the following sentence with the appropriate information:

> I'm looking for an executive (or business) coach to help me
> _____ . The person I'm looking to work with needs
> to _____ , should have _____ , and
> be able to _____ . [If applicable, add this sentence:]
> I only want to work with _____ .

For illustrative purposes, a completed version might look like this:

> I'm looking for an executive coach to help me <u>improve my team-building and conflict resolution skills.</u> The person I'm looking to work with needs to <u>be familiar with the semiconductor industry,</u> should have <u>a track record working with sales professionals,</u> and be able to <u>meet with me in the evening away from my office.</u> I only want to work with <u>someone who is at least my own age and preferably a little older.</u>

Note that both personal preferences and coach competencies are included.

Whether you canvass your personal network by e-mail, have some conversations with friends, or consult your human resource manager, being specific will save you (and everyone else) time and make for an efficient and effective search.

Your short list should contain at least two or three names of the most compatible candidates and preferably no more than five.

If you make initial contact with candidates by telephone, state up front what you hope to achieve in coaching. Then ask, "Is this within your scope and interest?" Eliciting an outright *no* allows you to move on to the next candidate name. Getting a *yes* or *maybe* response means a green light to arrange a meeting. Consequently, if you plan on delegating initial contact to someone else (for example, a personal assistant, human resource manager, or spouse), either brief that person well on what you're looking for or expect to spend time interviewing more candidates than you might otherwise have needed.

Are telephone interviews sufficient to identify and choose your Perfect Coach? If you anticipate that your entire coaching program will be done as distance telecoaching or that coaching will be brief, then the answer is *yes*. However, be sure to conduct a thorough telephone interview and request a complimentary session to preview the coach's personal style and methods. With any other kind of coaching, there is no substitute for a face-to-face interview. Indeed, a coach may reasonably insist on an in-person meeting to make his or her own determination of compatibility.

KEY POINT: Use trusted channels to identify potential candidates. If you delegate your coach search to someone else, be sure that person has your Perfect Coach profile for guidance.

STEP 5: EVALUATE COACH CANDIDATES

Conducting interviews is both a skill and an art. The key is preparation, and by now you are very well equipped to proceed.

Remember that coach selection is a compatibility exercise. Think of the interview as a guided conversation that will allow both you and the coach candidate to determine goodness of fit. If you would like a second opinion, consider inviting a mentor, boss, or your human resource manager to participate in the interview. This can add an element of expertise and objectivity to the process.

Essential interview subjects include those needed to confirm the coach's full-domain competency, plus fees and policies. Here are some sample interview questions:

- How long have you been a professional coach? What experiences and training have prepared you for a coaching career?
- Who have you worked with? What types of organizations and job positions [or professionals or entrepreneurs]?
- Do you specialize in a particular industry or area of coaching—for example, strategy, behavior change, leadership, career development, business growth, or work-life integration?
- Have you had people management responsibilities? Operational responsibilities?
- What is your approach to coaching?
- As a coach, what do you see as your primary role?
- Tell me about some of your recent client engagements and results.
- Can you give me an example of a program or situation similar to mine?
- What kind of assessment process am I likely to go through?
- As my coach, would you want to talk to other people? Who? Why?
- As I've described my coaching objectives, how long do you expect it will take to accomplish them? What factors would play into this?
- Can you accommodate my work schedule? How often would we be in contact? Would these be face-to-face meetings or by telephone?
- How available are you between appointments?
- How would we be able to recognize success?
- What are your fees? Do you offer a trial period?
- What are your policies about session cancellation, confidentiality, and information disclosure to third parties?
- Can you provide the names of some past or current clients whom I can contact?
- Will you sign a confidentiality agreement?
- Under what circumstances would you *not* work with someone?

Confidentiality requirements may prevent a coach from identifying current and past clients by name. Nevertheless, a coach should be able to convey ample descriptive information about client contexts and presenting issues, coaching methods, and results. If you feel the need, ask for third-party references, such as a human resource professional, business colleague, or former employer.

If your coaching will be employer funded, the candidates you interview may already have a service contract in place that details policies concerning confidentiality, fees, and session frequency. If this is the case, you should still inquire about these in your interview so that you make informed decisions going forward.

Red Flags

Pay attention to red flags during the interview that could be disqualifiers. Some common red flags are:

- The coach claims to be able to work with anyone on any issue or goal—a jack-of-all-trades.
- The coach uses excessive technical jargon or name dropping to impress you.
- The coach makes unrealistic claims or timetables for results.
- The coach talks more about himself or herself than focusing on you and your agenda.
- The coach does not offer new clients a trial period.
- The coach does not provide any client, character, or work references.
- The coach uses hard-sell tactics or pressures you for an immediate commitment.
- The coach has no clearly defined coaching method or program framework. (See Chapter Five for an in-depth discussion of this subject.)

Asking About Fees

Whether your coaching will be employer funded or private pay, be sure you understand how much the coach charges and what kinds of services and activities are included. Even if you will not be paying out-of-pocket, employer-funded coaching services get charged to a business or department budget, so you should be cognizant of the specific investment costs.

Two of the most common fee arrangements are time-basis and flat-fee.

Time-based fees are calculated at an hourly rate, much the way attorneys and accountants routinely charge for their services. Make sure you know what is billable. For example, in addition to direct face-to-face and telephone time, document preparation and review, e-mail and fax communication, and coach contact with third parties are also generally billable at the established hourly rate.

A flat-fee package usually allows unlimited contacts during a specified period of time. The period can be a week, a month, six months, or a year. Flat-fee packages function much like popular fitness club membership programs: you can be as heavy a user as you want for as long as you belong.

At the very high end of the market—for example, when the client is a Fortune 500 CEO or the head of a major international enterprise—coaching fees may consist of a base amount and a bonus component that is linked to specific metrics, such as the chief executive's annual bonus or the company share price.

Separate packages or fees may apply for assessment components, such as individual behavioral and multirater (360-degree) assessments, and other types of coaching-related activities and services. If substantial travel is involved, this too might be billable time.

Find out about payment terms. The options can vary significantly from coach to coach. The point is to identify likely fees and associated expenses. (Information about program agreements and terms is covered extensively in Chapter Four.)

Interviewing Candidates

In general, even if your first interview goes exceedingly well, resist the urge to end your search right then and there. Often you can learn a lot of useful information from these interviews about various coaching styles, methods, and fee arrangements. Exceptions do exist. For example, if you already know a candidate from a previous encounter or connection and he or she passes the compatibility test with flying colors, you might consider discontinuing the interview process.

Expect to devote at least one hour to each interview. This will enable you to have a broad-ranging discussion and observe the coach's interpersonal style in action. Then, while the experience is still fresh, use the following questions to evaluate the coach against your Perfect Coach profile.

- Does this coach have a track record of helping people in similar situations and with similar goals to mine?
- Do I have rapport with this coach? Does the coach possess personal and professional characteristics I would like to emulate?
- Is this coach prepared, positive, candid, and confident?
- Does this coach listen carefully and probe to make sure he or she understands my meaning, goals, and concerns?
- Are this coach's questions intelligent, pertinent, and insightful? Do they help me clarify or reassess my needs and goals? Expand my thinking?
- Does this coach provide references or examples of client successes?
- Does this coach clearly explain his or her coaching approach, as well as fees, confidentiality, and service guidelines?
- Are our schedules, availability, and contact requirements compatible? Does this coach subscribe to a written code of ethics?
- Will this coach sign a nondisclosure agreement?

Step 6: Choose Your Coach

Let's review the Perfect Coach formula:

Perfect Coach = Your Needs and Preferences + Coach Capabilities and Qualities

You may be surprised to discover that you relate well to more than one coach you've interviewed and the final choice is not obvious. Under such circumstances, completing the coach evaluation form in Exhibit 3.1 for each finalist can help you decide and, if need be, bring you back on course. The tipping point could be in how the coaches compare in the five competency domains, investment fee, or availability or start date. If you need to follow up with the finalists to clarify points or get additional information, do so without hesitation. Then make your choice in the knowledge that

EXHIBIT 3.1. CANDIDATE COACH EVALUATION FORM.

Coach's Name _____

Telephone Number _____

E-mail _____ **Date** _____

Ranking System Key:
1 = Superior; 2 = Satisfactory; 3 = Unsatisfactory

	Rankings			**Notes**
Coach Competency Domains	**1**	**2**	**3**	
1. **Experience-based knowledge** Real-world smarts Relevant work experience	☐	☐	☐	
2. **Education credentials** Formal education credentials Professional certifications	☐	☐	☐	
3. **Coaching competency** Formal training Experience coaching others	☐	☐	☐	
4. **Ethics based competency** Subscribes to formal code Provides written guidelines	☐	☐	☐	
5. **Personality and style** Trustworthy Clear communicator Good listener Positive attitude Self-confident Nondefensive Likable	☐	☐	☐	

Other Compatibility Factors	**Rankings**			**Notes**
Fee range and terms	☐	☐	☐	
Schedule compatibility	☐	☐	☐	

Summary Assessment

you have picked the Perfect Coach for you. You can look forward to reaping the benefits of a truly compatible relationship.

FINAL ANALYSIS

Things have to click before they can hum. Taking a compatibility approach to picking your coach definitely keeps the "science" in the selection chemistry. I've shown you how to use data-based decision making to cut through the hype, buzzwords, sales pitches, name dropping, and good intentions that often accompany the hiring of any service provider. If you've followed the six steps, you can be confident that you've made an excellent choice. Congratulations. You have your Perfect Coach. Now let's firm up the arrangement by taking an in-depth look at the details.

CHAPTER FOUR

TERMS OF ENGAGEMENT

More than two thousand years ago, Cicero observed, "In all matters, before beginning, a diligent preparation should be made." His advice certainly holds true in the twenty-first-century business world. Clarifying and documenting your coaching agreement is neither complicated nor time-consuming. And it's definitely diligent preparation.

You may be wondering: *Haven't I reached an agreement already?* You and your coach probably reviewed many details in the course of the interview preliminaries. For example, program logistics such as format, methods, duration, and contact frequency doubtless came up in discussion, as did fees and payment terms if you're the economic buyer as well. Or you may have a proposal in hand now.

If you generally like to know what you're committing to, the ins and outs of finalizing your coaching program will have intrinsic appeal. You're likely to scrutinize and negotiate terms carefully and ask questions to clarify anything you don't understand. If instead you routinely sign business waivers and medical releases without reading them, you may be tempted to give short shrift to the fine print. After all, you may reason, you've selected your Perfect Coach. Why not just leap into the pool and get wet?

One reason you should not is that a leap of faith can be a poor substitute for accurate information, such as how much water is in the pool and how chilly it is. As with business and professional relationships of all kinds, the more you know, the more you can influence and maximize a profitable outcome. This chapter will help you do just that by highlighting the key terms and conditions you need to understand and reach agreement on. Not only will this make you an informed consumer, but you will also avoid surprises later that could be the equivalent of diving into a pool of frigid water. I've also included checklists and sample agreements to make the process easy and, dare I say, positive and satisfying.

TWO PARTIES OR THREE? A RECAP OF WHO'S WHO

Let's briefly review private-pay and employer-based coaching as they relate to engagement terms and conditions. With private-pay services there are two parties: the client and the coach. The client is the economic buyer, that is, the person who authorizes and pays for services. Therefore, only a single coaching agreement is needed: one between the client and the coach.

By contrast, employer-provided services involve three parties: the client, the coach, and the employer. Whether the employer engages an external coach or an internal one to work with the client, there are still three parties. The de facto economic buyer is the employer. Top-level decisions concerning coach screening, fees, and program design and objectives are typically made by the economic buyer. Consequently, the primary service agreement is between the employer and the coach. For the coach and actual client to reach an understanding between themselves, a supplemental, or secondary, agreement is needed. Table 4.1 provides a comparison of these points and differences.

TABLE 4.1. COMPARISON OF PRIVATE-PAY AND EMPLOYER-FUNDED SERVICES.

Category	Private-Pay Services	Employer-Provided Services
Economic buyer	Client	Employer
Parties involved	Two parties: Client and coach	Three parties: Employer, coach, and client
Primary contracting party	Client	Employer
Primary agreement parties	Client and coach	Employer and coach
Secondary agreement parties	Not necessary	Client and coach

KEY POINT: A client–coach agreement is essential to achieving extraordinary results, regardless of who is the economic buyer.

Leading Minds on Beginnings

"Let no act be done at haphazard, nor otherwise than according to the finished rules that govern its kind."
—*Marcus Aurelius*

"Of a good beginning cometh a good end."—*John Heywood*

"Things bad begun make strong themselves by ill."
—*William Shakespeare*

"Undertake not what you cannot perform, but be careful to keep your promises."—*George Washington*

"Check small things."—*Colin Powell*

"Promises are the uniquely human way of ordering the future, making it predictable and reliable to the extent that this is humanly possible."—*Hannah Arendt*

THE PALEST INK BEATS THE BEST MEMORY

Samuel Goldwyn, the legendary movie mogul, had a reputation for business shrewdness and blunt speech. "A verbal contract isn't worth the paper it's written on," he remarked. Now you don't have to share Goldwyn's cynicism to appreciate the value of written agreements. In fact, I believe that a written document, whether brief or long, between you and your coach is an excellent practice and will go a long way to supercharging your coaching partnership from the start. This applies whether yours will be the primary contract or a secondary agreement.

Five Reasons to Have a Written Coaching Agreement

1. Confirm the partnership. The coach–client relationship is formalized, and key terms and conditions are delineated.
2. Specify key program logistics and policies. You will understand the services to be provided, the methods to be used, and poli-

cies regarding payment, session scheduling, and information sharing.

3. Provide structure to the program. The agreement sets a framework for coaching so that expectations and boundaries are clear. Having a predictable, reliable structure in place facilitates a strong, trusting relationship between you and your coach.

4. Maximize the return on investment. The more you know about how your coaching program will work, such as methods, options, and exclusions, the better equipped you will be to obtain the highest return on funds, time, and effort invested.

5. Ensure optimal service delivery. Written ground rules reduce the risk that misunderstandings or disputes will arise later because you have a reference document for consultation. You won't need to rely on memory or someone else's recollections.

Capturing key engagement terms in writing does not need to be a complicated or lengthy process. You may have a detailed proposal in hand already. Otherwise, many individual coaches and companies that offer coaching services have a standard boilerplate agreement that can serve this purpose or be modified to suit. Expect a typical agreement written in plain English to consist of one or two pages. By way of contrast and caveat, expect an attorney-drafted agreement to be longer and have words with legal meaning that you may have to have interpreted by another attorney.

Actually, you may have little choice but to sign *some* form of understanding. Even if your coaching is employer funded and the contractual arrangements are completely handled by human resource or purchasing staff, your coach may require an agreement between the two of you. The same applies if you will be working with an internal coach. In all cases, this is a sign of your coach's professionalism and desire to begin on a firm foundation.

BURNING QUESTION: WHY CAN'T HR TAKE CARE OF THESE DETAILS?

I'm often asked by those receiving employer-funded services if they can't just turn all contracting details over to their human resource professional or coach coordinator or purchasing agent. After all, engaging coaches and consultants is what these people are employed to do. My answer is a qualified one. If your organization has standard practices and procedures in place for hiring and paying independent contractors, then the coach (or the coach's company, if she is employed by one) will probably come to an agreement on the business terms with the designated representative. But even when this is the case, a separate written agreement between you and your coach that covers issues bearing directly on your coaching program is a great idea. Only in this way can you truly give informed consent and be an equal partner in what is, after all, *your* coaching program. In large corporate or institutional settings, it's common for a coach to have one general contract in place with the organization and then augment this with agreements with individual clients. In such instances, you probably don't need to know (or care) if your coach has workers' compensation insurance. But you should know if your coach is entitled to bill your employer for any in-person meetings you cancel at the last minute.

Of course, if you're paying for coaching out of personal funds or you're a sole proprietor or professional, you will be the point person for all aspects of the agreement. In either case, the information here will help you handle matters fast and well.

COACHING AGREEMENT TERMS 101

The following list sets out the key terms and conditions that I believe are most important to identify, understand, and include in negotiations and final commitment. Use this as a guide:

- Service provider information
- Service description(s)
- Service fees
- Payment terms
- Billable activities and expenses
- Information-sharing guidelines
- Proprietary information nondisclosure by coach
- Session cancellation policy
- Extension, renewal, and termination policies
- Dated signatures of contracting parties

Because individual circumstances and contexts are so diverse, I make no claim that this list addresses your unique situation. In addition, the following discussion is not a substitute for legal advice. If you have concerns or reservations about entering into a binding agreement, you should consult an attorney. If you will be making a substantial financial commitment, you may want to consult your financial adviser as well for peace of mind. By the same token, many people think that if they have clarified terms to their satisfaction, they don't need a lawyer simply as a matter of form.

SERVICE PROVIDER INFORMATION

The agreement should contain the names and contact information of the coach and the individual coaching client. The coach's firm or company should also be included if there is one. If you will be working with more than one coach (an unusual situation), then the agreement should list all coaches.

SERVICE DESCRIPTION(S)

The agreement should include a brief description of the services to be provided and program scope. This may be as basic as the generic term *coaching*. Some other commonly used service terms are:

- Executive or performance coaching
- Behavioral assessment
- Leadership and management development
- Stress management
- Career development

The purpose of coaching may or may not be assumed from the description or otherwise described. If a time period or session number and duration is known, this information can be stated.

SERVICE FEES

The specific investment fees associated with the described services should be listed. If the coaching program consists of multiple service components, such as an assessment battery followed by an extended coaching program, these may be itemized or combined.

If you have a preference for how this information is provided, let your coach know.

Common ways that coaches charge for their services are:

Time basis: A set hourly rate for services rendered. Fees are charged on the basis of professional time expended.

Fixed-program basis: A comprehensive set fee that covers a specified program or project.

Retainer basis: A set fee that covers service delivery during a specified time period or for an agreed-on number of hours.

If your coaching program is employer funded, fee structure and payment information are optional in the agreement between you and your coach; they may or may not be specified depending on your employer's policies and preferences.

PAYMENT TERMS

If you are the economic buyer, the agreement should state what fee amounts are payable at what time. Some coaches provide services on a prepaid basis only, while others may require an initial deposit and then invoice subsequently on a monthly basis. In the latter case, a discount may be available if you prepay services in full. Or you may have negotiated some other type of payment schedule. Whatever the terms are, these should be documented. Any penalty for late payment or overdrawn accounts should be clearly specified. Also, if you're arranging for long-distance telecoaching, the agreement should state who is responsible for telephone charges and call-backs.

If you're not the economic buyer and not involved with accounts payable, information about payment terms is optional and at your employer's discretion.

BILLABLE ACTIVITIES AND EXPENSES

If you will be paying for coaching on a time or retainer basis, it's important that you understand what activities are considered billable. These should be spelled out in the agreement.

There are basically two types of coaching-related services: direct client contact and nondirect collateral activities. For example, direct contact would include face-to-face and telephone sessions plus any electronic communications via e-mail and fax between you and your coach. *Collateral activities* is a catch-all phrase for all other kinds of effort and activities that a coach might legitimately perform in the course of providing agreed-on services to you. Coach preparation time is chief among these and can include the following:

- Assessment analysis and interpretation
- Ongoing program design and modification
- Session agenda development and record keeping
- Document review of materials and drafts that you provide

Additional collateral activities can include:

- Consultation with any sponsors, such as supervisors or HR staff, if coaching is employer funded
- Interviews with third parties, such as peers, bosses, staff members, and customers
- Report writing to sponsors

Knowing at the start what constitutes billable service time will prevent you (and your sponsor, if you have one) from an unwanted surprise later. Of course, if yours is a comprehensive fixed-fee program that includes all direct and collateral activities, you need not be concerned about these details.

If relevant to your situation, an explanation of expense reimbursement policies associated with out-of-town travel, lodging, or long-distance and international telephone charges incurred by the coach on your behalf should be provided.

INFORMATION-SHARING GUIDELINES

As the coaching client, you should know what information may or must be shared with third parties and under what circumstances. These terms should be clearly set out. With private-pay arrangements, there is little cause to be concerned that your privacy will be limited or compromised (but see the following section on electronic communications and coaching). By contrast, when coaching is employer funded, your organization has both an investment and an interest in the services provided to you. It's reasonable and appropriate that someone—a supervisor, human resource professional or other sponsor—ensure quality control. Thus, your privacy and confidentiality in coaching might be limited. The key is to clarify up front what types of information will and will not be shared.

For guidance purposes, information that a coach may reasonably be asked to provide to your employer includes:

- Program design, methods, and tools
- Goals and development plans
- Contact frequency, such as meetings and telesessions
- Progress reports and program summaries

Information that is generally not shared or disclosed includes:

- Results of any individual personality or psychological testing
- Interview and 360-degree survey data obtained by the coach, except in anonymous aggregate form

Note that information sharing may be either verbal or written.

Technology has made it possible to communicate just about anytime and from anywhere from a workstation, laptop computer, personal digital assistant, cell phone, and other handheld devices. Electronic mail and text and instant messaging can be convenient ways to share information in real time and when rapid review and response are vital. Coaching services that consist exclusively of tele-coaching also rely heavily on information technology to transmit client assignments and program materials across distances.

Let's review some important facts about e-mail communication:

- It creates a permanent record.
- It may be subject to electronic interception and therefore may not be secure.
- It may be archived or kept by third parties, such as Internet service providers.

- It can be subject to court orders. (Enron, Arthur Andersen, and Boeing's former CEO Harry Stonecipher are all cautionary examples.)
- Many employers retain the right to read their employees' e-mail.

The regulatory environment requires certain industries and government-related firms to observe strict electronic document retention policies. For example, the Securities and Exchange Commission requires that financial institutions archive instant messaging as well as e-mail exchanges.

Consider these facts when planning how you and your coach expect to use e-mail to communicate. If, based on your particular circumstances, there's anything distinctive or mandatory regarding your use of e-mail, let your coach know now so that the two of you can begin the way you want to continue.

Five Tips for Using E-Mail Wisely

1. Familiarize yourself with institutional policies and regulatory requirements regarding e-mail retention and review by third parties.
2. Comply with all institutional e-mail policies, including the appropriate use and transmission of sensitive and proprietary information.
3. If you are paying for coaching out of personal funds, ascertain whether you may properly use your employer's e-mail systems to communicate with your coach. Just because your coaching activities may involve work-related information and goals does not automatically mean you're entitled to use your employer's channels.
4. Clearly identify as sensitive or confidential any e-mail that you send to your coach, including attached files.
5. Never send e-mail when your emotions are high—to your coach or anyone else. As Confucius said, "When anger rises, think of the consequences."

PROPRIETARY INFORMATION NONDISCLOSURE AND NONUSE

Your coaching may well involve discussing and sharing sensitive business information, such as strategic plans, internal reports, presentation drafts, client lists, sales and revenue projections, and personnel data. A general promise from your coach to keep all information confidential, except as otherwise noted, may be assurance enough for you. Or you may want a more specific and explicit understanding. If your coach already has a nondisclosure agreement in effect at the institutional level, which is commonplace with employer-funded services, you need not be concerned with repeating these conditions in your individual agreement. However, if you are a private-pay client, you may want your coach to agree explicitly to nondisclosure and nonuse of your proprietary business information, intellectual property, and trade secrets. Similarly, you may want to stipulate that any materials you've shared are returned to you when your coaching ends.

SESSION CANCELLATION POLICY

The agreement should state policies and any penalties if you cancel a scheduled coaching session or meeting, whether in-person or in a telesession. Especially for cancellations made less than twenty-four hours in advance, you should know if your coach is entitled to charge a fee and, if so, how much.

BURNING QUESTION: IF I HAVE TO CANCEL COACHING SESSIONS SUDDENLY DUE TO CIRCUMSTANCES BEYOND MY CONTROL, WHY SHOULD I BE CHARGED?

If the agreement you have with your coach, either written or verbal, includes a session cancellation policy, you must abide by these terms. If you're liable, you're liable. Consider that your coach sets aside specific times to be available to you. Last-minute cancellations incur opportunity costs for your coach as a result of disrupted business activities. Therefore, even if you cancel for a good reason—say, because your best customer suddenly demands your presence on the opposite coast or the board of directors needs a revised report—you should not expect your coach to bear the financial consequences if your agreement states otherwise.

If the nature of your position or business is such that from time to time you're likely to have to cancel scheduled sessions with little advance notice, hopefully you've already discussed this possibility with your coach. It certainly merits a collaborative solution or agreement up front, as otherwise you might come to resent the coach through no fault of his own. Mind you, a sudden illness or family emergency is a different matter altogether. Most coaches will act with sensitivity and flexibility in such circumstances.

Extension, Renewal, and Termination Policies

Depending on your coaching program's particular format, the agreement may or may not include information about extending or renewing services. For example, retainer-based programs may include instructions regarding renewal terms and timing. First-time clients may be entitled to a trial period with an "off-ramp" clause, allowing them to terminate services early, and without penalty, if they decide that coaching or a particular coach is not for them. (There's no harm in inquiring.) Termination procedures, including the status of any unused prepaid fees or amounts due, should be clarified.

Client and Coach Signatures

A signed and dated agreement is desirable between you and your coach to formalize the engagement terms. For private-pay services, this is the one and only agreement you'll need. However, if services are employer funded, the coach-client agreement is supplemental to the primary contract between your coach and the organization. In this case, it's typically a good idea to provide your employer with a copy.

The list in Table 4.2 summarizes the terms and conditions I've discussed based on who's footing the bill. By now, the distinctions between private-pay and employer-funded programs should be

TABLE 4.2. COACHING CLIENT'S NEED-TO-KNOW LIST.

Details Needed	Private Pay (Primary Agreement)	Employer Funded (Secondary Agreement)
Service provider information	X	X
Service description(s)	X	X
Service fees	X	Discretionary
Payment terms	X	Discretionary
Billable activities and expenses	X	X
Information-sharing guidelines	X	X
Proprietary information nondisclosure by coach	X	Discretionary
Session cancellation policy	X	X
Extension, renewal, and termination policies	X	X

apparent. Items that are marked "Discretionary" refer to terms that your employer may or may not opt to share with you.

SAMPLE AGREEMENTS

We've gone over concepts, terms, and conditions. Now let's see how they might appear in an actual agreement between client and coach. I've provided three examples that address private-pay coaching, telecoaching, and employer-funded coaching, respectively (Exhibits 4.1 to 4.3). You will see that the first two are primary agreements, and the third is a secondary agreement. All three are intended for illustrative purposes only and to give you an idea of the many formats that are possible and common.

EXHIBIT 4.1. SAMPLE COACHING AGREEMENT FOR PRIVATE-PAY SERVICES.

Perfect Coach Services, Inc.
987 Anywhere Avenue
New York, NY 10017

Individual Coaching Services Agreement between (<u>Coach Name</u>) and
(<u>Client Name</u>).

To the Client: The following information describes professional
services and respective roles and responsibilities. Please review the
information carefully.

Service Description(s) and Related Fees

<u>Item 1</u>
Initial assessment battery, inclusive of administration, interpretation,
feedback session

- Fee for item 1: $ <u>XXXX</u>

<u>Item 2</u>
Individual performance coaching, inclusive of in-person and telephone
sessions and collateral activities

- Term   <u>6 months</u>
- Hours per month   <u>4</u>
- Start date   <u>May 1, 2006</u>
- Fee for item 2: $ <u>XXXX</u>

Terms and Conditions

1. *Payment Terms:* Assessment services are prepaid and nonrefundable
   once survey administration has begun. Coaching services are
   due no later than the first day of each month. Unused monthly
   coaching allowances have no rollover privileges and are not
   refundable. A discount of five (5) percent is offered on coaching
   services that are prepaid in full. Accounts more than 30 days
   overdue are subject to a late fee of 1.5 percent per month from
   the original due date.

EXHIBIT 4.1. SAMPLE COACHING AGREEMENT
FOR PRIVATE-PAY SERVICES, *continued*.

2. *Confidentiality and Nondisclosure:* The Coach agrees to hold client information confidential except as required by law or agreed by the parties in writing. The Coach also agrees to take all reasonable precautions to safeguard client information identified as *Proprietary Information* against loss, theft, or inadvertent disclosure and not derive any benefit from the Client's proprietary information. If the Client requests, the Coach will return any written, printed, digital, or facsimile client information the Coach possesses or delete same from computer files, on termination of services.

3. *Session Cancellation Policy:* If you need to reschedule or cancel an in-person session appointment, please give at least 24 hours' advance notice. In-person appointments cancelled less than one business day in advance will be charged against your monthly allowance.

4. *Additional Expenses:* Any extraordinary expenses such as those associated with out-of-town travel, lodging, and long-distance or international telephone charges will be billed to the Client on a pass-through basis and are due on receipt of invoice with documentation.

By signing this form, I acknowledge that I have read and agree to the above information and terms.

Signature _____

Printed Name _____

Address _____

Date _____

Organization _____

_____

EXHIBIT 4.2. SAMPLE COACHING AGREEMENT FOR TELECOACHING SERVICES.

(Coach Name)
Perfect Coach Services, Inc.
987 Anywhere Avenue
New York, NY 10017

Client Name _____

Client Address _____

Client Telephone Number _____

E-Mail Address _____

Coaching Term ___ Months, Start Date _____ End Date _____

Fee $ _____ per Month

Number of Telesessions per Month _____

Duration _____ (length of each telesession)

Terms:
1. Client telephones the Coach for all scheduled telesessions and is responsible for paying any and all long-distance charges.
2. Client pays all coaching fees in advance.
3. Client understands that coaching is designed to facilitate career, professional, or business goals and to develop and carry out a strategy or plan for achieving those goals.
4. Client understands that coaching is not a substitute for professional advice by mental health, financial, legal, or other qualified professionals, nor does coaching involve the treatment or diagnosis of mental health issues.
5. Client understands that information he or she discloses will be held as confidential unless he or she states in writing otherwise, except as required by law.
6. Client may choose to discontinue coaching at any time by advising the Coach of same. Prepaid coaching services that are not used are not refundable under any circumstances. However, Client may elect to freeze services for a period not to exceed 90 calendar days by so advising the Coach.

EXHIBIT 4.2.   SAMPLE COACHING AGREEMENT FOR TELECOACHING SERVICES, *continued*.

Please sign this agreement in the space below, indicating your acceptance of the terms and conditions set forth above. The Coach will return a countersigned copy to you.

I have read and agree to the above terms.

Client Signature _____

Printed Name _____

Date _____

Coach Countersignature _____

EXHIBIT 4.3.   SAMPLE COACHING AGREEMENT FOR EMPLOYER-FUNDED SERVICES.

Perfect Coach Services, Inc.
987 Anywhere Avenue
New York, NY 10017

Re: Individual Leadership Coaching Services

The following information describes what you should know about individual leadership development services and respective roles and responsibilities. Please review the information carefully. If you have any questions or concerns, please do not hesitate to discuss them prior to beginning this professional relationship.

Scope and Purpose of Services
You are receiving our professional services through your Employer for the purpose of improving your work-related managerial and leadership effectiveness. These services are not designed or intended to determine your level of responsibility, compensation, or the duration of your employment.

Information Disclosure and Confidentiality
Your Employer may be advised in general and summary terms of the nature, scope, methods, and objectives of your individual assessment

and coaching program. Prior to providing this information to your Employer, your Coach/Consultant will ordinarily discuss this with you before doing so. However, s/he is not obliged to do so.

If you undertake behavioral or personality assessment as part of your development program, the raw assessment data and related reports are confidential, and require your written authorization before they can be released to any third party, including your Employer.

Exceptions to Confidentiality

Privacy and trust are important aspects of the Executive-Coach relationship. There are, however, certain instances when information received from you must be disclosed as required by law, Employer's rules, or professional relationships. For example, any information that would compromise your Employer's interests, such as illegal activity or intent, is not protected. Any situations involving endangerment to yourself or others must also be disclosed, as required by law.

If You Need to Cancel or Reschedule a Coaching Session

Kindly give at least 24 hours' notice if you need to reschedule or cancel a session or appointment, and *two (2) business days notice prior to scheduled meetings that involve out-of-town travel.* Nonrefundable travel expenses due to cancellation on your part are billable to your Employer, as may be sessions that are cancelled less than one business day in advance.

By signing this form, I acknowledge that I have read and agree to the above information and terms.

Please sign the two copies of this agreement and return for counter endorsement.

_____	_____
Signature	Coach Countersignature
_____	_____
Printed Name	Printed Name
_____	_____
Organization	Organization
_____	_____
Date	Date

KEY POINT: If you don't understand an aspect of the proposed coaching arrangement, whether in written or verbal form, ask for clarification. If you would like something in your agreement to be added or modified, don't hesitate to discuss this with your coach and, where necessary, your coaching sponsor, supervisor, or coach coordinator.

FINAL ANALYSIS

I began this chapter by pointing out that people have different styles when it comes to the details. Don't confuse a written agreement with trusting or not trusting the other party. In fact, it would be foolhardy to embark on a coaching program with an executive coach you don't trust. The agreement provides structure, scope, and clarity to your coaching, as well as defining certain obligations and guidelines. You and your coach formally acknowledge a positive and exciting new relationship. Go ahead and test yourself now on the agreement summary checklist in Exhibit 4.4. By now you should be well familiar with these terms and able to respond with a "Yes" or "Not Applicable" to each of the nine questions. If your completed checklist contains any "No" responses, I recommend that you obtain the missing information so you know exactly what you and your coach are committing to. You can probably do so with a quick telephone call or e-mail.

Borrowing a famous phrase from Winston Churchill, you've now reached the "end of the beginning" that included assessing your coaching readiness, selecting your coach, and finalizing service terms and conditions. I've provided strategies, tips, and sample documents to guide you through these essential preliminaries. Next I'll share a terrific, time-tested coaching system with you. Imagine a model that's like shrink wrap: strong, transparent, and able to conform to almost anything.

EXHIBIT 4.4. AGREEMENT SUMMARY CHECKLIST.

Are the Following Details Covered?	Yes	No	Not Applicable
1. Service provider information			
2. Service description(s)			
3. Service fees			
4. Service payment terms			
5. Billable activities and expenses			
6. Program information sharing and confidentiality guidelines			
7. Proprietary information nondisclosure			
8. Session scheduling and cancellation policies			
9. Program extension, renewal, and termination policies			

CHAPTER FIVE

THE FIVE-STEP COACHING MODEL

"A theory," Albert Einstein said, "is the more impressive . . . the more different are the kinds of things it relates and the more extended the range of its applicability." What if a coaching model existed that was broadly applicable yet highly customizable—that could promote exceptional results whether your program was brief or extended, employer funded or private pay, face-to-face or telecoaching, a fix-it or improve-it situation?

This chapter introduces just such a tool, the Five-Step Coaching Model. Although it draws on scientific techniques, you don't have to be an Einstein to understand how it works. The model is powerful *and* straightforward. Why should you care? Because you will be smarter. Because you will maximize your coaching results. Because you will have a robust process for determining return on investment. Because you can more accurately evaluate your coach when the time comes. Over more than twenty years, I have used it to design hundreds of high-performance programs—for individuals, groups, and organizations.

I tell my clients to think of the Five-Step Coaching Model as the backbone of their coaching program. First, I will explain all five steps. Then I will dip into my client files to illustrate the model's versatility and effectiveness with several extended case studies. You will meet a midcareer banker, a growth-oriented entrepreneur, and a culture-shocked chief information officer.

INTRODUCING A SCIENCE-BASED MODEL

The Five-Step Coaching Model is a structured, data-driven approach to supercharging your coaching program and goals. It is based on sound scientific practices such as crafting clear definitions, obtaining reliable data, using relevant methods, conducting experiments, monitoring, and evaluation.

The five steps are shown in Figure 5.1. Let's look more closely at what each step involves:

- *Step 1: Define.* This involves defining top-level coaching issues, goals, and desired outcomes. I often ask clients, "What will success look like for you?" so we can uncover specific objectives and metrics. Otherwise we might not recognize victory when we achieved it. For example, if an associate-level attorney announced, "I want to make partner when I'm eligible in two years," this would be a clear and actionable goal.

FIGURE 5.1. THE FIVE-STEP COACHING MODEL.

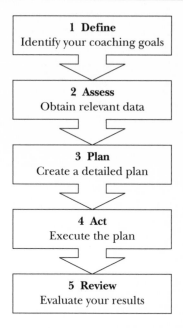

1 Define
Identify your coaching goals

2 Assess
Obtain relevant data

3 Plan
Create a detailed plan

4 Act
Execute the plan

5 Review
Evaluate your results

• *Step 2: Assess.* This step refers to analyzing your business or professional situation. I sometimes refer to it as the diagnostic phase. Data gathering can take many forms, such as reviewing annual performance reviews, conducting an individual behavioral assessment or needs analysis, interviewing third parties, and studying relevant business and organizational documents. The purpose of this step is to obtain valid, timely, and pertinent information on which to base subsequent coaching plans and activities.

• *Step 3: Plan.* This step involves developing your custom action plan. A major goal might get broken down into several component goals. In the case of the law firm associate looking to make partner in two years, her plan might consist of two goals:

1. Improve her rainmaking skills so she can secure at least half a million dollars of new business for the firm.
2. Increase her professional visibility among the firm's partners through strategic assignments and networking.

The plan serves as the coaching road map and consists of specific action steps and target dates for completion. Not only is a specific to-do list created, but accountabilities also get established. A method for measuring final results is also identified. (Chapter Seven will give you the inside scoop on winning action plan tips.)

• *Step 4: Act.* This is the execution phase, where the heavy lifting of achieving your goals occurs. Designated activities and tasks get accomplished. Your coach oversees and facilitates your progress. For example, in the case of the attorney seeking partner status, this could involve reading assignments, role-playing an initial customer meeting, and completing a certain number of new client appointments.

• *Step 5: Review.* The final step deals with evaluating your coaching results. Were your goals attained? Have you realized your definition of coaching success or moved significantly in this direction? If not, why not? In the case of the aspiring partner, has she acquired substantial new clients over the course of her coaching program? Has she raised her visibility and attracted positive attention among the partners in the firm?

In sum, this step determines how much progress has been accomplished. Your review component might also include recommendations for a follow-up strategy so that coaching wins are consolidated and fully capitalized.

WHY YOU SHOULD USE THIS MODEL

My Five-Step Coaching Model may seem familiar to you. Indeed, I hope it is. If you're up to speed with your project management and strategic planning skills, you may have recognized similarities between this model and standard data-based performance systems. What Einstein said about a good theory holds true for a good model: it's widely applicable. Regardless of what technique or tools your coach uses—or whether they are proprietary resources, or what they are called—your coaching program needs to include these five components to qualify for a triple-A rating. So if you're serious about achieving sensational, sustainable results, use this model and make it your own.

Enough theory. Let's look at applications to actual client situations. These include examples of brief targeted coaching, extended coaching, and consultative retainer coaching. In these examples, certain identifying information and attributes have been altered from the actual engagements to ensure client confidentiality. All client names are fictitious.

BRIEF TARGETED COACHING EXAMPLE: SLOWING DOWN TO ZOOM AHEAD

"What's the use of running if you are not on the right road?" a German proverb asks. What indeed. Yet the twenty-first-century workplace can seem like a series of sprints set within an endless marathon. If you're not careful, you can find yourself leading the pack but on the wrong racetrack.

SITUATION

Investment banker Andrew Beamon, an up-and-coming African American executive at a global financial firm, wanted to get the most out of his annual 360-degree survey feedback. His firm, which was deeply committed to talent development and constantly pushed personal advancement, made the services of an external coach available on request for just this purpose. From the organization's perspective, coaching was integral to its holistic approach to performance management and leadership development programs, yielding both short- and long-term dividends. An in-house coaching coordinator prescreened all coaches, coordinated requests and referrals, and oversaw the coach's orientation to the firm and business unit. The firm's standard coaching package was for a maximum of fifteen hours of coaching services provided over three months. Coaches were primarily used to help employees interpret their 360-degree feedback surveys (fully described in Chapter Six) and to create and launch their individual development plans.

When I first met Andrew, he exuded confidence and capability. He was also eager to talk about his 360-degree results, a copy of which I had already read. "Did you see the comment about me being like the Energizer Rabbit?" he asked. "That's definitely me. I just keep on going," he said with obvious pride.

Andrew clearly had a lot going for him. The youngest person his firm had ever sponsored for a prestigious executive M.B.A. program, his early years at the firm had been spent as a stock trader. When his immediate boss and mentor switched to the private banking division, Andrew soon followed. Now in his late thirties and a newly minted managing director, he knew he was one of the firm's designated "100 next-generation leaders."

After telling me about his background and work context, Andrew and I went over his 360-degree survey results. In virtually every category—business acumen, interpersonal relationships, organizational citizenship, developing others—he scored well above average and frequently in the "Outstanding" top 10 percent category. When we'd gone over the entire report, including quantitative rankings and reviewer comments, I asked him about his coaching goals.

"I want to work on my weaknesses," he replied, flipping to the sections he had highlighted.

"Even your lowest ratings are relatively high," I pointed out. "How large an effect would moving the needle on these scores have on your performance and career targets?"

The question took him aback. "I've always gotten better by hammering away at my weaknesses," he said, a perplexed look on his face. "I preach this to my people, and I've always practiced what I preach."

I suggested that we switch tactics briefly. I asked him what he wanted to do next at the firm. Where did he see himself in two or three years?

Andrew proceeded to describe his career ambitions with enthusiasm and clarity.

"Okay, I think I get it," he told me. "I've had tunnel vision. I shouldn't automatically assume that coaching should always focus on the weakest link. I'd be better off focusing on what I'll need to move up to the next level."

APPROACH

Andrew was a top producer for his firm who, true to his Energizer Rabbit reputation, never stopped doing. A power talker whose high energy, industry knowledge, and passion won over clients and colleagues alike, he was accustomed to using his annual 360-degree report as a remedial scorecard even when his lowest ratings were still very strong. He had never considered how to interpret and integrate his survey results with his big-picture strategic goals. This realization uncovered a new and compelling issue for him. "I need to become more aware of what I'm keeping score of," he said. "If something doesn't advance my business or personal goals, I shouldn't be doing it, period."

With this insight, Andrew went back and reread his 360-degree feedback with new eyes. He concluded that his highest-value coaching goal involved becoming more strategic in advancing the business and his career, not just tackling whatever found its way to his PDA. He would need to acquire new habits of reflection and strengthen his time management skills. He also wanted to apply his current strengths, including his leadership abilities, to next-level opportunities. With a three-month time framework, we could get a detailed action plan in place and rolled out. However, I pointed out that we'd need to incorporate procedures and additional partners into the program so he could continue to progress without me. He was fine with this.

With Andrew's permission, I interviewed his supervisor, human resource manager, and executive assistant to build a more comprehensive data mirror on which to design an action plan. Three themes emerged from my fact-finding that underscored and complemented his 360-degree feedback. Andrew should:

- Select business priorities and then stay with them.
- Delegate more responsibility and tasks to subordinates.
- Reduce the number of departmental meetings he called.

Interestingly—and perhaps not surprisingly—these suggestions meshed nicely with his coaching goals, especially in terms of freeing up time to think strategically about priorities and options. Andrew drafted an action plan that consisted of two discrete goals:

- Improve time management skills to allow regular reflection time into his schedule to improve strategic and critical analysis.
- Reengineer the roles and responsibilities of his five direct reports to facilitate delegation of work.

For each goal, he identified specific action steps, people he needed to include in the process (his change partners), and target completion dates.

As it turned out, Andrew accomplished both goals within our program's time framework. Consequently, in our last session, we discussed specific ways to reinforce and support the new attitudes and skills he'd acquired. Lasting change requires a disciplined approach and lots of practice. Andrew worried about slipping back into his old ways of handling whatever problem or request was right in front of him. The biggest benefit of coaching, he told me, was not what he'd expected when he made his initial request: "Going in, I thought I'd work on my weakest areas. But now I'd have to say that learning how to slow down and become selective in my choices and actions has changed my whole approach to realizing my aspirations."

FIVE-STEP COACHING MODEL APPLICATION

Here's how the model informed Andrew's program:

- *Step 1: Define.* Andrew initially defined coaching success in terms of improving his lowest-rated 360-degree performance areas. However, with discussion and reflection, he characterized coaching program success in terms of improved effectiveness in areas with the highest professional payoff.

- *Step 2: Assess.* Several assessment methods were used. First, there was Andrew's 360-degree survey, which his firm had administered and processed. My initial meetings also yielded important information about Andrew's personality and change readiness and his take on departmental dynamics and business drivers. Finally, the interviews I had with his supervisor and key support professionals fleshed out his 360-degree results and the organizational context in which he needed to be successful.
- *Step 3: Plan.* After reviewing all assessment findings collaboratively, Andrew identified two short-term goals with long-term value and impact. Together we crafted a detailed action plan to guide him to achieving them. Andrew then showed the plan to his manager and his manager's manager. Both heartily supported it. His manager in particular was excited about the reengineering of business team roles that Andrew proposed to implement.
- *Step 4: Act.* Andrew got busy executing specific action steps. He brought his direct reports into the reengineering process, which proved to accelerate (rather than impede, which is what he feared) the initiative. His executive assistant was an eager partner in optimizing his time management skills and daily schedule. During our regularly scheduled coaching sessions, some by telephone and some in person, we discussed Andrew's progress.
- *Step 5: Review.* Because this was a brief, three-month program, expectations for progress and change were kept modest. Even so, progress indicators were very positive. Andrew successfully completed both goals associated with his action plan in record time. Aware that his accomplishments were new and still superficial, he used our final meeting to refine a follow-up action plan that would keep him on course.

RESULTS

Andrew subsequently was tapped to head one of the firm's overseas private banking offices, a recognized grooming position and stepping-stone to the "top of the house." While abroad, he developed and rolled out a new investment product that generated millions of dollars in new revenue for the firm. He has been writing his own ticket since.

EXTENDED COACHING EXAMPLE I: GROWING PAINS

"Entrepreneurs are simply those who understand that there is little difference between obstacle and opportunity," Machiavelli noted five hundred years ago. The following story shows how the Five-Step Coaching Model informed one gifted entrepreneur's extended program.

SITUATION

Tom Peterson, the CEO and owner of a thriving specialty electronics company, loved to ride his Harley-Davidson to work. Little did he know that when he bought out a competitor, he was shifting gear from incremental to radical growth. Overnight, his company, which had net sales of $18 million the previous year, almost doubled its head count and increased its customer base by 40 percent. The acquisition also meant taking on long-term debt for the first time, something Tom was still adjusting to psychologically. Even so, he brimmed with enthusiasm and optimism. "I'm really excited about the possibilities, but we need to reorganize and reach cruising speed quickly," he told me. "There are a number of big contracts coming up that we have our sights on. Plus, now that we're well past the fifty-employee mark, we're subject to all sorts of new regulations, so there's more bureaucracy. At times there just doesn't seem to be enough of me to go around."

Everywhere Tom looked he saw decisions to make about company integration: business tracking and accounting systems, production and inventory monitoring, employee benefits, new marketing initiatives. To top matters off, his trusted number two person, whom he'd intended to promote to chief operating officer, had decided to return to his native Australia. The number of business advisers he needed had also mushroomed.

Several members of his local presidents roundtable shared their own experiences with leadership coaching and suggested that he work with an executive coach.

"Who'd have thought I'd work with a consultant to help me deal with all the other consultants I'm working with," Tom told me. A fit, methodical man in his late fifties, he wore the official high-tech uniform: open-collared shirt and khakis. "I've grown up with this industry. I know it inside out," he continued. "I've always had a good nose for where it's heading. That's why I knew we had to scale up through acquisition to stay competitive. 'Eat or be eaten.'"

"What's your greatest concern? What keeps you awake at night?" I asked.

"My greatest concern is this: How do I continue to run this show on a daily basis? I sure don't want to spin out at the first sharp curve in the road."

APPROACH

With his company's rapid growth through acquisition, Tom knew he needed to make a quantum leap in his leadership and change management skills to stay successful. Until this point, he had relied on his trade association and business roundtable group for continuing management education. Now he needed intensive, rapid assistance to make good on his company's enhanced business platform. Since he was both the economic buyer and the coaching client, there were only two parties to the program agreement. (True, technically this was an employer-funded program since the company paid for coaching services. However the distinction between private-pay and employer-funded arrangements can lose its significance when dealing with small business owners and entrepreneurs. In this instance, for practical purposes Tom and the company were one.)

The challenge Tom faced was akin to learning how to drive his motorcycle not on smooth highway tarmac but off-road under constantly changing conditions. Accelerating his leadership skills so he could accelerate his company would take a commitment of approximately twelve to eighteen months, I told him, and maybe more. Mergers and acquisitions typically take this long or longer to complete and are notorious for being messy under the best of circumstances. Besides, who knew what management and business issues might emerge along the way?

"You're not just my business coach," he replied evenly. "You're part of my overall risk management strategy."

FIVE-STEP COACHING MODEL APPLICATION

Here's how the model guided Tom's extended program:

- *Step 1: Define.* For starters, Tom defined coaching success broadly to mean that he would be able to oversee the integration of the two companies in a timely fashion and without losing any key talent. Success for him meant that he'd be able to do what he needed to do to execute his business plan over the next two to six business quarters.
- *Step 2: Assess.* Tom undertook a personalized behavioral assessment battery, the better for both of us to understand his professional and personal background and particular work, thinking, and communication styles. Two days of shadowing Tom at work yielded additional valuable information. I interviewed a cross-section of company stakeholders, including employees and lead customers, plus other interested parties such as business peers. We reviewed the accumulated data to identify Tom's strengths, behavioral style preferences, and potential blind spots. Tom was surprised to discover that staff perceived him to be conflict avoidant when it came to handling people problems in the company.
- *Step 3: Plan.* Tom's first action plan draft reflected his eagerness to race ahead with company integration and assimilation activities. He listed six individual goals, not the suggested two or three, which read like an execution to-do list. Although these were all pragmatic and sharply focused on business objectives, I suggested that he might want to take a step back and consider the "what" before the "how." For example, what kind of leader did he want and need to be? Could he articulate his vision for a high-performance culture in the postmerger company? What leadership competencies would get him there? Tom went back to the drawing board and produced a very different action plan consisting of the following goals:

1. Upgrade his communication style and habits to keep employees and customers fully engaged
2. Strengthen his skills to build and lead a winning management team
3. Improve his ability to make tough or unpopular decisions in a timely and transparent manner

We now had a clearer picture and road map to coaching success. Tom's program included both structured elements, such as scheduled sessions and related assignments, and a just-in-time feature for us to communicate on an as-needed basis.

• *Step 4: Act.* Our coaching work took into consideration the fluid nature of his role and responsibilities as company owner and chief executive officer. To jump-start his learning, I prepared a customized reading list that targeted skills or issues he wanted to master. Multiple detailed action steps created a path to accomplishing each goal. We used his operational to-do list as the basis for action learning experiments. Real-time consultation and debriefing augmented our regularly scheduled coaching sessions. In this way, Tom had a sounding board and got "news he could use" when he actually needed it. Of course, he had no shortage of opportunities to try out new behaviors and approaches.

• *Step 5: Review.* Given the extended nature of Tom's coaching, both interim and summary reviews were built into his program. At six and twelve months, we examined the progress indicators he had identified at the start in his action plan. At the twelve-month mark, Tom put himself on the line by undergoing his first-ever performance evaluation. Although he worried that his management team would be less than candid with their feedback, this proved not to be the case. Moreover, his survey results provided a rich catalogue of specific instances and examples of performance excellence. Especially noteworthy were his strong ratings in communication and motivating others, areas that were vital to the company's post-merger business and management success.

RESULTS

At the time his custom program ended a year and a half later, Tom was celebrating on several fronts. The loss of his number two person had actually proved a blessing in disguise, since it allowed Tom to build a more balanced senior management team. He hired outsiders to oversee the human resource and information systems functions. He devoted significantly more of his time to being the outward face of the company with clients and the community. He came to relish and seek out public speaking opportunities for the first time in his life. A new multimillion-dollar contract was in the bag. A competitor was sending out feelers about a possible sale. Venture capitalists and bankers were constantly trying to get on his calendar. "You know you're successful when they need you more than you need them," Tom wryly observed. Some months later, his regional trade association recognized him as their Business Person of the Year.

Tom embodied many characteristics of the successful entrepreneur: dedication, resilience, flexibility, and hard work. When I asked him to calculate the return on investment of his coaching program, he looked at me over his reading glasses and shook his head. "If I did, I'd have to call one of those VCs [venture capital firms] in order to pay you."

Extended Coaching Example II: Reboot Camp

When it comes to major change, whether it involves individual, team, or organizational performance, things can sometimes look like a failure in the middle. Indeed, Winston Churchill went so far as to characterize success as "the ability to go from one failure to another with no loss of enthusiasm." This next case required the client to relinquish core beliefs and acquire a more appropriate (and effective) repertoire of interpersonal skills. Progress was by no means linear. In fact, performance even dipped for a short period.

Situation

Val Martinez was the new chief information officer (CIO) at a nonprofit multisite health care organization. Her track record on upgrading information technology (IT) systems had impressed the chief executive officer and board at a time when they were considering a multimillion dollar investment in next-generation equipment and software. However, after two executive sessions where she castigated other attendees, the CEO called her on the carpet. Her style needed to change pronto. "She has a tendency to put people down to make her point," the director told me by way of background. "That might have worked for her in her last job, but it doesn't play here." He characterized her as a "diamond in the rough."

Val saw things otherwise. "I've been remanded to charm school," she said by way of breaking the ice at our first meeting. While skeptical about how coaching could help her, Val had prepared for our meeting by doing an online search of the subject. When I asked her what she would consider a successful outcome, she quickly replied, "To do the best possible job. Second-best is not an option." In her next breath, she recited a litany of the many obstacles in her way, including "lazy" staff, poor standards and work quality, and too many meetings. "How am I supposed to be successful under these conditions?" she asked plaintively.

What followed was a wide-ranging discussion of the challenges of her new job, what she saw her mandate to be, and her former job experiences. Prior to joining the nonprofit organization, Val had spent her entire professional life in industry, working her way up the corporate ladder at a pharmaceutical company widely known for its intense, competitive culture. Bitterly disappointed when an outsider was hired over her for an officer-level position, she had decided on a radical career change to the nonprofit world. Her strategy in taking the CIO position was to become a bigger fish in a smaller pond.

Though in her early forties, Val had known only one other employer—her previous company. In her former position, projects typically got done by "ordering or shouting, or sometimes both." Consequently she'd been exposed to only one management style: command and control.

She interviewed several coaches before expressing a desire to proceed with me. I pulled no punches with her before agreeing to be her coach. I pointed out that similar to a computer reloading its operating system to start afresh, she needed to reboot as a manager in order to succeed.

APPROACH

This engagement was first and foremost an "on-boarding," or executive transition, project. A newcomer to both hospital administration and nonprofit operations, Val was a stranger in a strange land. Like many other strangers, she brought her own beliefs and customs with her. (Consider that the words *alienate* and *alien* both derive from Latin roots meaning "set apart" or "different.") She needed to acquire an understanding and appreciation of the organization's distinctive culture or risk being rejected by it. In short, she needed to think and act differently. These objectives involved a substantial learning agenda, not the least because Val would have to unlearn attitudes and habits that had served her well until now. Furthermore, based on her many criticisms of her administrative and technical staff, I wondered if Val really saw her own behavior as ineffective or problematic.

In any case, the CEO and board were both enthusiastic about supporting Val's success in the job. Even she sounded more positive as we got under way. "My husband also thinks I can be too sharp," she said sheepishly. "I guess I'm not aware of how I come across."

FIVE-STEP COACHING MODEL APPLICATION

Val's program was pegged at twelve months, with the option of extension on an as-needed basis. Here is how it unfolded:

• *Step 1: Define.* Val and her supervisor, the CEO, defined coaching success collaboratively to mean that she would be able to develop and promote effective working relationships with her superiors, colleagues, and staff. "I'll know it when I see it," the CEO told me.

• *Step 2: Assess.* Val completed a personalized behavioral battery that included emotional intelligence and general personality surveys. Given the interpersonal nature of her coaching goals, opinion data were obtained from everyone who interacted with her regularly. In addition, I observed her in a variety of work settings, including her own departmental meetings. The feedback from others was remarkably consistent: Val was perceived as a talented "technician" who bullied people and made them feel stupid. The "B-word" tentatively reared its head in connection with her. Observing Val in action, I saw firsthand how she could use her tongue as a blunt instrument when she was frustrated with someone or something. These were automatic behaviors born of habit. Plenty of work lay ahead for us. Fortunately, Val's keen intelligence, curiosity, and achievement orientation were powerful allies.

• *Step 3: Plan.* Val's action plan could be summarized by the phrase, "Out with the old, in with the new." She needed to jettison outmoded behaviors, and the attitudes and beliefs that drove them, and replace them with a more functional repertoire. Her specific goals were:

1. Acquire effective communication techniques and strategies for building critical working partnerships
2. Improve her own coaching skills to enhance staff morale and performance

She decided to go public with her goals and shared them with her direct reports. This had an immediate, salutary effect, as they regarded her disclosure as the first signs of trust and positive regard.

• *Step 4: Act.* Val was out to prove that she could change. Nevertheless, she found that modifying her behavior was difficult and stressful. Her habits and reactions reflected her ingrained attitudes and values. We had to uncover and test cherished assumptions she held about what constituted acceptable work standards, commitment, and professionalism. Val, it turned out, held many "shoulds" to be self-evident. She tended to apply perfectionistic standards globally, whether the situation or solution warranted it.

With the aid of a journal, she kept track of events that triggered reactions and responses that she wanted to eliminate. Insight into cause-and-effect caused her to reevaluate the validity and usefulness of her attitudes, allowing her to look with fresh eyes at how things there were done. For example, she stopped using her former employer as her standard of comparison. These were all important progress indicators.

In the early months of executing her action plan, Val hit a wall. With insight, she became extremely self-conscious about everything she did. She was aware of how she didn't want to act, but did not yet have a full-functioning repertoire of replacement skills to use instead. This learning lag is common and temporary in coaching, and one that peak performers like Val often have a hard time tolerating. She complained about feeling stymied and second-guessing herself. At one point she was so frustrated with how she handled a presentation to the board that she talked about chucking coaching altogether. The CEO's support and involvement at this juncture proved critical. A pep talk from him restored her confidence and fortitude. She persevered through and out of her performance dip, showing courage and risk taking in the process.

• *Step 5: Review.* Val's program lasted nineteen months. A 360-degree-style survey was administered at the sixteen-month point. Feedback revealed significant improvement in the areas of team building, developing others, and leading by example. The remainder of

the program focused on consolidating and reinforcing these accomplishments. Val's greatest lesson learned, she said, was, "Being a
drill sergeant is not the same as being a leader."

RESULTS

Val underwent nothing short of a seismic attitude shift in how she
viewed herself as a supervisor and leader. Her coaching program
guided her through the acquisition of an entirely new leadership per-
sona. Once she stopped behaving in ways that undermined people's
self-esteem and trust, a different interpersonal vista opened before
her. She was able to get into sync with her department, her peers, and
the organization's culture. Discharging her business role and responsibilities then proceeded on all cylinders. Val exceeded timetables
and expectations in rolling out a scalable and cost-effective information systems upgrade. Word got out of her successes, and she was fea-
tured in a prominent industry publication. Several foundation
directorships followed. Eventually she returned to the for-profit arena
as the chief information officer of a public company.

CONSULTATIVE RETAINER EXAMPLE: SOUNDINGS

Retainer-based arrangements are commonplace in many professional services, including law, accounting, and management consulting. Typically the client pays a set fee for so many hours of expert
service or advice per month, or one flat fee for unlimited consultation during a specified period of time. In return, the client has access to the professional's (or the firm's) "smarts." (I'm not using the
term *retainer* to mean an initial deposit payment against total expenses incurred.)

When it comes to executive and business coaching, retainer arrangements usually occur after an initial coaching program has
ended. A solid foundation of trust and regard is already in place.
The client has been able to determine the coach's value-added
contribution and seeks to continue the relationship, though in a
less structured or intensive format. Retainer arrangements work
especially well when the client wants real-time, on-call contact with
a coach on an as-needed basis. I call these arrangements "consultative retainers" because clients get support, advice, and account-

ability around emergent issues and events. For a coach to be highly effective in this role requires prior knowledge of the client and the client's business context.

To show how the Five-Step Coaching Model informs a retainer-based program, we turn back to Tom Peterson, CEO of a fast-growing electronics company whose extended coaching program has already been described in this chapter. Let's fast-forward a few years and pick up Act Two of Tom's story.

SITUATION

A lot changed for Tom and his company after we worked together. He engineered two more acquisitions, one of which extended the company's product line into a completely new market. He had turned sixty the previous year. His oldest son, a certified public accountant, was now chief operating officer (COO) and ran the business day-to-day.

When he called me one day, Tom sounded upbeat and satisfied. "I've got a few things on my radar, though," he said. "Some decisions about the company's future. We went public, did you know? Closely held, of course. I'm still the principal owner."

He came straight to the point when I asked how I could be of help. "There are things about the business I'm not ready to discuss with my son. And my wife is certainly not objective on this score either. I got to thinking that I could use a sounding board now and then, someone who knows how I think and doesn't pull any punches. So what do you say?"

APPROACH

Tom had no preset coaching agenda. Rather, he wanted to be able to contact me on an occasional, as-needed basis. "Coaching Lite," he called it. In any case, this scenario was ideal for a retainer-based program.

FIVE-STEP COACHING MODEL APPLICATION

Although this engagement was unstructured and even free form compared to Tom's previous coaching program, it nevertheless drew on the Five-Step Coaching Model format:

- *Step 1: Define.* Tom defined his program goal in terms of improved strategic thinking and decision making. He equated coaching success with rendering optimal business decisions on select issues.
- *Step 2: Assess.* Tom and I spent a session in which he updated me on significant personal and business developments. Together we composed a list of pertinent background documents for my review. These included management committee minutes, strategic plans, organization charts, and a recent employee climate survey. In this way I had current reference points for our work together.
- *Step 3: Plan.* The phrase "PRN basis" is most commonly associated with administering medical treatments. An acronym for the Latin phrase *pro re nata,* it means "as the situation demands." It's also an apt description of Tom's coaching program, since he was responsible for initiating contact as the situation required or he saw fit. We did build in a fallback mechanism, agreeing that I would get in touch if I did not hear from him every six weeks. We also agreed that in-person contact was the optimal communication mode, with the understanding that this might not always be possible or practicable.
- *Step 4: Act.* Tom sought an expert, confidential, and unbiased third party to discuss the occasional complex or thorny issue. In the following months, we explored a number of sensitive business and career decisions, including:

- Specific interactions with the company's other major shareholders
- Top-level business succession planning
- First thoughts about preparing an exit strategy for himself

Being a highly self-directed person, Tom used our retainer relationship as a means to test and refine his thinking. He was able to discuss complexities associated with the family business life cycle and to preview various strategies and approaches. My role in this process was as sounding board, cheerleader, and devil's advocate. Contacts ranged from telephone calls to scheduled half-day meetings.

- *Step 5: Review.* Tom found this consultative retainer approach suited both his business needs and his personal preference for "just-in-time" access. In this case, rating the program's success involved one person's subjective opinion: his. Tom had stated at the start a desire to optimize his strategic thinking and decision making on an issue-by-issue basis. Did he think the retainer program had helped him achieve this goal?

As it happened, Tom's evaluation was very positive. He cited high satisfaction with what coaching had provided for him. Although he positively thrived on what he did, being the boss had a lonely side, he remarked. Having the opportunity to engage in open and deep dialogue from time to time was just what he wanted. "The actions I *didn't* take as a result of talking things through were just as important as the ones I did," he noted.

RESULTS

Tom backed away from plans to retire any time soon. Instead, he and his son worked together on a long-term strategic succession plan for the company. Tom oversaw its actualization, all the while keeping an eye out for additional business growth opportunities.

FINAL ANALYSIS

You've discovered a powerful and adaptable framework in the Five-Step Coaching Model. You've been introduced to the exciting possibilities of made-to-measure leadership development through sample coaching vignettes. You know what components a high-octane program—yours—should include. If you and your coach use this systematic approach, no matter by what name, the two of you will recognize success when you see it. You will also be able to demonstrate bottom-line value to yourself and any sponsors.

J. P. Morgan once said, "The wise man bridges the gap by laying out the path by means of which he can get from where he is to where he wants to go." I've laid out a time-tested path out for you. Let's take a closer look at what you need to master the individual steps or phases. We've already discussed step 1, defining your goals, in earlier chapters dealing with coaching readiness and coach selection. We have traction. Now we'll take the mystery (and anxiety) out of the remaining four steps, starting with the assessment phase.

CHAPTER SIX

ASSESS FOR SUCCESS

Whenever the stakes are high, operating on the basis of hard data, not instinct or selective impressions, is essential. Indeed, a robust fact-finding process is necessary to produce the best possible plans and outcomes. Physicians use clinical diagnostic tests, attorneys have the pretrial discovery process, and pilots perform preflight checks. Athletes and their coaches pore over videorecordings. The same principle applies to your coaching program: a comprehensive fact-finding phase is key to achieving maximum results.

We will take an in-depth look in this chapter of what assessment, the second phase of the Five-Step Coaching Model, involves. I will show you what types of performance-related data are commonly important to obtain, and why. I'll give you a clear overview of common assessment methods and tools and the rationale behind them. I will also give you pointers on what to expect with personality and 360-degree surveys. Finally, you will hear what three leaders from very different backgrounds shared with me about the importance of self-knowledge. Along the way I'll tell you about exciting developments in leadership and behavioral research. My bet is that you'll come away with an appreciation of the benefits and advantages that robust diagnostics bring. Plus, you'll get every ounce of value from your coaching program.

THE ASSESSMENT ADVANTAGE

You might ask, "Why bother with assessment activities when I already have a good picture of my coaching goals and situational context? Besides, I know myself better than anyone else does."

Let's be clear that gathering additional information is not about doubting you or your opinions. Rather, it's about complementing your subjective appraisal with additional expertise, data sets, and interpretations. For instance, when you see your physician about some complaint, you may have an idea of what's going on. However, your doctor is likely to want objective criteria, such as an X-ray or blood analysis, to confirm or rule out conditions with greater certainty. Diagnostic tests might even reveal something unexpected or additional. Similarly, if you work with a golf or tennis pro to improve your game, he or she will want to see you in action, not just proceed on the basis of your verbal analysis.

When it comes to executive coaching, many accurate diagnostic tools exist that will enable you and your coach to obtain important data efficiently. The time and expense associated with this second step of the Five-Step Coaching Model will pay off handsomely. Here's how you can specifically profit:

Eight Benefits of an Assessment Phase

1. Establish your baseline performance levels so you can chart progress over time.
2. Ascertain that your coaching goals are accurate and attainable.
3. Confirm that your objectives are the highest-value ones to pursue.
4. Test your assumptions, perceptions, and beliefs against other data points.
5. Identify your personal style and relative strengths and weaknesses.
6. Differentiate between performance symptoms and root causes.
7. Reveal blind spots or systems barriers that can have an impact on goal attainment.
8. Incorporate specific behavioral and situational considerations into your program.

No matter how well you know yourself and your coaching goals, yours is still only one perspective, one point of view. William James, a pioneering American psychologist (and brother of novelist Henry James), is commonly credited with saying, "Whenever two people meet, there are really six people present. There is each man as he sees himself, each man as the other person sees him, and each man as he really is." Your coaching program is more certain of success the more it incorporates multiple perspectives. Otherwise you run the risk of acting on faulty or incomplete information, wasting time and money, and achieving subpar results. To make the case further, I'll quote another celebrated nineteenth-century figure, Benjamin Disraeli: "To be conscious that you are ignorant of the facts is a great step to knowledge."

To operate at a peak performance level you need a feedback-rich system. Consider your views and opinions as valuable, but remember that they're a narrow slice of the panoramic vista known as reality.

It's a 360-Degree World

Assessment can contribute to your self-awareness and self-knowledge, thereby improving your professional effectiveness and scalability. What types of data are important to obtain? Based on my twenty-plus years of hands-on management consulting experience, I believe you and your coach need data drawn from three areas:

- Personal context—how you see yourself
- Interpersonal context—how others see you
- Situational context—your professional and career context

With this information in hand, you and your coach can create a comprehensive 360-degree data mirror (see Figure 6.1).

A 360-degree perspective enables you to see things that you might otherwise not see. Imagine that you're driving in rush-hour traffic and about to change lanes when suddenly a loud warning honk comes from nowhere. You quickly swerve back into your lane, aware now that another car is traveling in your side mirror's blind spot. Remember that moment of panic when you realized that you might have caused an accident? While you didn't mean to endanger anyone, you were operating on the basis of incomplete information. You needed to be able to see the situation from all angles. You needed a full 360-degree perspective.

Similarly, with respect to your coaching program, a 360-degree data mirror produces the fullest perspective for decision making and planning. Let's take a closer look at the types of information your data mirror should ideally capture and reveal:

FIGURE 6.1. 360-DEGREE DATA MIRROR.

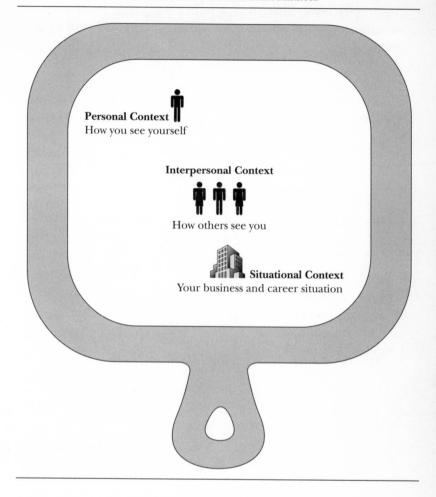

- *Personal context.* Information regarding your personality, sense of self, aptitudes, learning and working styles, beliefs, perceptions, values, life experiences, and lifestyle falls into this category.
- *Interpersonal context.* What do other people think of you? This category includes perceptions, opinions, and beliefs that others have of you.
- *Situational context.* What are your actual professional roles and responsibilities? Your operational realities at work? This

category encompasses organizational and broader market conditions. It can also include personal lifestyle and family variables as they pertain to your on-the-job performance and prospects.

Don't be daunted if this seems like a massive amount of information. In actuality, your coach will do much of the sifting and synthesizing, so the two of you can zoom in on what really matters to you.

Circumstances may not always permit creating a complete 360-degree data mirror. However, the wider the angle is, the more thorough your assessment will be. Among the standard information-gathering methods and collateral documents your coach may consider are these:

- Interviews
- Opinion surveys
- Direct observation
- Personality and behavioral assessment
- Position descriptions and performance appraisals
- Business documents

As you can see, some of the resources on this list are likely to be sitting in a file cabinet or on a computer hard drive, ready for consultation. Now let's take a closer look.

- *Interviews.* Sitting down with people one-on-one or in small groups is a common fact-finding technique. For starters, your coach may put you through a structured interview to develop a comprehensive profile of your past and current activities, accomplishments, and aspirations. Your coach may meet with others as well, such as your manager, business partners, subordinates, peers, board directors, mentors, and customers. Under certain circumstances, family members might be interviewed.
- *Opinion surveys.* When it comes to opinion surveys, the sky's the limit concerning what they can address. For coaching purposes, surveys that capture information from people you work with

or other stakeholders, such as customers, clients, and sponsors, can be helpful. Other types of opinion surveys include customer satisfaction studies, organizational climate and culture studies, and the popular 360-degree feedback report (also known as a multisource or multirater feedback survey). Depending on the specific nature of the survey, your coach can discover how others see you (the interpersonal context) or get a handle on business issues affecting your professional performance (the situational context). For example, someone coaching an executive or line manager would be interested in reviewing the results of any recent company climate or employee satisfaction studies.

• *Direct observation.* Often direct observation is the hands-down choice for collecting key information. There's no substitute for seeing you in action, whether in practice or on the job. While this option may not always be part of your coaching arrangement or objectives, it can be a powerful and efficient assessment technique. Much like a sports or musical coach, a skilled executive coach can identify what's working well (and develop it) and what needs to change. If you're doing strictly telecoaching, videotaping may be a next-best option if your coach is amenable to reviewing the material.

• *Personality and behavioral assessment.* Are you an extrovert or an introvert? Action oriented or reflective? Cued into other people's moods or clueless? A wide range of assessment tools is available to help determine your personal style and work traits in areas such as communication, problem solving, and conflict resolution. These range from off-the-shelf products to state-of-the-art customized assessment suites. They can be extremely valuable in shedding light on how you see yourself (your personal context). Depending on your coaching objectives, the scope of your program, and your coach's professional training, scientifically validated surveys, also known as psychometric tools, are available that look at key personality factors, emotional intelligence, stress management, occupational preferences, communication and conflict resolution skills, and other areas.

• *Position descriptions and performance appraisals.* What are your roles and responsibilities? Have they recently changed, or are they about to change? A position description can explain important aspects of your situational context. Your annual performance appraisal can show how others, and particularly your manager, regard your ability to execute against expectations. Both can be useful.

- *Business documents.* Strategic plans, analyses, and internal reports can provide situational context. They flesh out the operational realities (or potentialities) that your coaching program is intended to facilitate and enhance. If, for example, part of your job mandate is to roll out a new business model, your coach would want to know the game plan in as much detail as possible (assuming there *is* a game plan; the "build-it-as-you-go" management challenge is one reason that "just-in-time" coaching is so valuable).

Of course, assessment methods vary depending on the scope of your program. Not all methods may be appropriate or feasible in your case. This is especially the case with telecoaching and certain types of highly targeted or time-limited engagements.

KEY POINT: Your data mirror should capture and reflect information that's specific to your coaching goals. Relevance is key. Seasoned coaches know what's important at this stage and how to obtain it.

LEADER SPOTLIGHT
Kevin Roberts
Global Chief Executive Officer, Saatchi & Saatchi

Kevin Roberts, CEO of the giant global Saatchi & Saatchi advertising agency, is passionate about self-knowledge. Born and raised in England, his first job was with Mary Quant, a fashion icon in the 1960s. Senior positions at Gillette and Procter & Gamble followed. Before taking the helm at Saatchi, he was CEO of Pepsi-Cola in Canada. Sitting in his Manhattan office overlooking the Hudson River, Roberts spoke about his personal career and leadership philosophy.

"If you don't know yourself, what are you going to do? How are you going to change, coach, nurture, mentor, and inspire unless you've done that for yourself? It really is about getting your personal purpose sorted and then linking that to the purpose of the company to see if they're in sync or not. A lot of the times they're not.

"There are really only two questions I have to ask of myself. First, when am I at my very best? Second, what will I never do? Here at Saatchi & Saatchi, we share these questions with everyone we work with. Asking people when they're at their very best is an amazing thing because you spend the first two hours on that question listening to rubbish. 'Well, I'm at my best at times of crisis,' which nobody really is. Yeah, great, probably not true but nonetheless very interesting. *Now when are you really, really at your best?* The Peter Principle is right [in an organization, each person rises to the level of his own incompetence]. It's driven by people not digging deep into their hearts about when they're at their best—and then not sharing that with their job director and with their people. So that's why you've got great salesmen and great marketers who become lousy general managers. Nothing is worth becoming second to yourself."

I asked Roberts to answer these two questions himself, which he did with enthusiasm and candor.

"I'm at my best when I'm in a team as long as I'm the captain of the team. So I look for situations where I can play with a team and influence people because I'm really good at it.

"I'm at my best when I don't have a boss but when I have a coach or mentor." He laughed. "I am definitely not my best when I'm on my own without one. Hopeless. I have a hands-on mentor who works with me forty-five days a year. He provides me with counsel, guidance, perspective, and support. And I tell him everything."

He continued. "Now about the other question: *What will you never, ever do?* Myself? I would never leave New Zealand where my family lives now. So when I was asked to run the global company and it was suggested I could live in New York City, I said 'I can't.' Why? Well, I've got this list. It says, 'Things I'll Never Do.' I'll never leave New Zealand. So we sorted that out and I still live in New Zealand."

Roberts, who at age seventeen was captain of a prominent English rugby team, also shared his view of the leader as coach: "My success is actually making someone leave my room vow to do something that they never dreamed possible, or just perform better than they did when they came in. That turns me on more than anything in the whole world. I think that there's nothing better than seeing someone just do something they thought they couldn't. You go, man, look at that, that was so great!"

Leading Minds on Self-Awareness

"The unexamined life is not worth living."—*Socrates*

"Everyone should know his character and inclinations, and should be a rigorous judge of his strengths and weaknesses."—*Cicero*

"He who knows others is clever; he who knows himself is enlightened."—*Lao Tzu*

"Knowledge of the self is the mother of all knowledge." —*Khalil Gibran*

"Not to have control over the senses is like sailing in a rudderless ship, bound to break to pieces on coming in contact with the very first rock."—*Mahatma Gandhi*

"Too many people overvalue what they are not and under-value what they are."—*Malcolm S. Forbes*

"I think self-awareness is probably the most important thing towards being a champion."—*Billie Jean King*

"Know yourself. Don't accept your dog's admiration as con-clusive evidence that you are wonderful."—*Ann Landers*

◆ ◆ ◆

BURNING QUESTION: WHAT IF I DON'T WANT ANYONE TO KNOW I'M WORKING WITH A COACH?

Complete privacy may be feasible if you're paying for coaching personally or if you're both the client and the sole economic buyer. In either case, you can arrange to meet away from your business premises or opt exclusively for telecoaching. Otherwise, at the bare minimum whoever is funding your coaching—supervisor, mentor, or human resource manager—is bound to know. A key question to consider is this: Would a total blackout serve your coaching goals? If you're evaluating your career direction or strategy, getting input from others may not be essential. But if you're looking to improve your negotiation skills, working with a coach under wraps can be like painting a room in the dark: you might get the job done, but the results are likely to be spotty and inconsistent.

Without multiple viewpoints and feedback, you and your coach are working with a very narrow, and possibly distorted, data mirror. Truth be told, we're not always the most accurate or reliable observers of our own behavior. If secrecy is important to you, ask yourself why. Is it for a legitimate reason, such as career or employment transition, or does it concern irrational fear or misplaced pride?

Sometimes you need to take a risk to become more than what you are now.

THE POWER OF PERSONALITY ASSESSMENTS

You have to be self-aware before you can understand yourself. This is where personality and behavioral testing comes in. Although they're commonly called "tests," there are no right or wrong answers. You can't "fail." I'm emphatically not referring to ink blots, dream analysis, IQ tests, clinical screening, or pop psychology quizzes. I'm talking about personality and style inventories that measure normal traits, preferences, and work-related behavior. Think of these surveys as comparable to a baseline diagnostic, such as a routine electrocardiogram. You have no cause for trepidation or worry.

Literally hundreds of proprietary assessment tools are available for just about every conceivable career and work-related purpose. I will mention a few of the most popular surveys. I'm not endorsing any particular instrument or set of instruments. Just as different vitamin manufacturers can produce equally effective products, so too can different test developers produce valid and reliable personality surveys. In both cases, it's product quality that is important. And appropriateness. After all, if you need vitamin C, taking vitamin E won't do the trick.

One group of surveys takes a "type" approach to personality, identifying a person's traits and preferred style across several dimensions. Two of the better-known type surveys are the Myers-Briggs Type Indicator (MBTI) and the Fundamental Interpersonal Relations Orientation-Behavior Survey (FIRO-B).

LEADER SPOTLIGHT
John H. Marburger III
U.S. Presidential Science Adviser and Former President,
Stony Brook University

Over a distinguished four-decade career in science and academic administration, John H. Marburger III has served as president of Stony Brook University and director of Brookhaven National Laboratory. In 2001 he became presidential science adviser and director of the White House Office of Science and Technology Policy. I had the privilege of working with Marburger during his tenure at Brookhaven National Laboratory. From Washington, D.C., he shared his views with me about the importance of self-understanding to effective leadership.

"You need a vision of what you personally want out of a leadership role," he said. "Do you want to make history? Do you want to make the organization more effective? Is there one big project you want to accomplish? Do you want to build foundations so the organization will be more effective in the future? Do you just want more money? How you conduct yourself as a leader depends on what you are trying to do. Your own personality and personal experience will affect and limit your choices here."

According to Marburger, effective leadership is always situational leadership. "Effective leadership doesn't occur in a vacuum. Leadership qualities differ in different organizations or institutions. Successful leadership as an environmental advocate, for example, requires a very different pattern of behavior from leadership as a legislator or as the CEO of a small company. So it's necessary to have some vision of the type of organization in which your career path will develop.

"The most difficult challenges to leadership are always personal weaknesses," he said. "My own natural inclination is to analyze when I should be acting. I try to overcome this by having action-oriented people on my staff who continually propose specific proactive measures I could be taking.

"I believe in conscious competence. I think unconscious competence is dangerous. That's the real pitfall when you think you've just got it right. You're sort of instinctively flowing along in a Zen-like state performing excellently. That's when your competitors are out there doing something else that you hadn't thought of."

Other personality assessments commonly used in coaching situations are the NEO Personality Inventory (NEO-PI), the 16 Personality Factor Survey (16 PF), the Guilford-Zimmerman Temperament Survey (GZTS), and the Hogan Development Survey (HDS).

Career and occupational planning surveys include the Strong Interest Inventory and the Campbell Interest and Skill Inventory. And surveys of emotional intelligence include the Bar-On Emotional Quotient Inventory (EQ-iTM) and the Emotional Competence Inventory (ECI).

These are just a few of the many personality and interest tools available to trained professionals. Among popular off-the-shelf products that anyone can administer or take is the DISC Profile, an acronym for the four dimensions of Dominance-Influence-Steadiness-Conscientiousness.

Most personality surveys are multiple-choice questionnaires that can be completed securely online at a convenient time and place. Expect to spend between fifteen and forty-five minutes, depending on the instrument. A comprehensive battery of several complementary surveys can take several hours to complete, a solid investment comparable to undergoing an intensive health or financial checkup. Usually you will receive one or more explanatory reports that you and your coach can review and discuss together.

How do you benefit? First, your signature style and traits are clarified. Second, understanding your style and preferences can optimize your coaching learning agenda. For example, someone who's analytical and introspective by nature might learn faster or deeper with one approach, while someone who's intuitive and spontaneous might benefit from a different format or methods. Third, identifying relative strengths and blind spots can refine your coaching goals. This is because diagnostic testing moves beyond visible behavior to underlying attitudes and motivations.

Imagine, for instance, that you're an entrepreneur or account executive who is responsible for new client acquisition. Your assessment shows that you tend to seek approval from others and have a low tolerance for rejection. How might these characteristics support or limit your ability to close new business? If you're not a natural-born salesperson, can you develop a style that's effective and not stress generating? If your coaching program were to focus on sales skills without considering your individual personality, this missing link could compromise your overall results.

Seven Points to Know About Personality Assessments

1. Survey results are based on your own opinion (self-report), that is, on how you answer multiple-choice items or questions. They capture subjective data (how you see yourself).
2. No one or two personality surveys will capture your unique characteristics 100 percent fully or accurately.
3. A battery or suite of complementary surveys provides more information than any one survey (just as a full blood workup yields more information about your body chemistry than any single test).
4. Cross-cultural differences may affect or even invalidate results, as all assessments are not culture-neutral tools.
5. If you're not fluent in English or you prefer test administration in a different language, tell your coach.
6. Advanced psychometric assessments, including many adult personality tests, typically require specialized graduate education or professional certification to administer.
7. Not all executive and business coaches have an interest in personality assessment or are qualified in this area.

I never cease to marvel at the "aha!" moment many of my clients experience when they read their first assessment summary. Whether the information creates new insights or confirms what they already knew about themselves, they take away an appreciation of their special traits, strengths, complexity, and particular blind spots. (And we *all* have blind spots.)

Granted, coaching programs do not always include a separate personality assessment or battery component. For starters, it may not be consistent with a program's specific objectives. Situations in which you're working on a very targeted basis, your coaching is part of a defined enterprise-wide initiative, or funds are limited fall into this category. However, if you've never had an in-depth individual assessment and you're in a position to do so with a qualified professional, the activity can be a highly profitable investment.

How the Subjective Becomes Objective

If you love to get "under the hood" to learn how things work, you may be interested in knowing more about how personality surveys generate the results they do. Scientifically developed tests are typically *norm based,* meaning they compare your answers to the typical range of responses by people similar to and different from you. For example, if you repeatedly answer questions on a survey in ways that suggest you see yourself as independent, the degree to which you get a high score on "independence" is not just based on how high your score is, but also on how much higher it is compared to the average person in your comparison sample group. Your score is also based on the degree to which people in the comparison group vary above and below the average. For instance, if most people in your comparison group score relatively low and there is little variation between people above and below that low average, then your relatively high score on "independence" is interpreted as a "very high" score.

Personality Testing and Confidentiality

By their nature, personality test results contain highly personal information. As a rule, even if personality testing is employer funded, the actual assessment information, including raw data and interpretive results, is provided only to you, the coaching client. A confidentiality clause to this effect may appear in your coaching agreement or guidelines. If you're unsure, clarify this point in advance, or ask your coach to do so.

If you want to show your assessment results to other people, such as a spouse or friend, this is fine. The decision, however, should be yours to make. In fact, your coach might ask for your written permission before releasing assessment material to any third party even if you initiate the request. These are all safeguards intended to protect your privacy and promote a trusting, collaborative relationship with your coach.

Web-based technology, with password protection and secure servers, makes test taking convenient and safe. However, transmitting assessment results electronically is a questionable practice, no matter whether coaching services are private pay or employer funded.

Electronic files can be corrupted or go astray. Data in your e-mail in-box could inadvertently be accessed or broadcast by someone else, or wind up stored on a company hard drive or remote server. Re-member that this is personal, and potentially sensitive, information.

My preference is to send assessment results and reports as hard copies, either hand-delivered or posted by courier service, to the client's preferred address, business or home.

Both the American Psychological Association and the American Counseling Association have detailed ethical guidelines regarding testing practices and test confidentiality and disclosure. These guide-lines apply to their respective members. Other professional and cre-dentialing organizations may or may not have stated policies. If you're likely to be completing a personality profile or battery and want to know more about record keeping and information sharing, ask your coach before you get under way. You're entitled to full dis-closure and peace of mind.

EMOTIONAL INTELLIGENCE AND PEAK PERFORMANCE

Emotional intelligence, sometimes called EI or EQ for short, refers to your ability to recognize your feelings and those of others and manage your own emotions and those of others. The term was coined by psychologists Jack Mayer and Peter Salovey in 1990.

Emotional intelligence is distinct from IQ, which refers to cog-nitive abilities, such as critical reasoning, verbal knowledge, and memorization. Currently, behavioral scientists have put forth sev-eral models of EI. The school of thought led by Reuven Bar-On considers EI as a set of *personality traits* that promote personal well-being and self-actualization. Another group views emotional intel-ligence as a *range of competencies* that includes self-awareness, self-management, social awareness, and social skills. Best-selling author Daniel Goleman is a leading proponent of the latter model. Several psychometric EI tests are available that assess a person's abilities in these four areas.

Behavioral research continues to show just how critical EI com-petencies are to effective leadership, management, and entrepre-neurship (to say nothing of interpersonal effectiveness in general). To be able to control your feelings is essential to your effectiveness as a professional. Similarly, the ability to accurately gauge other people's feelings and relate to how they're feeling—in other words, to show empathy—is a distinct interpersonal advantage. If you're able to develop rapport, and motivate and inspire others, you have a higher probability of being able to achieve results through others. After all, leaders need followers.

I am not saying that emotional intelligence is the only ability that current and aspiring leaders need to cultivate and demonstrate. Rather, what the research to date suggests is that EI competencies, whether innate or learned, result in a significant performance advantage at work.

In his book *Working with Emotional Intelligence* (1998), Goleman cited competency research in over two hundred companies and organizations worldwide. The findings suggest that about one-third of the difference between average performers and top performers was due to technical skill and cognitive ability, while two-thirds was due to emotional competence. At senior-most leadership levels, over four-fifths of the difference between average and top performance was due to emotional competence.

Research reported by Ruderman, Hannum, and Leslie (2001) at the Center for Creative Leadership found that the primary causes of executive job derailment were deficits in emotional competence. The three primary causes were poor interpersonal relations, inability to work well in a team, and difficulty in handling change.

The question of whether emotional intelligence can be taught or enhanced with executive coaching or by watching others remains a lively research subject.

Because self-awareness and empathy have been known success traits since ancient times, emotional intelligence is sometimes described as "old wine in new bottles." The bottom line is that you can't readily know what's going on inside others—employees, customers, shareholders, patients, or the public—if you don't know what's going on inside yourself.

KEY POINT: You can have a charismatic personality like Virgin Atlantic's Richard Branson or a self-styled type B personality like Time Warner's Richard Parsons and be successful all the same. Research suggests that this is not the case if you lack emotional intelligence.

LEADER SPOTLIGHT
Theresa Gattung
Chief Executive Officer, Telecom New Zealand

While still in her teens, Theresa Gattung decided she would one day lead a public company. In 1999, at age thirty-seven, she become CEO of Telecom New Zealand, the country's largest corporation. Today she figures among *Fortune* magazine's "50 Most Powerful Women in Business."

A dynamic, fast-talking "Kiwi," as New Zealanders style themselves, Gattung has studied the lives of leaders, past and present, ever since she was a girl. She has strong opinions about how personality factors and technical knowledge affect career and leadership potential.

"I used to think that being a leader was about leading from the front," she told me. "Because I'm an extrovert, I had a picture in my head that good leaders were extroverts. What I've come to understand over time is that it's not about personality. I've now worked with some fantastic leaders who were extroverts and some who were introverts. I think there are leadership styles that work best in different situations.

"You can have different types of personality and still lead effectively. But what is absolutely nonnegotiable is character. I came to the view a while ago that truth rings true. People see through people who are unauthentic. The most important thing is to be your authentic self—not to be someone else's version of a leader but to really try and understand your own self and do it your way.

"You know, hubris is a huge problem. In business, and probably in life, you can't achieve without having a strong ego. How you balance that with people who will always tell you the truth is a real problem for a CEO. You've got so much power and everybody wants to play to you. The media write you up. The PR team gets these nice profiles and airbrushed photos of you. But at the end of the day you're still just an ordinary person. I've had people work with me for over ten years. We've gone through a range of things together. They will always tell me the truth."

Gattung continued, "Emotional intelligence is really important in a leader. People have so many choices now. If they choose to stay in a situation, they have to be linked in at the heart level as well as the head level. So it's important that leaders intuit what's going on and adjust their style based on how they come across and what people need to be coached or managed. I remember when Daniel Goleman's book *Emotional Intelligence* came out [in 1995]. I thought, 'Oh yeah, here's a management fashion. We'll have that for a few years until the next one.'

But it's always been true that integrated human beings actually are best able to be leaders. I've always looked for it in the people I've hired.

"But to be honest, I look for that second. The first thing that I look for is obviously technical competence in what they're doing, and the second thing is having their egos well under control. I just think too much ego is such a killer. It leads to poor judgment at some point and ruins teamwork." She ticked off her priorities: "Technical competence, having an ego under control, and then dealing with people. Being a member of a team, taking responsibility, really, really having the stamina for the long haul, and not being in it for the glory. I'm a big believer that no one person has everything that you need, but a team definitely can. I've always thought emotional intelligence is a key part of teamwork."

THE MIGHTY 360-DEGREE FEEDBACK SURVEY

Organizations worldwide have embraced the 360-degree feedback survey as a "best practice" tool for performance management and development. It's also called a multisource or multirater survey because you're provided with feedback from a full range of your work relationships, or sources. The people polled include your immediate supervisors, your peers and direct reports, yourself, and sometimes other stakeholders as well. This 360-degree scope provides a diverse mix of work interactions and viewpoints. In a nutshell, you're rated across a range of work-related criteria that typically include leadership and business performance, teamwork and team building, and corporate citizenship. Using advanced technology, test developers can customize surveys for a specific organization or person and distribute them to be completed online. Individual feedback reports are then computer generated. The reports often have two parts: a statistical score summary and an anecdotal or comments section. The statistical part shows aggregate and comparative data. For example, you might rate your problem-solving skills as "very good," while your direct reports rate you on average as only "good" in this category. Your boss rates you as "good" and your peers rate you on average as "very good." Ratings from your direct reports and peers are typically aggregated to maintain the anonymity of individual respondents, thereby encouraging candor.

Unlike individual personality testing results, 360-degree feedback data may not be completely private and confidential, especially if the survey is part of an enterprise-wide performance management program.

The 360-degree feedback survey has long been recognized as a valuable assessment tool because multiple feedback sources are typically more reliable than just one source. Also, getting input from people in different roles and reporting relationships means that a person's performance and capabilities are evaluated across a wide range. Consequently, the person being rated can have greater confidence in the validity and relevance of the data. In other words, if your boss, colleagues, and direct reports all rate you as a highly effective project manager, in all probability you are. By the same token, if a 360-degree survey yields uniformly unfavorable feedback about your project management skills, the chances are good that you do indeed have a deficit in this area.

Used properly, the 360-degree feedback survey is a mighty and impactful assessment tool because it sheds light on the personal context (how you see yourself), the interpersonal context (how others see you), and the situational context (your business and career situation).

I don't believe a 360-degree survey by itself is equivalent to a 360-degree data mirror. However, I do believe it can make a substantial contribution to the mirror.

Low-tech versions of the multisource survey exist. For instance, I often opt to do structured one-on-one interviews in person rather than use a computerized format. This way I get to know the players as well as their opinions.

Multisource feedback tells you what you're doing well on the job and what you can improve. Any discrepancy between how you rate your performance compared to how others rate you is especially valuable. Also, research studies show that feedback recipients who overrated themselves on their surveys subsequently improved more than those whose self-ratings were in line with their raters.

Many coaching clients develop their coaching goals on the basis of their 360-degree survey feedback. Today, organizations worldwide link their leadership and executive coaching programs to their annual 360-degree performance reviews. They engage coaches to help their executives and managers interpret feedback results, set development goals, and then achieve them.

Research by Smither and colleagues (2003) further shows that those who participate in coaching or some other development activity after getting their 360-degree feedback improve more than those who do not. In other words, coaching maximizes the effectiveness of the feedback.

Key Point: Fear of negative feedback comes with a high price tag. Criticism, Aristotle observed, is something we can easily avoid by "saying nothing, doing nothing, and being nothing."

Case in Point: The Newcomer

Efferem had intellectual firepower to spare. With a Ph.D. in electrical engineering and more than twenty scholarly articles to his credit, he was an acknowledged expert in his field. After testing the waters as an outside special consultant to a national manufacturing company, he had signed on as a salaried senior manager. This transition from outside subject matter expert to inside supervisor and project manager involved a completely new role and people management responsibilities.

Nothing in Efferem's background had prepared him to lead and supervise other people. As an individual contributor and subject matter authority, he was supremely confident in his abilities. As a newly minted manager, he was acutely aware of what he did not know. He saw executive coaching as a lifeline and was overjoyed to receive just-in-time assistance.

It was too soon to obtain multisource feedback from Efferem's coworkers, since they didn't yet know him well. Instead, the assessment phase of his program involved one-on-one interviews with his manager, direct reports, and colleagues to understand their expectations, company values, and individual personalities. Efferem also undertook a comprehensive behavioral battery, his first ever, which shed light on his thinking, communication, and interpersonal styles. I made a point of studying his position description, projects docket, and six-month performance targets. In this way, we were able to build a panoramic data mirror that captured all three performance-related contexts: individual, interpersonal, and situational.

An interesting corollary emerged from this fact-finding phase: Efferem's group was seriously understaffed to complete an upcoming $10 million project on time. Conducting a thorough assessment at the beginning of his coaching program meant that Efferem, his team, and the company were all able to succeed in a big way. This discovery alone was arguably worth a hundred-fold the company's investment in his coaching.

FINAL ANALYSIS

The greatest benefit of an assessment phase is increased self-awareness. The more you know about yourself, about how others perceive you, and what situational factors are critical to your success, the easier it is to remain "consciously competent." The more you understand your own motivational drivers, talents, and behavioral styles and preferences, the more purposeful and strategic you can be in setting and achieving goals at any time and anywhere.

Furthermore, the more successful you become, the more self-aware you need to be and the more you need to know your strengths, limitations, and blind spots. As Bill Gates told *Fortune* magazine, "You have to be careful, if you're good at something, to make sure you don't think you're good at other things that you aren't necessarily so good at" (Schlender, 1998). Overconfidence combined with ambition and excessive ego can be a disastrous combination.

In Shakespeare's comedy *Much Ado About Nothing*, the story's hero, Benedick, overhears his friends criticize his arch and prideful ways. Once he gets over the shock of hearing his closest associates describe him negatively, Benedick rouses himself to take corrective action. "Happy are they that hear their detractions, and can put them to mending," he says.

In real life, not everyone shares Benedick's attitude: only champions and those who aspire to be the best they can be assuredly do. Becoming accustomed to constructive criticism—indeed, asking for it on a regular basis—is essential to sustainable excellence. This is why peak performers in so many fields, including sports, the performing arts, and business, rely extensively on coaches for evaluation and preparation purposes. Your learning curve becomes steeper.

Next I will share proven strategies and tips for transforming your coaching goals into concrete and implementable activities.

CHAPTER SEVEN

YOUR POWERHOUSE ACTION PLAN

Planning brings us to the third phase of the Five-Step Coaching Model. Plans are the tools for getting from goals to results. "The secret of getting ahead is getting started. The secret of getting started is breaking your complex overwhelming tasks into small manageable tasks, and then starting on the first one," Mark Twain said.

We're familiar with strategic plans, business plans, performance management plans, crisis management plans, and so forth. Yet Twain's advice on how to get ahead often goes unheeded. I hear a good deal of ambivalence and even skepticism expressed about planning activities: "Why have a plan when everything can change tomorrow?" or "Why have a plan when I might change my mind? When I operate best on gut instinct?"

The savvy professional, however, knows that today's white-water business conditions make a compelling case for effective personal planning skills. Self-mastery, self-direction, and a sound decision-making system are more important than ever before to both individual and enterprise-wide success. You need to be able to focus, but more important, you need to have a focus. "If you chase two rabbits, you will not catch either one," a Russian proverb points out.

I'm going to be explicit in this chapter and lay out everything you will need to co-create not just an action plan but a Powerhouse Plan with your coach. I will reveal advanced techniques that make the difference between an action plan that positively soars and one that never achieves liftoff. I'll provide step-by-step guidance, sharing insider tips along the way that come from two decades' worth of helping exceptional people realize their ambitions. You will also learn how to troubleshoot potential mental traps and other derailers. I'm confident that the knowledge and tools you acquire here will serve you well in a variety of situations, not just in your coaching program. You will become more adept at planning activities for yourself, for your team or business, and in coaching others. Along the way, you will hear from two seasoned CEOs on the merits of coaching and planning.

COACHING PLAN BASICS AND BENEFITS

A Powerhouse Plan doesn't take a lot of time or effort to create. However, if you're unclear about what precisely is involved, you're not alone. After all, converting strategic, complex, or big-picture goals into a series of executable tasks may not be patently obvious. So let's start with an overview of action plan basics and benefits.

WHAT'S A COACHING ACTION PLAN?

A coaching action plan is tactical, not strategic, in nature. It's concrete, not abstract. And, notably, it's a joint venture with your coach. Together you will build a unique, made-to-measure blueprint for achieving maximum results. After all, no one else is exactly like you, shares your special aspirations, or operates in the same environments that you do. Your coach is your ready, expert partner. Just as an architect has the expertise to transform a variety of inputs—owner specifications, site conditions, building material properties, and so forth—into a winning blueprint, your coach knows how to work with you to produce the right plan for you.

An action plan has these features:

- It's a written road map.
- It lists one or more personal top-value goals.
- It identifies specific action steps toward achieving each goal.
- The specific steps may or may not be interrelated.
- It identifies who is responsible for what and by when.
- It measures progress and results.
- It is brief.

Eyes sometimes roll when I mention the SMART goal-setting method because it has been around forever. SMART is an acronym referring to five goal characteristics:

Specific: detailed, concise

Measurable: quantifiable

Achievable: realistic, feasible

Relevant: high value, profitable, desirable, practical

Time-based: timely, finite

The SMART method is an old workhorse that remains effective, based on proven principles of adult learning. By way of illustration, compare these two goal statements:

Statement 1: I want to get a leadership position in some community business association.

Statement 2: I want to become president of my local chamber of commerce within the next three years.

Statement 1 is vague and seems more like wishful thinking than an actionable objective. (It may remind you of some New Year's resolutions you've made.) By contrast, statement 2 meets the SMART goal criteria. It's detailed enough in terms of what and when, so that discrete action steps (how) can be developed to move the goal forward. This statement not only has a focus; it is focused. In other words, you have enough information to begin to determine how to implement the goal.

How a Coaching Action Plan Adds Value

The benefits of a personalized action plan are numerous. I believe a formal written plan is essential to most coaching programs because it:

- Converts your strategic goals into executable tactical goals
- Makes your goals "real" by documenting them in writing
- Integrates information from your assessment into your program objectives

- Provides detailed direction and structure
- Facilitates desired knowledge and skill acquisition
- Establishes accountabilities for activities and results
- Ensures that you, your coach, and any sponsors share the same road map
- Primes your motivational pump

I sometimes refer to this last benefit as a "stealth advantage" because people don't routinely think about leveraging motivational forces. The wise individual knows better. "There is in the act of preparing, the moment you start caring," Winston Churchill observed. The psychological boost you get from producing a high-value, detailed game plan will fuel your enthusiasm and commitment.

BURNING QUESTION: IS A WRITTEN ACTION PLAN ALWAYS NECESSARY OR DESIRABLE?

I can think of three coaching situations that are legitimate exceptions to the action plan rule. First, if you're working with a coach for a short period of time, say, for a month or less or a few sessions, a detailed action plan may be overkill. Your goals can probably be captured just as easily in your initial coaching agreement. After all, brief contact typically is targeted and structured by its very nature. Second, if you are working with a coach to create an action or development plan, then creating a plan for the plan would be nonsensical. For example, many organizations arrange for coaches to help managers and other high-potential individuals create their annual development plans. By the end of the coaching engagement, the client has a detailed plan to implement without further assistance from the coach. Third, if your coaching arrangement is retainer based, such as I described in Chapter Four, then no goals in a conventional sense exist for which a plan is necessary. Rather, you're accessing your coach's "smarts" on an as-needed basis.

If your coaching program does not fall into one of these categories, then an action plan is key to realizing extraordinary results.

Leading Minds on Planning

"Nothing comes of nothing," *Shakespeare wrote for his title character King Lear. Forethought and focus have been the hallmarks of excellence across the centuries.*

"Before beginning, plan carefully."—*Cicero*

Benjamin Franklin devised a week-by-week plan to improve his character by working on thirteen virtues, including temperance, order, industry, and moderation. "By failing to prepare, you are preparing to fail," *he said.*

"One never notices what has been done; one can only see what remains to be done."—*Marie Curie*

"Give me a stock clerk with a goal and I'll give you a man who will make history. Give me a man with no goals and I'll give you a stock clerk."—*J. C. Penney*

"To tend, unfailingly, unflinchingly, towards a goal, is the secret of success."—*Anna Pavlova*

"Once I am set on a goal, it becomes difficult to deflect me."—*Albert Einstein*

Thomas Watson, founder of IBM, used to write his goals on signs and hang them everywhere so that every day he would reinforce himself.

"A life that hasn't a definite plan is likely to become driftwood."—*David Sarnoff*

"Whatever failures I have known, whatever errors I have committed, whatever follies I have witnessed in private and public life have been the consequence of action without thought."—*Bernard Baruch*

ANATOMY OF A POWERHOUSE PLAN

What transforms a so-so action plan into a Powerhouse Plan capable of supercharging your coaching program? For starters, let's look at the typical components of a standard-format plan.

Standard Coaching Plan Components

Goal statement: What do I want to achieve?

Action steps: What specific tasks or activities must I perform to get there?

Performance measures: How will I know I've completed this step?

Plan or change partners: Whose help will I need to complete this step?

Due date: By when will I complete this step?

Some barebones versions don't even include all of these categories. For example, they lack specific performance or progress metrics or even specific action steps. They're simple-minded, not just simple, and distinctly subpar. Avoid them.

My Powerhouse Plan version dramatically enhances the standard format by adding a motivational component and a troubleshooting component. Together they act like twin booster rockets. I've highlighted the additions.

Powerhouse Plan Components

Goal statement: What do I want to achieve?

Benefits of goals: How will I be better off? How will my organization be better off?

Obstacles to goals: What's likely to prevent me from achieving this goal?

Solutions to obstacles: How will I remove or overcome these obstacles?

Action steps: What specific activities or skills do I need to get there?

Progress measures: How will I know I've completed this step?

Plan or change partners: Whose help will I need to make this happen?

Due date: By when will I complete this step?

The Benefits section category, with its explicit value proposition, is the motivational component. Your action plan should include this information. First, this section confirms that a goal you thought was important back when you were just considering coaching is still worthwhile. You should be able to list expected rewards and advantages or reevaluate the goal's relevance. Second, a documented set of benefits is a powerful source of ongoing encouragement and positive reinforcement. At times when you ask yourself or your coach, "Now, why am I doing this?" you will have a ready reminder. You will be able to answer these perennial bottom-line questions: What's in it for me? What's in it for my business?

My Powerhouse Plan format also contains a robust troubleshooting section. The Obstacles category requires you to take a proactive approach to problem identification:

- What external factors or situations could prevent you from reaching your goal?
- What personal traits or tendencies could get in the way or make reaching the goal that much more difficult?

Reflecting on these questions is akin to a downhill racer's identifying the treacherous aspects of the ski run well in advance of the race. Flagging potential threats to your goals is important to neutralizing them.

Common obstacles that coaching clients cite include:

- Lack of time or poor time management skills
- Travel schedules
- Work load and responsibilities
- Family obligations
- Insufficient resources, such as budget or head count
- Ingrained habits

The issue is not that obstacles may exist but rather that you and your coach are prepared to deal with them. Here's where the Powerhouse Plan's Solutions category comes into play when it asks, "How will you overcome the problem or barrier?"

If, for instance, departmental understaffing is likely to derail your goal of improving delegation skills, you need to solve or eliminate this issue. Otherwise your goal is likely to be dead on arrival. One of my coaching clients compared the troubleshooting piece of his plan to clearing land mines: "It pays to check the road for booby traps before setting out," he said.

Exhibit 7.1 shows how to set up a Powerhouse Plan. As you can see, the information you need can be written on one page per goal. If you have more than one coaching goal, which is often the case, repeat the exercise a second (and possibly a third) time.

THE ASSESSMENT CONNECTION

In Chapter Six, I noted that relevant data are collected from a variety of sources in the assessment phase. You and your coach are then in a position to devise a comprehensive, or 360-degree, data mirror that reveals how you see yourself, how others at work see you, and your situational context at work.

Here are specific ways your assessment results inform your coaching action plan. We'll look at each Powerhouse Plan component in turn:

- *Goals.* Are the goals you've selected the highest priority based on business needs, others' feedback, and how your performance will be evaluated? Has any key performance deficit or opportunity been identified? Are your goals realistic when tested against the facts? Do you and your coach have solid assessment data for making decisions?
- *Benefits of goals.* What are the probable rewards, tangible and intangible, associated with your goals? When you have third-party and benchmarking data available, the value of attaining your goals is clarified—and often quantified, too.
- *Obstacles to goals.* Assessment information can be used to pinpoint potential threats to your action plan. For example, how can you achieve goal X if there's no budget for it or if it involves confronting people, which you typically avoid doing?
- *Solutions to obstacles.* By the same token, your assessment results may provide the information necessary to find solutions to barriers or threats. If not, they may still point the way to the sources and resources you will need to consult.
- *Action steps.* You achieve a coaching goal by undertaking certain tasks and activities that involve behaving in new or different ways. Your assessment results often indicate or confirm what behaviors or

EXHIBIT 7.1. POWERHOUSE ACTION PLAN.

GOAL Number ___ (State as Specific, Measurable, Attainable, Relevant, Timely)

Benefits of Achieving This Goal	
For Me:	**For My Organization (if applicable):**
Obstacles to Achieving This Goal	**Solutions to the Obstacles**

Action Steps	**Progress Measures**	**Change Partners**	**Target Due Date**
1.			
2.			
3.			
4.			

_____   _____   _____

Today's Date   **Goal Completion Date**   **Approved By (if applicable)**

capabilities you need to acquire. For example, if a negative verdict has been rendered about your conflict-avoidant style, then taking a negotiation workshop would be a helpful and worthwhile action step. Furthermore, if your coach has a clear picture of your personal learning style, these preferences can be incorporated into your program. Some people prefer to read books; others prefer to watch an instructional video or attend a seminar.

- *Progress measures.* The methods and tools used for your initial assessment can inform how your progress is measured. For example, follow-up interviews or multisource surveys can be used to compare before and after behavior. Metrics relevant to your particular goals, such as sales or customer acquisition rates, project milestones, or employee retention, can be compared against your initial baseline levels.

- *Plan or change partners.* Besides your coach, who else is important to achieving your goals? A supervisor or sponsor? Your direct reports or administrative assistant? A counterpart in another department? Your assessment data will help to identify your change partners.

- *Due dates.* Interim and final due dates are set realistically and fit into your life and lifestyle. Milestones may be synchronized with known enterprise-wide evaluations, such as annual performance reviews.

KEY POINT: A given destination can usually be reached by different paths. Similarly, there are usually multiple possibilities and options, not just a single right choice, to developing your action steps.

PREPARING THE POWERHOUSE PLAN WITH YOUR COACH

Executive and business coaches have different approaches to preparing action plans. There is no set division of roles and responsibilities. Some write the first draft for you, basing this on your goal-setting discussions to date. Then the two of you refine this draft together. Other coaches expect you to write any and all versions of the plan yourself, limiting themselves to oversight and editing activities. Still others have no set protocol and collaborate based on the particular circumstances and your preferences. With all types of coaching arrangements, not just telecoaching, preliminary drafts may be e-mailed or faxed back and forth.

I prefer to have my client write the initial draft after we've gone over the Powerhouse Plan format and template because ownership is involved. This is the client's coaching program and plan, not mine. I want to discover what he or she picks as top goals, benefits, obstacles, action steps, and so forth. Then we can flesh out points and add, modify, or delete to end up with a comprehensive blueprint. As a coach, I'm the equivalent of a program architect. I have the expertise to design and build an optimal plan, but the plan is ultimately the client's.

If you're allergic to writing things down or have a tendency toward "analysis paralysis" or perfectionism, consider using the following guided conversation approach. Based on the eight Powerhouse Plan components, it is highly interactive, low anxiety, and gets the job done.

In this approach, your coach asks you questions based on the eight Powerhouse Plan components, and you answer them. One of you needs to take notes, or you can audiotape the conversation and have it transcribed. Either way, when you're done, you will have a first draft. By now, these questions should be familiar:

1. What is your goal?
2. What are the benefits of achieving these goals? To yourself? To your business or organization (if relevant)?
3. What obstacles or barriers can prevent you from achieving your goals?
4. What are the solutions to these obstacles?
5. What specific action steps will move you toward each goal?
6. For each action step, are other partners involved?
7. For each action step, how will you measure your progress?
8. By what date will you accomplish each action step?

If your action plan consists of several discrete goals, answer all eight questions for your first goal, then go back and repeat the process for your second goal, and so forth.

Once you and your coach have a draft on paper, refining and finalizing your working version usually is a simple back-and-forth process. A completed sample plan consisting of one goal is shown in Exhibit 7.2.

EXHIBIT 7.2. SAMPLE COMPLETED POWERHOUSE PLAN.

GOAL Number __1__ (State as Specific, Measurable, Attainable, Relevant, Timely)

I want to be able to manage conflict effectively among my direct reports.

Benefits of Achieving This Goal	
For Me:	**For My Organization (if applicable):**
• More time to focus on the business • Ability to delegate more responsibilities • Less personal stress	• Improved teamwork, fewer turf wars • Increased productivity divisionwide
Obstacles to Achieving This Goal	**Solutions to the Obstacles**
• I habitually avoid dealing with interpersonal differences until I'm forced to. • My team is accustomed to coming to me to referee their disputes.	• Go public with my coaching goals so I'll feel accountable to my team. • Explain to my direct reports why the status quo is unacceptable and how we'll all be better off.

Action Steps	Progress Measures	Change Partners	Target Due Date
1. Tell direct reports of my coaching goals and how my progress will be measured.	I've made the announcement.	Direct reports	1 week (next meeting)
2. Read negotiation and assertiveness articles and books.	Books have been read and discussed with coach.	Coach will supply reading list	3 weeks
3. Attend a multiday negotiation skills course.	a. Course completed b. I'm able to use techniques in real time.	Boss must approve funds and time away	2 months
4. Keep critical incident log of conflict, disputes, and my responses.	Debrief and analyze with my coach.		Monthly review for 3 months

(Now)	_(+ 4 months)_	(Manager)
Today's Date	**Goal Completion Date**	**Approved By (if applicable)**

LEADER SPOTLIGHT
Howard Putnam
Former Chief Executive Officer, Southwest Airlines and Braniff International

Howard Putnam, a seasoned leader in commercial aviation, knows firsthand that getting coached from the sidelines can make a huge difference in high-stakes situations.

"One thing about coaching, you've got to know when you need it," Putnam, the former CEO of Southwest Airlines, told me. Currently a speaker on leadership and business issues, he is active in mentoring entrepreneurs and nonprofit leaders. In his opinion, developing a high-performance organization involves lots of individual attention and encouragement. "You can't build a culture in a group. It takes one-on-one work to find out what people have really learned."

At a critical point in his career of running airlines, Putnam got some winning advice about planning strategy from an unexpected source: he was coached by a football coach.

"I left Southwest to take on the task of saving the financially troubled airline, Braniff International. At the time we didn't know the books had been cooked, like Enron, and we had only ten days of cash left. Our job was to save it or restructure it through Chapter 11, which is eventually what we had to do.

"One of our good customers was the New Orleans Saints NFL football team. When the day came that we had to shut the airline down and put it into Chapter 11, I called their colorful coach, Bum Phillips, and tried to explain what Chapter 11 meant and that we wouldn't be able to operate the charters for the New Orleans Saints in the fall of that year. I told him we would arrange alternate air charter transportation.

"Bum didn't understand all the legal jargon. His mind quickly turned to football, which was his life and his reference for leadership decision making. He said: 'So you lost yardage on the last down. Hell, Howard, just call another play.'

"Braniff was out of cash and grounded. Our only play was to reorganize it under the rules of Chapter 11, work out payment plans with all the creditors, and get it flying again. That is what we did, and it flew again two years later."

Putnam is emphatic about the importance of continuous planning to professional success. "Do you have another play in your playbook in preparation for the day you lose yardage? Do you have a contingency plan? Look at your playbook. Are you ready?"

I'll never forget Bum saying: 'Hell, Howard, just call another play.'"

ELIMINATING MENTAL TRAPS

Faulty beliefs can interfere with goal setting. I call these faulty beliefs "mental traps" because they limit a person's professional growth and prospects much the way a trap ensnares its victims. Often these mental traps operate outside one's awareness, springing to the surface only when they're triggered by some external influence, such as a planning or goal-setting requirement. Over the years, I've found that the surest way to dispatch a mental trap is to challenge its faulty reasoning and replace this with accurate information.

Five Common Mental Traps

1. Setting goals will limit my options and therefore my success potential.
2. Accomplishing easy goals is better than going after difficult goals.
3. Having a set of general goals in my head works just as well as writing them down.
4. Modest expectations of success yield better results than high expectations.
5. Action plan goals should be laid out as long-term objectives.

Let's examine these statements. For each mental trap, I've provided the correct and corrective information about goal setting. Check these against your own beliefs and assumptions.

TRAP 1: SETTING GOALS WILL LIMIT MY OPTIONS AND THEREFORE MY SUCCESS POTENTIAL.

Fact: An all-too-common misconception goes like this: creating a plan involves a commitment written in stone. Mental trap! First, setting goals does not mean they can't be altered or even jettisoned if circumstances require. Your options are not limited in a negative way. Rather, your priorities get defined and focused. For example, writing a grocery list helps you to shop efficiently and effectively. Otherwise you might have to walk up and down every supermarket aisle, carefully studying the shelves in the hope that you will recognize what you needed. Maybe you will or maybe you won't. You'd certainly spend much more time and energy in the process.

Second, research clearly shows that goal setting enhances rather than limits success potential. For instance, one study involving sales professionals found that the more they set goals and planned their efforts, the more sales they made and the more commissions they collected (Van de Walle, Brown, Cron, and Slocum, 1999). In fact, setting goals accounted for a whopping 60 percent of their sales success. This result is consistent with what sports and exercise research studies show: goal setting leads to significant performance enhancement.

Bottom line: You're limiting your success potential, as well as your current performance, if you're not setting actionable goals for yourself. This is the case whether you're working with a coach or not, whether you're salaried or self-employed, whether you're a CEO or a front-line manager.

TRAP 2: ACCOMPLISHING EASY GOALS IS BETTER THAN PURSUING DIFFICULT GOALS

Fact: On the surface, there's something deceptively logical and appealing about this mental trap. After all, if we perceive something as easy, we're more likely to be successful in accomplishing it. Therefore, we should be more inclined to do it. However, research shows that accomplishing difficult goals produces better performance results than completing easy or moderate ones (Campbell and Ilgen, 1976; Locke and Latham, 1990).

Imagine doing arm curls with a one-pound weight. You can do lots of repetitions because you're not taxing yourself. But you're not accomplishing much in terms of strength building, and because you're not challenging yourself, the activity becomes boring very quickly. Once you're bored, motivation declines and you're likely to quit. There's some truth in the maxim, "No pain, no gain."

Michelangelo warned against this mental trap: "The greater danger for most of us lies not in setting our aim too high and falling short; but in setting our aim too low, and achieving our mark."

Bottom line: If you're looking to achieve maximum results, set goals high while still keeping them attainable.

TRAP 3: HAVING A GENERAL SET OF GOALS IN MY HEAD WORKS JUST AS WELL AS WRITING THEM DOWN

Fact: Specific, as well as difficult, goals prompt better performance than vague or "do your best" goals (Latham and Locke, 1991). Then there's the oft-cited Harvard Business School survey of its 1979 M.B.A. graduates. Asked if they had clear written goals with plans for their career when they left school, only 3 percent answered in the affirmative. Thirteen percent had goals they had not written down and did not necessarily have a plan. Eighty-four percent had no goals at all. Ten years later, Harvard did follow-up interviews with the following results: the 13 percent who had goals were earning on average twice as much as the 84 percent with no goals at all. The 3 percent with written goals were earning on average ten times as much as the other 97 percent put together. (I have yet to locate a published version of this study. M. H. McCormack [1986] refers to it in his book *What They Don't Teach You at Harvard Business School.*)

Without written, specific plans, how can you and your coach partner effectively to measure progress or be certain you're on course? Steve Bennett, CEO of software giant Intuit, pointed out the importance of documenting plans when he told the *New York Times,* "I learned that if you're going to be a big-time leader, you have to be able to get things out of your brain and into writing."

Bottom line: Goals that exist only in your head are wishes, not actionable objectives. You and your coach need a shared document so that the two of you are literally, as well as figuratively, on the same page.

TRAP 4: MODEST EXPECTATIONS OF SUCCESS YIELD BETTER RESULTS THAN HIGH EXPECTATIONS

Fact: This mental trap operates in anticipation of failure. The rationalization goes like this: if you don't get your hopes too high, then you don't feel too disappointed or frustrated (or guilty). In fact, this attitude doesn't protect you against disappointment as much as sets you up for mediocrity. You wind up paying a high price in output when you reduce the "octane power" of your expectations. Of course, you and your coach need to be realistic in setting goals. However, assuming you have the right tactics, tools, and resources, holding high expectations of success is the equivalent of having "high-test in your tank."

Self-efficacy, a concept associated with psychologist Albert Bandura, refers to people's beliefs about their capabilities to produce designated levels of performance that affect their lives. Those with high confidence in their capabilities approach difficult tasks as challenges to master rather than as threats to avoid. They sustain their efforts in the face of failure, which they're likely to set down to insufficient information or effort. After winning the women's singles tournament at Wimbledon in 2005, Venus Williams told the media, "I was the fourteenth seed. I wasn't supposed to win. . . . But I always bet on myself." That's the power of talent combined with effort and self-confidence.

Bottom line: Set your expectations as realistically high as you possibly can. You have a support system and safety net in your coach.

TRAP 5: ACTION PLAN GOALS SHOULD BE LAID OUT AS LONG-TERM OBJECTIVES.

Fact: Action plans should include short- and mid-range activities. This is not to say you shouldn't have long-term goals. In fact, the superordinate goal or goals that drive many executive coaching programs, particularly when clients are top-level managers or entrepreneurs, are often long term in nature because strategy and performance cycles at this level are usually measured in quarters and years rather than in months. There's a world of difference between big-picture strategic objectives and the specific actionable goals to get there.

World-class athletes may have their eyes on an Olympic medal, their ultimate goal, but the route to this goal is a series of tactical plans. Remember that coaching action plans are tactical plans. Achieving early wins is essential to building confidence and fueling motivation. Segmenting or breaking down extensive tasks into incremental activities also produces better performance outcomes.

Losing thirty pounds can seem like a daunting task compared to losing ten pounds, then another ten, and then the final ten. Success at shedding the first ten pounds gives you a sense of achievement and competence. You're motivated to stay with your weight-loss program.

Bottom line: Ideally, action plans should have a time framework of six months or less or, alternatively, contain interim goals that allow for early wins and positive reinforcement. Action plans can be sequenced or iterative.

Winning Action Plan Tips

In summary, keep these proven pointers in mind:

- Set a small number of goals—no more than three.
- Set short-range targets for your goals, knowing you can always build on these later.
- Set goals to be challenging but not impossibly high.
- Be strongly positive and enthusiastic about achieving your goals.

Plain Talk About "Resistance Persistence"

Mental traps around goal setting are fairly common. Usually they can be eliminated with straightforward education. But resistance to goal setting can exist for other reasons too:

- *No intrinsic motivation.* If coaching is part of a lockstep enterprise-wide program or if someone is mandated into coaching against his or her wishes, the individual's intrinsic motivation level may be zero. Without personal buy-in, goal-setting activities have little or no perceived value. The person may even resent the "help."
- *Fear of failure.* Fear of failure can haunt the offices of even smart, industrious people. Shaky self-esteem, paralyzing perfectionism, or excessive egotism can prevent a person from trying new things or becoming a novice again. Someone who is risk or change averse or whose self-image doesn't allow for taking baby steps may feel distinctly uncomfortable when the time comes to draft an action plan.
- *Fear of success.* A close cousin of fear of failure is the fear of success. Here too self-esteem issues are typically involved. The person doubts whether he or she is worthy of greater accomplishment, recognition, or success. Psychological issues prevent the person from getting down to business.

- *Personal style or habits.* Remember the Myth of Universality that says, "Everyone is coachable"? Let's take a moment to recognize the awesome diversity of human personality, attributes, interest, and experience. We need to accept reality: not everyone is a prime candidate for executive coaching any more than everyone is a prime candidate for elected office. Some people are constitutionally intuitive, in-the-moment types. Others thrive on the rush of imminent deadlines, of snatching victory from the jaws of defeat. Still others possess highly creative, free-form personalities. Some push back at any type of outside direction. (One of the benefits of a thorough behavioral assessment is to identify a coaching candidate's behavioral orientation and preferences.) Working on something as structured as an action plan may well be inconsistent with a person's worldview, ingrained habits, or personal value system.

No matter the reason, you simply can't push a rope. This is why determining one's coaching readiness up front is so important, as I stressed in Chapter Two. Any of these four circumstances can result in "resistance persistence," a pattern of stalling, rationalizing, or outright avoidance. My purpose here is not to blame or criticize anyone; rather, I want to emphasize that even with the best of intentions, counterindications to coaching may not surface until the action planning phase.

LEADER SPOTLIGHT
Robert Danzig
Former Chief Executive Officer, Hearst Newspaper Group

Robert Danzig went from office boy to CEO at Hearst Newspapers and led the multibillion dollar company of six thousand employees for twenty years. Today Danzig continues to be a committed activist in developing people to their fullest potential. He serves as dean of the Hearst Management Institute, the company's executive development program, and also works individually with senior executives to improve their leadership effectiveness. Through writing and public speaking, he shares his remarkable personal story: from growing up in five foster homes to being mentored by a number of wise and caring managers.

LEADER SPOTLIGHT
Robert Danzig, *continued*

Danzig told me about his own coaching philosophy and planning approach. "At one time I was asked to work with a new company president. He needed more insight into his behavior and how he could be more effective. 'People perceive me as inscrutable,' he said. When I checked with his people myself, they told me, 'He doesn't give any feedback.' So our coaching goal for him was to go from being inscrutable to scrutable. We identified a number of options he could try, and in particular how he could show appreciation. Making gestures of appreciation was a key step in the plan. We also built incremental gains into the plan so he could grow in confidence and enhance his existing strengths.

"When it comes to developing executive skills, technical skills are a given. Leadership—really growing your destiny—involves unleashing a full range of individual capabilities. Coaching focuses a spotlight on personal growth; it can expand a person's insight and opportunities. From a company's perspective, coaching is also a way of showing unique interest in a person. You grow loyalty when you grow your people."

Having increased cash flow one-hundred-fold and acquired $2 billion in new business while running Hearst Newspapers, Danzig knows the bottom-line value of developing and retaining high-performance talent.

KEY POINT: If you're having serious trouble moving forward at this stage, be courageous and tell your coach (if she hasn't inquired already). In this way, the two of you can reevaluate the situation together and determine what makes sense.

ACCOUNTABILITIES AND APPROVALS

"Writing things down primes the pump for taking responsibility," George Morrisey told me. The author or coauthor of nineteen books related to strategic and tactical planning, Morrisey describes planning as "laying out the sequences of events that have to occur for you to achieve your goal." He is a strong advocate of the written plan because having one establishes and reinforces accountabilities: "It's a way of getting people to own both the process and the outcomes. Agreement by all parties is critical to success. Leaders not only must be accountable themselves; they need to reinforce accountability in others."

When you and your coach have arrived at a viable draft, usually after one or more revisions, you have identified a preliminary set of accountabilities. Why only preliminary? Because even with one-on-one coaching, a supporting cast is usually needed and involved. You need to speak with those you have listed under "Change Partners"—for instance, your boss, administrative assistant, or human resource manager. Make sure they understand what you're trying to accomplish; what you're asking them do, support, or facilitate; and why you're asking them to do it.

Ask for their help; don't demand it. For example, you may need your manager's permission to attend an off-site program or hire temporary staff. Or you may want a colleague to signal you at meetings if you begin to drone on. Be as specific as possible with your request. Don't be surprised if they offer to do more or make helpful suggestions you hadn't considered. Of course, express your gratitude. Explain or remind them that you're working with a coach, who will be your principal resource.

Finally, if your coaching program is employer funded, you must get your key sponsor to review and approve the final draft. This person may be your supervisor, your supervisor's boss, a human resource professional, or someone else. Getting your sponsor's green light ensures that you're all in agreement about program goals, accountabilities, progress indicators, and completion dates.

That's it. You're ready for a powerful, well-aimed launch into your actual program. Here's a program plan final list by way of review:

- Clear, high-value goals identified
- Written Powerhouse Plan format
- Plan reviewed and refined with your coach
- Mutual agreement on goals, methods, outputs, and time lines
- Plan partners consulted and on board
- Approved by coaching program sponsor (if applicable)

Final Analysis

One way of thinking about your coaching plan is this: it describes what success looks like, so you'll know it when you see it. If you and your coach use the Powerhouse Plan components and format, you are poised and prepped to get under way. Your sense of purpose and motivation are elevated. You're psyched and emotionally engaged.

The plan's the thing! "Plan the work, then work the plan," the saying goes. In the next chapter I will tell you what really goes on in coaching sessions behind closed doors. You will get an insider's view of the methods and science behind the magic.

CHAPTER EIGHT

ACTION AND IMPACT

You have approached your executive coaching program and partnership with purpose and passion. Now great things are going to happen. I often compare the first three coaching stages (define, assess, and plan) to setting up a laboratory. Now that you've equipped it with what you will need, you're ready to put it to good use. The action phase of your coaching program is akin to having your own learning and performance improvement laboratory. It is a place for observation, practice, and experimentation. The hard work associated with your action steps and any other coaching-based execution occurs here and now.

I will take you behind the scenes in this chapter to show you what typically goes on in a coaching session. For starters, you will learn about common coaching methods and formats and when they're likely to be used. Being familiar with these will help you to get the most from your program. However, in my view, the "what" of action coaching takes a back seat to the "why" and "how" aspects. The really big story I will focus on—the one that will enable you to appreciate the added value of executive coaching—deals with your brain and how coaching improves it. My psychologist's bias is showing here. So too is my unswerving commitment to helping you achieve consistent, extraordinary results. Methods are tools to learning. The heavy lifting in your action phase needs to be grounded in heavy learning. I will show how your coach facilitates the latter so you can do the former better. Case studies and leader spotlights round out the chapter.

ACTION COACHING NUTS AND BOLTS

The action phase of coaching is frequently called the heart of coaching because this is where behavior and performance actually change. Let's consider how you benefit from your coach's involvement during this stage.

Five Ways Your Coach Supercharges Your Action Phase

1. Accelerate learning. Your coach provides an expert, facilitative environment for you to discover untapped talents and acquire new knowledge and capabilities. You also get fresh thinking on strategies, opportunities, and solutions directly relevant to your success.
2. Maintain focus. Your coach helps by monitoring completion of action steps in an effective and timely fashion. If circumstances warrant, your coach suggests refinements or adjustments to your plan.
3. Tell the truth. Your coach supplies critical information and feedback that others may not tell you (or dare to tell you). Your coach has no agenda except your success.
4. Oversee accountability. Your coach holds you responsible for commitments made, thereby helping you stand by your goals and plan.
5. Reinforce motivation. Your coach keeps your motivation strong, and provides inspiration and support so you can take any setbacks in stride.

BEHIND (NOT SO) CLOSED DOORS

A great coaching session is like having a great conversation, tutorial, and major league pep talk all wrapped into one. You come away from it with new insights, clear direction, and renewed confidence and purpose.

The format of a coaching session can vary, as can the methods your coach uses in interacting with you. Coaching is highly flexible and responsive to your needs and goals. You can usually execute your Powerhouse Plan and action steps successfully by a variety of approaches and techniques.

SESSION FREQUENCY

One of the most frequent questions I'm asked about executive and business coaching is how often coaching sessions should occur. Industry surveys tell us that the most common arrangement, whether face-to-face or by telephone, is weekly contact. Sessions typically range between thirty and sixty minutes in duration. With telecoaching programs you may have a regular session time, say, on Thursdays at 8:00 A.M. The same dedicated scheduling may apply for in-person coaching, especially if yours is a brief, targeted program. In both instances, consistency and regularity provide structure and oversight to ensure steady progress.

If your calendar is in constant flux, as is the case with many CEOs, profit center executives, and technical professionals, a fixed, recurring appointment may not be feasible. Instead you and your coach may arrange to have one longer session, anywhere from ninety minutes to a half-day, every few weeks complemented by as-needed contact in between. This scheduling format works best with extended coaching arrangements, where goals and action steps have completion dates that are several months or business quarters away. Of course, numerous variations are possible. Once you've had a few sessions, you and your coach may tweak the logistics so they work as well as possible.

At the start of the execution phase, I recommend that coach and client be in weekly contact to ensure that "liftoff" is smooth and sustained. However, if your coaching program is retainer based or otherwise does not include a formalized coaching plan, when and how you're in contact with your coach depends on your particular agreement terms.

SESSION LOCATION

The two most common locations for in-person coaching sessions are your business premises and your coach's office. If you're likely to be distracted by telephone calls, e-mails, intercoms, staff, or other interruptions, your own office is not an ideal meeting venue. Instead, arrange for a small conference room or office in another area or building, the better to focus your attention and be assured of privacy. Similarly, if privacy is a key concern, you may want to meet off-site, for example, at your coach's office, a private club, or a rented conference room. There can be more exotic meeting locations as well—for example, a private home, a chauffeured limousine, or a corporate jet.

If you're paying for coaching out of personal funds, meeting at your workplace may or may not be appropriate. Much depends on your coaching goals. If you're a business owner or self-employed entrepreneur or professional, you're probably fine. However, if you're a salaried employee, be sure that having your coach on-site does not create a real or perceived conflict of interest. In other words, if you have a private-pay coaching arrangement and want to explore all possible career and employment opportunities, you and your coach should probably meet off-site.

SESSION FORMAT

Coaching sessions involve either scheduled or ad hoc contact. In this respect, they reflect the realities of other mainstream professional interactions, such as communicating with your colleagues or with a trusted adviser such as your attorney or physician.

Scheduled Sessions

Scheduled sessions are planned in advance. Whether a scheduled session occurs face-to-face or remotely (that is, by telephone or videoconference), the agenda is co-created by you and your coach. It is usually based partly on your written plan and partly on emergent events, needs, and opportunities. Past, present, and future matters are all likely to be covered.

- *Past events.* Your coach will be eager to know what you've been up to since your last session. Your coach may ask:

What action steps from your written plan have you taken?

What other work-related developments have occurred in the interim?

- *Present analysis and interpretation.* Collaboratively the two of you review what you've reported in your update. Your coach evaluates what you've described, elicits additional data to flesh out key points, and helps you analyze and make sense of the results. Your coach may test your thinking and guide you through the discovery and consolidation of new information and perspectives. Your coach may ask:

How did your efforts turn out? What were the results?

Did you achieve your aim? If not, why not?

What do the results mean?

How did [or do] you feel? What have you learned?

What will you do differently next time?

- *Future planning.* Together you will look at what's next on your Powerhouse Plan and upcoming work demands. Your coach will help you identify practice opportunities to apply what you've learned. Time-sensitive skill and knowledge needs are identified. Your coach may ask:

What pressing issues or performance concerns are coming up for you?

What tools, capabilities, or resources will you need to be successful?

What action steps or activities associated with action steps will you do next?

When and where can you practice or try out what you've learned?

To be sure, the questions your coach asks (or their equivalents) will occur in the context of a conversation; they will not be a cross-examination. Furthermore, the tidy chronological sequence I've outlined here would, in an actual coaching session, almost certainly be an amalgam of time events, with much hopping among past, present, and future. You're likely to utter the phrase, "And that reminds me . . . ," often in your coaching sessions as you make linkages between what has happened and what will happen, and between abstract know-how and real-life application.

KEY POINT: Be sure to start your sessions with a working agenda so that time gets allocated properly. Otherwise key issues or breaking developments may get short shrift, especially if your coach doesn't know about them yet.

Ad Hoc Sessions

An unexpected development, a sudden crisis, or an urgent decision deadline are typical situations when a "just-in-time" coaching session can profoundly influence desired results. With ad hoc sessions, *you* initiate the meeting and set the agenda. Consequently, the role your coach plays—such as sounding board, clarifier, troubleshooter, co-strategist—depends on the presenting situation. Ad hoc sessions are, by their nature, often conducted by telephone. Many executive coaches include ad hoc contact in their service offerings to provide clients with maximum responsiveness and value. For example, retainer-based programs and those that offer unlimited coach access during the specified time period typically do. By comparison, short-term and targeted programs that consist of a fixed number of sessions or cumulative hours may or may not include impromptu contact. (See Chapter Four for a full discussion of engagement and program terms.)

Since ad hoc sessions are prompted by you and stem from a time-sensitive need, they tend to be highly focused and consultative. Consequently, you, not your coach, may be the person who asks questions first. You might ask your coach:

"How should I . . . ?"

"What do you think about . . . ?"

"What's a good way to . . . ?"

For instance, you might seek an objective opinion or a chance to try out an approach and get feedback, or learn specific how-to tips. Here are examples of completed questions:

"How should I tell my second in command that he's not getting promoted?"

"What do you think about letting the committee set the strategic goals instead of me?"

"What's a good way to convey these talking points clearly?"

Depending on the situation and its complexity, an ad hoc session can last a few minutes or much longer.

KEY POINT: A mix of scheduled and ad hoc coaching sessions can be a knockout combination. I call this the "Over Time and Over Night" medley. When coaching provides you with tools and solutions to immediate needs, you're in the zone for achieving extraordinary results. Your capabilities and confidence mushroom. Your motivation to see your coaching goals to conclusion is strengthened.

Case in Point: From Sounding Off to Sound Choice

Laura was a smart, no-nonsense Wall Street executive. Like many other type A high-flyers, she had a tendency to pull the trigger first and ask questions later. Our coaching relationship was several years old, funded by her firm, and currently retainer based. We met quarterly for a half-day tune-up session. In between, she contacted me on an as-needed basis.

One day I received an urgent message from her assistant. Could I speak with Laura that same afternoon? She was on a business trip in Rio de Janeiro but did not want to wait until she returned to the States to talk.

When she phoned later, Laura got straight to the point: "I got a nasty e-mail from my boss yesterday. and I'm really annoyed."

Her boss, I knew, was the division CEO.

The e-mail in question involved a key appointment in her group, which she intended to fill with an internal staff promotion. In it, her boss had expressed his disapproval bluntly, if not absolutely.

"I know my business better than he does," she fumed. "I know who and what I need to fill this seat."

I asked Laura to tell me more about her decision process. What made her candidate the best choice? What were his qualifications and track record?

When she was done making her case, which seemed a reasonable one on the surface, I asked her to weigh the pros and cons of overriding her boss's wishes. Specifically, what were the likely costs she'd pay in terms of their working relationship?

I could sense Laura analyzing the situation long distance. From her tone and hesitation, I could tell she was having second thoughts. "I need to think this over some more," she said and signed off.

When we followed up a few days later, Laura had returned from her trip and had already retained a headhunter to help fill the position with an outside candidate. Being the action-oriented person she was, I wasn't at all surprised.

"Thanks for slowing me down long enough to think strategically," she told me. She was having lunch with her boss to mend any broken fences.

COACHING METHODS AND TECHNIQUES

Although nothing mysterious or ultratechnical happens in a coaching session, something quite remarkable does occur: learning. At any moment the human brain receives about 100 million pieces of information through the nervous system. Even as we strive to do our best, we're usually not mindful of how we're able to continue expanding our talents and capabilities. Conversations, new experiences, a provocative book, an operational audit, a passing remark or chance encounter: any and all of these are learning opportunities. Indeed, the difference between activities that are mundane and those that yield exceptional outcomes can often be described in one word: focus. We learn when we're focused and motivated.

Coaching methods are pathways to learning and top-flight performance. Executive and business coaches use methods and techniques that you probably use yourself as a leader, manager, or professional. However, where you might use these methods casually or haphazardly, your coach uses them purposefully and systematically.

Put another way, your coach uses common methods to produce uncommon results.

You have experienced a number of these methods already in earlier phases of your program. (See, for example, the discussion of assessment methods in Chapter Six.) As you will see from the descriptions that follow, some of the methods overlap, while others work in tandem or close proximity.

Eight Winning Coaching Methods

1. *Discussion.* Dialogue, whether face-to-face or by telephone or videoconference, is the linchpin of coaching. This highly interactive and versatile method allows powerful two-way communi-

cation and new insights. You and your coach can review assignments, situations, and events; you can brainstorm, troubleshoot, and prepare. The possibilities for promoting learning and positive change with this method are practically limitless.

2. *Active listening.* A corollary technique to discussion is active listening. People speak at 100 to 175 words per minute but can listen intelligently at 600 to 800 words per minute. Consequently listeners' minds can wander. Your coach, however, intentionally focuses on what you say and how you say it in order to understand you fully.

3. *Assigned activities.* You may be asked to keep a journal or log, read an article or book, prepare a draft summary, or try new behaviors and approaches. Assigned activities may come directly from your written plan in the form of action steps, or they may be supplemental homework in response to new developments and opportunities.

4. *Instruction.* Your coach may provide tutelage, informational materials, or other resources with the aim of transferring knowledge to you rapidly and in a timely fashion. If, for example, you're about to conduct midyear employee evaluations, getting a "key points" briefing from your coach on how to give effective feedback could be extremely valuable.

5. *Rehearsal.* Your coach may help you ace an upcoming event by putting you through your paces in advance. Indeed, if you have a high-stakes meeting, a difficult conversation, or an important interview looming, preparation is critical. The same applies if you're attempting to improve an existing skill or acquire a new one. Guided practice and role playing are two standard rehearsal techniques.

6. *Direct observation.* Not all coaching methods occur behind closed doors. To the contrary, if circumstances permit, your coach may watch you in action to see firsthand how you're doing. If you're speaking to a large group or your team knows you're working with a coach, it's often possible for your coach to observe you. Shadowing is another type of observation technique. As the term suggests, this approach involves following you as you go about your regular business activities so that your coach learns more about your routine, business context, and

interpersonal style. Of course, real-life observation is not possible with telecoaching. Even so, reviewing video recordings of you in action might be an option.

7. *Adjunct communication.* Your coach may be in touch with you in between sessions to request (or provide) information, feedback, and updates. These activities do not always require face-to-face interaction—or, in the case of remote coaching, a telephone conversation. E-mail or fax communication can often get the job done efficiently. (Note, though, the points I made about electronic communication and confidentiality in Chapter Four.)

8. *Communication with others.* With your prior knowledge, your coach may meet or confer with collateral parties such as your manager, direct reports, team members, colleagues, or even customers. In fact, if you have a Powerhouse Plan guiding your execution phase, anyone you listed as a change partner is a potentially valuable feedback source on how you're progressing.

In actuality, your coaching session is likely to be a dynamic encounter drawing on a variety of methods. Usually there are multiple pathways to achieving a desired or necessary outcome. Whether your program is employer funded or private pay, brief or extended, in-person or remote, flexibility and adaptation to your learning preferences and situation are standard. Of course, one approach may be better or faster or more effective for you than another.

When you're actively engaged in your coaching session, you won't be thinking about specific methods, nor should you be. Rather, being familiar with the techniques and approaches you're likely to encounter allows you to relax and focus on what's really important. You're also better able to indicate any preference for one approach over another, thereby partnering fully with your coach.

KEY POINT: No amount of expertise on your coach's part can substitute for candor and accuracy on your part. You must be truthful and complete in what you say. Withholding important details or massaging the facts to protect your ego ultimately won't serve you and your lofty goals. The ability to confront reality, especially when it's uncomfortable, is an essential leadership trait.

HOW COACHING HELPS YOU LEARN

When you're motivated by ambition or high stakes, you approach learning seriously. You're emotionally as well as cognitively involved. Coaching sessions are structured to provide the proper atmosphere for serious learning. Things are slowed down long enough for you to catch your breath and really pay attention. You're in a safe, positive environment where trial-and-error experimentation is encouraged. Remember, this is your own unique learning lab.

Coaching actually changes your brain. In order to learn, your brain must perform three distinct operations, as illustrated in Figure 8.1:

Task 1: Remember. You create a memory of the new information.

Task 2: Recall. You recall the information at will.

Task 3: Apply. You put the information to use.

FIGURE 8.1. HOW YOUR BRAIN LEARNS.

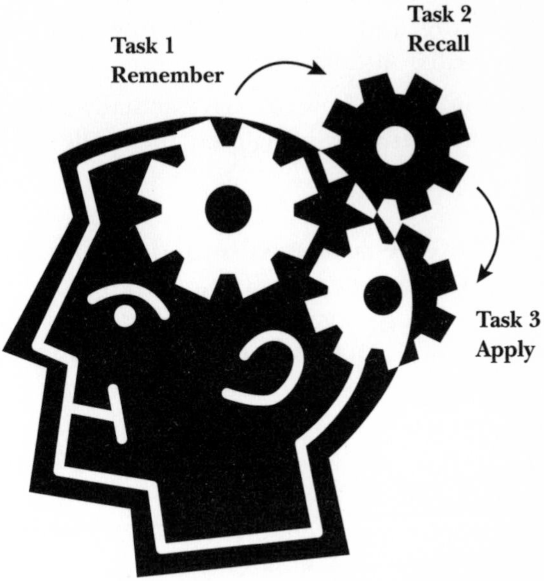

Task 1
Remember

Task 2
Recall

Task 3
Apply

Your brain consists of about 100 billion nerve cells, or neurons, that are constantly sending and receiving electrochemical impulses. When you concentrate, you strengthen certain patterns of connection, making each connection easier to create the next time. In this way memory develops, and habits and skills do too. They all become embedded in your brain as frequently activated neural networks. If you stop performing an activity, the corresponding neural networks fall into disuse and eventually may disappear. The principle of "use it or lose it" definitely applies (as most adults who took high school trigonometry know).

Coaching encourages and reinforces the creation of new neural sequences (that is, new learning) inside your brain. In so doing, you acquire new attitudes, knowledge, and capabilities. You develop new habits, shed maladaptive behaviors, and elevate your performance in much the way a champion athlete perfects his or her performance through intensive, repetitive practice.

Here is how your brain works in coaching sessions:

Task 1: Remember. You are optimally prepared mentally and emotionally to pay attention to new information and evaluate existing information.

Task 2: Recall. You have extensive opportunities to practice retrieving, interpreting, and connecting the new information to current needs, skills, and objectives.

Task 3: Apply. You review how you have actually performed. In so doing, you start a new learning cycle that builds on the preceding one.

In other words, you prepare, practice, and perform. "We are what we repeatedly do," Aristotle said. The coaching methods and formats I've described here organize and enhance this mighty learning cycle. The result is that you're able to perform much more effectively and confidently—and faster too!

KEY POINT: Execution involves performance. Performance involves behavior. Behavior involves learning. Learning involves focus. Your brain might appreciate the acronym FOCUS as a memory tool—it stands for "Follow One Course Until Successful."

Leading Minds on Focus

"If I have ever made any valuable discoveries, it has been owing more to patient attention than to any other talent."—*Isaac Newton*

"The shorter way to do many things is to do only one thing at a time."—*Wolfgang Amadeus Mozart*

"You've got to stick at a thing, a particular thing, until you succeed. I feel that's the only way to succeed—by concentrating on something in particular."—*Betty Cuthbert, Australian Olympic track champion*

"You must be single-minded. Drive for one thing on which you have decided."—*George S. Patton*

"Nothing focuses the mind better than the constant sight of a competitor who wants to wipe you off the map." —*Wayne Calloway*

"What is success? I think it is a mixture of having a flair for the thing that you are doing and knowing that it is not enough, that you have got to have hard work and a certain sense of purpose."—*Margaret Thatcher*

"On the day I'm performing, I don't hear anything anyone says to me."—*Luciano Pavarotti*

"Nothing will work unless you do."—*Maya Angelou*

SUPERCHARGING YOUR "KNOWING-DOING" CYCLE

I have compared your coaching sessions to a learning laboratory. Within this laboratory, your coach acts as your personal catalyst. The dictionary defines *catalyst* as "an agent that provokes or speeds significant change or action." This catalytic role is especially significant in supercharging your knowing-doing cycle, the dynamic process by which we become smarter and more capable (see Figure 8.2). We think and then we do. We do and then we think about what we've done. This interplay between reflection and actual experience is sometimes called *experiential learning*.

As adults, we seldom stop and think about how we continue to learn new things. It can even feel a little artificial or uncomfortable to analyze something we take for granted. However, the more you know about proven tools and methods for performance improvement, the better equipped you are for superb on-demand execution. For example, superstars as diverse as iconic CEO Jack Welch, Tour de France champion Lance Armstrong, and opera diva Renée Fleming are all on record as to how they produce the results they want. They are exceptionally gifted people, to be sure, but they've also mastered their personal knowing-doing cycles.

With your coach as catalyst, your knowing-doing cycle becomes highly concentrated. He or she points you toward key information that expands both your insight (knowing) and performance capabilities (doing).

Of course, we must always keep sight of the big picture: what happens inside your coaching sessions should relate directly to your activities outside coaching. After all, locker room strategizing and feel-good pep talks mean nothing if players don't deliver in the game. Extraordinary executive coaching results mean demonstrable real-world results. Figure 8.3 shows the myriad ways your coach's catalytic role speeds improvement where it counts.

You prepare and practice inside your coaching sessions, and then you perform outside your coaching sessions. This is the executive coaching "triple-play." In the process, you complete your actions steps, modify and refine your coaching plan as needed, and achieve your coaching goals.

FIGURE 8.2. THE KNOWING-DOING CYCLE.

Knowing
- Reflection
- Lessons learned
- Detect patterns
- Generalize results
- Strategize next steps

YOU

Doing
- Actual experience
- Concrete events
- Act and interact
- Test hypotheses
- Real-life experiments

FIGURE 8.3. HOW YOU ARE COACHED TO LEAD.

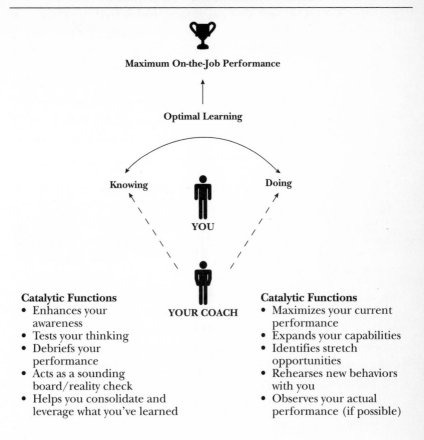

Furthermore, you and your coach can replace completed goals with new ones, creating a rolling Powerhouse Plan.

You are truly coached to lead.

Case in Point: Closing a Knowing-Doing Gap

Scott, the executive director of a private research institute, was known throughout his organization as a voracious reader of business and management best-sellers. Although widely respected and liked, he had a reputation as a micromanager.

Intellectually, Scott knew that his meddling tendencies sapped morale and trust. Replacing these with more appropriate and effective approaches was his primary coaching goal. A strong believer in transparency and leading by example, Scott enlisted his entire senior team as change partners in his program. Indeed, he and I built plenty of feedback loops into his Powerhouse Plan so we could monitor his progress with these key people.

But old habits die hard. Scott and I were both aware that he had to tackle the root cause of his overcontrolling style, not just the overt behaviors. We devised a series of experiments that involved Scott's absenting himself from certain management meetings and decisions. He recorded his reactions to these episodes in a log, which we then reviewed together.

Over time, Scott saw a pattern to his log entries. Trust, or more properly, the lack of it, was a recurrent theme. There was no surprise here.

However, a major breakthrough came when Scott realized that he lacked trust in himself.

"I've been making everyone crazy around here because I'm not sure of myself," he said, in utter amazement.

Scott's "aha!" moment, the result of guided discovery over time in his coaching sessions, cleared his path forward. Subsequently we could focus on the real driver behind his micromanaging: his shaky self-confidence. With this new awareness, real change began to occur. He joined a president's organization where he could benchmark his own leadership capabilities against a peer group. He was pleasantly surprised at how he stacked up.

As his self-confidence grew, Scott was able to close the gap between knowing what he should do (get out of his people's way) and actually doing it. He and his direct reports collectively celebrated what became known throughout the institute as "Scott's extreme makeover."

"I knew I could do better. I just didn't know how to get there on my own," he told me toward the end of his coaching program some fourteen months later.

He passed another milestone when he let his book club subscriptions lapse.

"I don't feel the need to read everything under the sun anymore," he said. "So don't count on me for new book recommendations."

With time and confidence to spare, Scott went on to spearhead the institute's first major fundraising campaign.

LEADER SPOTLIGHT
Maurice Lévy
Chairman and Chief Executive Officer, Publicis Groupe

Since taking the helm of Publicis Groupe in 1987, Maurice Lévy has acquired over one hundred companies, transforming what was a highly respected French advertising firm into the world's fourth largest communications conglomerate. *Fortune* magazine has cited Publicis Groupe as one of the ten best companies to work for in Europe. Listening to Lévy describe his operating philosophy and values, you quickly realize the central roles that coaching, mentoring, and aggressive learning play.

"I work by rolling up my sleeves and being in the forefront with the team," he told me, describing his leadership style. "I think the best way to work is never to be satisfied, always overdemanding, and never complacent. We live in a changing world. We have to deal with clients who are evolving and consumers who are evolving. So if we stick to our old knowledge, and our old schemes, and our old way of work, we are just dead.

"A quality that is well embedded in our organization is what we call the 'human touch.' You must believe in people, in the human spirit. Ever since our firm's inception, we have always taken pride in encouraging people to grow, to bloom, to learn, to become better. With this approach, we have also been able to deliver better worth to the client, because when our people are confident and curious, they find better ways of communicating."

Lévy noted that the Publicis paradigm involved a delicate balancing act: "There is a kind of paradox in the way we work. We try to be very efficient. We are very demanding in what we ask from our people. We are uncompromising with performance. At the same time we have this one overarching rule: we give permission to fail. It's something that I believe is very important. First, I think we learn more from failure. Second, I think that if we want our people to act fearlessly, to take initiative and be entrepreneurs, they should feel they have permission to fail. People have a second and a third chance here. This is something that is highly appreciated. They are accountable, and at the same time they can take new responsibilities."

Lévy, who is in his early sixties, identified his primary role now as working with his firm's next generation of leaders: "I spend a lot of time trying to advise and share information. It's important to give people a feeling of confidence that they can deliver. But I know that your own experience is far better than the experience you learn from others. You never learn the same way from somebody else's stories and anecdotes that you learn from doing things yourself.

"I'm still always looking. I'm trying to learn. I believe the day you stop learning you become really old."

IN PRAISE OF UNLEARNING

I want to call attention briefly to one aspect of the action coaching phase that is often overlooked: the challenges you may encounter in unlearning.

HABITS

"A nail is driven out by another nail. Habit is overcome by habit," Erasmus observed more than four hundred years ago.

When you learn something new, you acquire new behaviors. If the behavior or skill is brand new, you're doing the equivalent of hammering a nail into virgin wood. Nothing was there beforehand. However, if you're replacing an existing behavior or set of behaviors with more effective ones, you have to unlearn as well as learn. Practically speaking, you and your coach may need to hammer away for some time before the existing "nail" (the outmoded or problem habit) is displaced and replaced.

I say this not to discourage you, but rather to alert you to what to expect. Habits are intransigent by their very nature. The neural networks associated with them are well established in your brain. They resist modification. In general, this is not a bad thing. After all, habituated behaviors enable us to function efficiently. For instance, you wouldn't want to have to concentrate intensely every time you performed routine tasks such as brushing your teeth or preparing scrambled eggs. Instead, habits allow you to do them without much conscious effort.

Even when you're highly motivated, ingrained behaviors take time to eliminate. Consequently, you may feel frustrated or even a bit discouraged during your "hammering" phase. This is perfectly normal. The important point is to stay the course. Be patient with yourself and the process. The more you practice and repeat new learning—in other words, the more you "hammer"—the more quickly you form new habits and advance your goals.

Be prepared for some temporary frustration where habit breaking is involved. If you travel two steps forward and one step backward, you're still achieving a whopping 50 percent gain.

TRAPEZE MOMENTS

Another challenge you're likely to experience with unlearning involves a situation I call the "trapeze moment." In order to swing from one trapeze to another, the circus artist must relinquish his grip and fly through the air for several heart-stopping moments. Similarly, in the course of abandoning old behaviors and acquiring new ones, you can experience one or more trapeze moments: temporary performance gaps caused when you have to let go of the old and familiar but have not yet attained comparable proficiency at the new.

For example, trapeze moments can occur when you are changing from a command-and-control style to a consensus-based approach, moving from an individual contributor role to a managerial position, or adapting to a new organization's culture and norms.

In my experience, trapeze moments are among the trickiest aspects for a coach and client to navigate successfully. No one wants to feel deskilled, especially not people with high expectations of their own performance. Very senior and accomplished individuals are particularly likely to feel uncomfortable or stressed because with a significant track record to their credit, they're not used to anything less than stellar execution every time. They are also accustomed to being in control. Therefore, the psychic costs associated with a performance dip, even a temporary one, can seem disproportionately high.

You can't grasp the trapeze in front of you without letting go of the one you're on. By the same token, unlearning means you have to relinquish your old ways.

Trapeze moments can be unsettling and frustrating in the short run. They require personal courage and perseverance, traits that leaders and those aspiring to leadership positions have to cultivate on a regular basis. You have to dare, to stretch yourself, if you want to continue learning and growing. But remember that you have a safety net: your coach.

In dealing with trapeze moments, you first should know what they are and that they can happen to you. In fact, if you don't encounter them during your action phase, your program is probably not challenging enough. Second, keep your big-picture goals in mind. What holds true in the business world also holds true in coaching situations: sometimes performance must decline in the near term in order to improve dramatically in the long term. Third, tell your coach if you're feeling seriously deskilled or are worried about a transient performance dip.

I find that when clients are introduced to the concept of trapeze moments early on, they're far better prepared to take them in stride later. Maintaining a sense of control is important, as is knowing what and where the obstacles are likely to be.

KEY POINT: You can't learn to fly and keep one foot on the ground. You can't learn to swim and remain on dry land. Coaching helps you manage and reduce learning risk in ways you cannot easily replicate elsewhere.

LEADER SPOTLIGHT
Rhonda J. Brown
President and Chief Executive Officer, Nine West Footwear Corporation

Rhonda Brown started her career in the fashion industry as an assistant buyer at Macy's and never looked back. As the CEO of Nine West, a division of Jones Apparel, she runs an international footwear, accessories, and retail group with annual revenues approaching $2 billion. Amid the bustle of an industry market week in Manhattan's Garment District, Brown talked about her personal experiences of mentoring and coaching. She is a firm believer in lifelong learning and parachuting out of one's comfort zone. "All the experience I picked up along the way culminates in this wonderful place I'm at today," she told me.

Brown considers herself fortunate to have a long-term mentor whom she still consults from time to time. About mentoring in general, she said, "It only works if the mentor is serious, because if it's not genuine, it never works. There are very few people I've worked with who have enough self-confidence and self-esteem to share those hidden secrets or advice."

She offered an unconventional twist to what is commonly associated with mentoring and coaching activities. "Some people are serious mentors, and some are 'little mentors,' she said. "A little mentor is somebody who may do something you don't like and you vow that you'll never do that. I really believe that negative experience or witnessing poor or bad behavior is a type of little mentoring. For instance, I had a couple of bosses who were evil twins. In many ways they taught me a lot about business, but I also learned what not to do. I think that's mentoring—accidental mentoring—but really, really key all the same. I can count on my hands those individuals who touched me in a negative way as well as a positive way: what I don't do today and what I do today as a result."

Speaking about her own mentoring and coaching styles, Brown said, "When business is good, that's usually when I'm my toughest. It's easier to push expectations and standards then. When things are tough, I go more into teaching mode so that people can bubble up problems and solve them, as opposed to being afraid and not telling me about the problems.

"My whole focus in the job I do today is the future. My ultimate goal, no joking, is to replace myself. What I do for a living is ever-changing. How can I grow if I don't have someone who can do what I do now? If you're in a senior position, you have to be flexible. But you also have to be inquisitive. If you're not curious, you can never get to the next thing. Some people can do it, and some will never be able to do it. But those people I believe can do it, I'm constantly pushing them a little harder."

FINAL ANALYSIS

"The doer alone learneth," Friedrich Nietzsche said. What goes on between your ears is the most critical activity that occurs during your action phase. You learn. You transform new information and insight into output. You elevate your game. And you unlearn. You abandon ineffective, self-limiting attitudes and behaviors. This dynamic process, whether it takes place over weeks or months, is guided, accelerated, and monitored by your coach.

When you realize or exceed your coaching goals, pride in personal accomplishment is richly deserved. Your heavy lifting produces valuable results. You have scaled up.

I will show you how to evaluate both your coaching program and your coach in the next chapter.

CHAPTER NINE

REVIEWING RESULTS THAT MATTER

result n. *The consequence of a particular action, operation, or course. A favorable or concrete outcome or effect.*
AMERICAN HERITAGE DICTIONARY (4TH ED.)

"However beautiful the strategy, you should occasionally look at the results," Winston Churchill said. With the fifth and last phase of the Five-Step Coaching Model, we have arrived at just this point. It's time to measure what matters.

Executive coaching is a performance-based activity and service. For coaching results to qualify as extraordinary, they need to pass the acid test of raising your performance. The bar needs to be set high and the threshold needs to be met or exceeded:

- Did you accomplish your coaching objectives?
- What can you do now that you could not do before?
- Are you demonstrably more effective?
- What is the proof?
- What are the tangible benefits?

My promise in this book was to show you how to achieve extraordinary results with executive coaching. We have focused on enhancing your leadership capabilities: those attitudes, behaviors, and competencies that enable you to achieve with and through others.

You have gone the distance. You've entered the fifth and last phase of the Five-Step Coaching Model. It's time to review what you have accomplished. Given all that has preceded in terms of planning, action learning, and ongoing monitoring, I think you will be pleasantly surprised at how straightforward evaluating your program can be.

Remember the Fuzzy Results Myth that says there's no way to measure outcomes from executive coaching? Often this objection arises because people don't know how to evaluate results. This does not apply to you. With the pointers and checklists I provide here, you will learn how to determine if your results qualify as extraordinary. In other words, are they:

- Evidence-based?
- Measurable?
- Practical?
- Sustainable?
- Value-added?
- A good deal?

Finally, putting the finishing touches on this review phase of the Five-Step Coaching Model includes evaluating your coach as well as your results. I will give you the know-how and tools to do so easily and confidently.

WHY EVALUATE YOUR COACHING PROGRAM?

How often have you attended a workshop or completed a program only to move immediately on to the next pressing matter on your calendar? If you're like most other overworked managers today, I'll bet this happens fairly often. The temptation is strong to just get on with things. It's even more tempting to keep on moving when you're not sure how to evaluate what you've just been through.

Why is it important to hit the brakes and do a formal review of your coaching program? Here are five compelling reasons:

Five Reasons to Review Your Coaching Program

1. Decide if your coaching objectives were met. How will you know whether you achieved your coaching goals unless you take a hard look at what occurred? When you review your program, you confirm your actual progress and successes. If you modified your original objectives, which is certainly possible given today's

kinetic business environment, did you and your coach do so consciously? By way of illustration, consider a small-craft pilot who sets out to fly to San Francisco but lands in Oakland instead. Now there may be any number of good reasons that this flight deviation occurred. However, the pilot should be aware that he or she is in Oakland and not San Francisco.

Have you reached your coaching destination? Reviewing your flight plan will tell you if (and where) you have arrived.

2. Satisfy yourself and any sponsors that the investment was a profitable one. Value is in the eye of the beholder. Can you justify the investment in coaching—to yourself and to any funding sponsors—in terms of identifiable outcomes and outputs? Was your coaching program worth the money, time, and effort? How have you benefited? Was it a good deal?

3. Identify how to sustain and extend your coaching results. When you entered college, you might have taken a math or foreign language placement exam. If you scored above a certain cutoff level, you placed out by demonstrating a satisfactory level of proficiency. If you chose to take a more advanced course, this was because you had a particular reason for doing so. Similarly, when you review your program, you do two operations: first, you determine your current performance levels; second, you determine if you have placed out. If you find that you have reached an optimal "cruising altitude" where your new capabilities are concerned, you will want to be sure you can maintain them over time. Or you might want to leverage these capabilities further on your own—for example, to new situations and opportunities.

4. Determine if a program renewal is warranted. Extraordinary results can create a real hunger for ongoing improvement. High achievers are never satisfied; they don't rest on their laurels. Besides, the competitive landscape is constantly changing. When you look back, you're also positioning yourself to look ahead. You can make an informed decision about whether a program renewal makes sense. You might want to continue to elaborate on or refine your current agenda. You might want to add to your repertoire of leadership competencies or prepare for your next career step or assignment. When you clearly identify any outstanding performance goals, you can project the

value-added of renewing your program and consider the options. For example, a retainer-based program might serve your needs better than a more structured format.

5. Use program evaluation findings to evaluate your coach. It stands to reason that your coach's performance is directly linked to your own. After all, Joe Torre's standing as an effective manager depends in large part on how the Yankees perform over the season. No World Series, no kudos. To evaluate your coach accurately and fairly, you need to complete your own scorecard first.

Leading Minds on Results

"Everybody, soon or late, sits down to a banquet of consequences."—*Robert Louis Stevenson*

"I think one's feelings waste themselves in words; they ought all to be distilled into actions which bring results."—*Florence Nightingale*

"The only true measure of success is the ratio between what we might have done and what we might have been on the one hand, and the thing we have made and the things we have made of ourselves on the other."—*H. G. Wells*

"Try not to become a man of success but rather to become a man of value."—*Albert Einstein*

"The measure of success is not whether you have a tough problem to deal with, but whether it is the same problem you had last year."—*John Foster Dulles*

"It is much more difficult to measure nonperformance than performance."—*Harold S. Geneen*

"We will be judged by only one thing, the result."
—*Vince Lombardi*

"Champions keep playing until they get it right."
—*Billie Jean King*

SUCCESS INDICATORS: A MULTILEVEL APPROACH

Success indicators are tools for gauging your coaching results. When the time comes to review your coaching program, you are likely to consider these five dimensions or levels (Figure 9.1):

Level One: Personal Satisfaction

Level Two: Learning

Level Three: On-the-Job Application

Level Four: Business Impact

Level Five: Return on Investment

Most of the time, people are unaware of the distinctions I've just listed. However, you cannot determine the total accrued value of

FIGURE 9.1. PROGRAM EVALUATION REVIEW LEVELS.

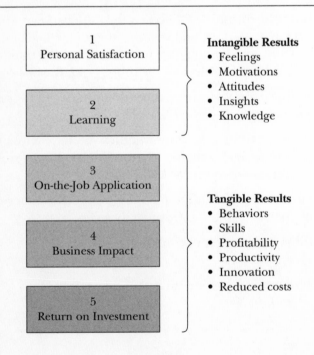

your coaching program unless you know on what levels you're doing your evaluation. Now I will explain what these levels mean and cover (Table 9.1 summarizes the distinguishing characteristics of the levels).

LEVEL ONE: PERSONAL SATISFACTION

Level One evaluation deals with subjective emotional experience. Simply stated, did you like your coaching program and your coach? Do you feel that you accomplished something worthwhile? Appraisals at this level are generally impressionistic and tend to be based on feelings (that is, gut instinct) rather than thoughtful analysis. Of course, the value of positive emotional and motivation

TABLE 9.1. CHARACTERISTICS OF COACHING EVALUATION LEVELS.

Evaluation Levels	Who Decides?		Tangible Evidence?
	You	Others	

Level One: Personal Satisfaction
   What do you think of your coaching
      program?
   Did you like it?
	X	No	No

Level Two: Learning
   What specific insights and knowledge
      did you acquire?
	X	No	No

Level Three: On-the-Job Application
   How did you apply what you learned?
   What specific behaviors and skills did
      you use?
	X	X	Yes

Level Four: Business Impact
   What are the top- and bottom-line
      consequences?
   What is the evidence?
	X	X	Yes

Level Five: Return on Investment Was your program a good deal?	X	X	Yes

states can border on priceless, a point I'll return to shortly. Peace of mind knows no price tag whatsoever. Still, while you can estimate a *perceived* value at this level, and a stratospheric one at that, you cannot point to a tangible result or benefit.

Sample Personal Satisfaction Statements

"I feel more confident."

"I liked [or disliked] my coach."

"Coaching was definitely worthwhile."

Key Point: Personal satisfaction is a notoriously unreliable success indicator. Consider that the most challenging college professors—the ones who stretch their students' thinking and performance—often receive low student feedback evaluations. Conversely, you can like your coach and yet experience little or no change or improvement.

Level Two: Learning

Level Two evaluation also calls for your subjective opinion. However, at this level, you can identify program results in terms of learning outcomes. What do you know now that you did not know before? To answer this question, you must reflect on what actually occurred. Without a doubt, new insights and knowledge can be precious takeaways. However, being intangible, they are difficult to appraise and often involve a good deal of subjectivity and relativity.

Sample Learning Statements

"I realize now that I want to shoot for a place on the executive committee."

"I know how to use consensus building to jump-start my team."

"I've learned that I can't do everything myself."

Level Three: On-the-Job Application

Level Three evaluation moves into the realm of concrete data and observable performance. We're now dealing with tangibles. Evidence-based judgments are possible. How did you use what you learned? What specific behaviors and competencies did you demonstrate? Where and when? At this level, not just you but other people too can ascertain if your coaching objectives and targets were attained.

Sample On-the-Job Application Statements

"I realize now that I want to shoot for a place on the executive committee, so I volunteered to spearhead the annual golf fundraiser.

"I used consensus building to jump-start my team and get the project done without additional head count."

"I learned that I can't do everything myself, so I turned all new client presentations over to Marketing."

LEVEL FOUR: BUSINESS IMPACT

Level Four evaluation addresses the business results of your performance. Here too you're dealing with tangible outcomes. How have your coaching results translated into top- and bottom-line outputs? What is the evidence to support your value-added claims?

Sample Business Impact Statements

"I realize now that I want to shoot for a place on the executive committee, so I volunteered to spearhead the annual golf fundraiser. We got national media attention, raised $4 million, and I'll be joining the board in January."

"I used consensus building to jump-start my team and get the project done without additional head count. The company saved half a million dollars in recruitment and compensation costs."

"I learned that I can't do everything myself, so I turned all new client presentations over to Marketing. I now have time to focus on potential multibillion dollar markets in Asia."

LEVEL FIVE: RETURN ON INVESTMENT

Level Five evaluation looks at the monetary cost-benefit ratio. Did your coaching program return a satisfactory payoff? For a handy calculation method that often suffices, consider using or adapting this formula:

Return on Investment (ROI) = $\dfrac{\text{Program Results} - \text{Program Costs}}{\text{Program Costs}}$

For example, a school superintendent whose coaching goal was to improve her negotiation and influencing skills persuaded the school board to rebid the district's electric utility contract. As a result, the district was able to reduce its electricity expenditures by $163,000 over two years. The total cost of her coaching program was $25,000.

Let's do the math:

$$\text{ROI} = \frac{\$163,000 - \$25,000}{\$25,000} = \frac{5.52}{1} \times 100 = 552 \text{ percent}$$

Based on this single on-the-job application, the return on investment for the superintendent's coaching yielded a return of roughly 5 to 1, or 552 percent.

This ROI formula is approximate, not precise. Those of you with advanced financial or economics expertise know that total program costs typically include opportunity and administrative costs, not just coaching fees. If you (or your chief financial officer) require nothing less than an exhaustive ROI analysis, then by all means call in the accounting whizzes. ("Taking into account the isolated benefits minus the program costs, adjusted for inflation . . ."). However, be sure to factor in the additional cost!

Sample ROI Statements

"I saved three times what my coaching program cost by acting strategically and restructuring rather than automatically increasing head count."

"We doubled our repeat business last quarter. Our net profit was almost twenty times what the firm paid my executive coach over the same period to help me manage my time more effectively."

"I invested $15,000 in personal funds to work with a coach on upgrading my career strategy and managerial skills. The merit increase I received this year comes to about the same amount, *and* it's ongoing."

In my extensive experience, and the research backs me up, when you work with a competent professional and a robust program model, executive coaching generates a better return than government bonds, the stock market, and most real estate ventures too. Here is some additional ROI food for thought:

- Total replacement costs for senior management and high-knowledge professionals easily range from 40 to 100 percent or more of their annual compensation.
- Star producers are worth their annual quota or revenue, not just their annual salary.
- Lost clients or customers can add more than 100 percent to the direct and opportunity costs of employee turnover.
- Coaching fees are one-time, whereas better performance and business impact are annualized and ongoing.

MORE ABOUT INTANGIBLE COACHING RESULTS

You might wonder whether I am saying that intangible coaching results have no value.

No, not at all. Intangibles such as feelings, attitudes, and insight can be among the most valuable and enduring results of your coaching program, far surpassing any monetary gains. To be sure, if you feel more confident or enthusiastic or in control of your destiny, you have obtained a precious takeaway.

But consider this: your intangible benefit is very likely the product or by-product of a tangible result. For example, when you have successfully applied a new skill, you are likely to feel more confident. Using our definition criteria, applying a skill is a tangible result, whereas feeling more confident is intangible.

To illustrate my point, consider these examples:

- When you have delivered a project on time and on budget, you feel less stressed.
- When you receive a promotion, you revise your view of what you can accomplish.
- When you devise a cost-savings solution, you think differently about your creative potential.
- When you delegate and your team delivers, you become more trusting.

In each instance, the intangible result comes from a tangible result. In other words, it is born out of an observable and measurable action or application.

I often tell clients and sponsors to compare intangible and tangible coaching results to smoke and fire. We know that where there is smoke, there is usually fire. When you can identify a high-value intangible coaching result, I'll bet that you and your coach can identify one or more contributory tangible results.

Let's refashion the above examples as questions and answers:

Question: "Why do I feel less stressed?" Answer: "I got the project done on time and under budget."

Question: "Why do I feel more ambitious?" Answer: "I got the promotion based on what I accomplished and have my sights set on another."

Question: "Why do I feel more creative?" Answer: "My ideas have practical implications and rewards."

Question: "Why do I feel more motivated?" Answer: "I scored one touchdown with this hire; I can do it again."

Question: "Why do I feel more trusting?" Answer: "I behaved in a different way, and the team productivity soared."

Just follow the smoke back to its source. Your coach should be able to help you do this.

LEADER SPOTLIGHT
Robert Erburu
Retired Chairman and CEO, Times Mirror Company

Robert Erburu joined the Times Mirror Company as a young attorney and retired as its chairman and chief executive officer in 1996. He currently serves as nonexecutive chairman of the board of Marsh & McLennan Companies and chairman of the board of trustees of the National Gallery of Art. The Huntington Library, where he is chairman emeritus, recently dedicated its new art gallery building to Erburu and his wife Lois in honor of their many years of dedicated leadership.

Looking back on his career at Times Mirror (parent company of a news media empire that included the *Los Angeles Times* and *Newsday*), Erburu talked about lessons learned on the road to becoming an effective leader. He identified strong communication and team-building skills as important capabilities.

"One of the things I always pushed, and still do, is how important it is in an organization to have a group of people really work together," he told me. "The best way to get them to work together is to make sure that they talk to one another. If you're the boss, you can do a lot about that. Not everyone will think that's the most important thing, but if the boss thinks it's the most important thing, it's likely to get done.

"When I arrived at Times Mirror, I was the youngest fellow there. I didn't know anything about the business. There were a couple of older men I worked with who knew a lot. One thing I learned very quickly was never to surprise people. Never not tell them what you know they will want to know. If they think you're going to keep them on the right level, you're going to get more cooperation, and more things will get done. If you communicate with people on a 'Well, I'll talk with him today, but I won't talk with her,' you can get yourself into a lot of difficulty because then others think it's okay for them to do the same thing."

According to Erburu, good communication assumes an even larger role in leading change successfully in companies and nonprofit institutions.

"I've always tried to organize things so that when change was going to happen or an important step was going to be taken, by the time we got to the point of acting, no one would be surprised. Everyone would say, 'That makes sense.' This isn't always easy to do because not everyone will agree, but you just have to make every effort to keep the group with you. The best way to do this is to make sure that as you take steps, you take them with you."

Erburu noted that many people helped to shape his career path and growth, among them the journalism professor who urged him to go to law school to learn to think logically. Later, the Chandler family, which owned the Times Mirror Company, figured prominently as sponsors and mentors.

Still, he made this observation about the developing leader's journey toward autonomy:

"One thing that leaders can't be is replicas of each other. When I became president of Times Mirror, whenever I had a problem I would say to myself, 'What would Al [Casey, a former company leader] do?' Then one day—fortunately it wasn't too long—I said to myself: 'Wait a minute, Bob. You're asking yourself the wrong question. It's not "What would Al do?" It's "What would *Bob* do?" Bob is Bob, and Al is Al.' Pretty soon people said, 'Hey, Bob, you figured out the right thing. We like you to be you.'"

Review Methods

Extraordinary coaching results are fact based and data driven. How then do you and your coach obtain the information to decide:

- If your behavior changed in the desired ways (Level Three)?
- If your changed behavior improved business results (Level Four)?
- If coaching services were a good deal overall (Level Five)?

The Powerhouse Plan Approach

If you used the Powerhouse Plan approach described in Chapter Seven, your review process should be a breeze because much of the information needed to answer the three critical review questions is literally at your fingertips. Your Powerhouse Plan contains:

- SMART goals: goals that are specific, measurable, actionable, realistic, timely
- Clearly identified benefits, both to yourself and, if relevant, to your organization too
- Individual action steps
- Specific progress or performance measures and completion dates

I've highlighted these elements on a sample plan for illustration purposes (see Exhibit 9.1).

With your coach, review your Powerhouse Plan (or other equivalent detailed action plan). Did you achieve your goals? If you can honestly answer "yes," go ahead and verify the "Benefits" section. You might be pleasantly surprised at how much you can augment benefits you expected with what you have actually achieved.

But then consider whether you and your coach are the sole judges in deciding if you reached your goals. Look at the "Progress Measures" section of the plan. Much depends on your program's purpose and how it was initially set up. Consider any additional understandings that were made up front about how your program would be evaluated. If, for example, your coaching has been highly confidential or a private-pay arrangement, you're probably not going to seek input from third parties now. Rather, look to your

EXHIBIT 9.1. POWERHOUSE PLAN EVALUATION METHOD.

GOAL Number ___	(State as Specific, Measurable, Attainable, Relevant, Timely)
	✔

Benefits of Achieving This Goal For Me:	For My Organization (if applicable):
✔	✔

Obstacles to Achieving This Goal	Solutions to the Obstacles

Action Steps	Progress Measures	Change Partners	Target Due Date
1. ✔	✔		✔
2.			
3.			
4.			

_____   _____   _____
Today's Date   **Goal Completion Date**   **Approved By (if applicable)**

Powerhouse Plan. Did you achieve your goals? Did they yield the expected benefits? Expect your coach to explore, test, and expand your subjective report. When feedback sources are limited, a second party's critical eye is that much more important.

If you have had "change partners"—that is, people who were involved directly or indirectly in initiating or implementing your action plan—then your review should incorporate their opinions, not just your own. As I pointed out in Chapter Six, multisource feedback tells you about your real-world effectiveness. In general, it is more reliable and accurate than single-source information. It is objective in a way that self-evaluation and self-report are not.

Whenever possible, your program review should include third-party feedback. You and your coach will want to know:

- Have others noticed a change in your behavior?
- Do others associate your behavior change with improved on-the-job performance?
- Do others believe these changes are contributing to operational or business effectiveness?

The methods used to obtain this information should be familiar to you by now, since they include techniques used during your initial assessment phase. The aim is to assess performance change by doing a before-and-after comparison:

- *Interviews.* Your coach consults change partners and collateral parties such as your supervisor and human resource manager. These can be one-on-one or group sessions.
- *Opinion surveys.* Your coach obtains current feedback from others. A follow-up 360-degree survey is often administered for this purpose. Organization climate surveys and customer satisfaction surveys are other possible tools.
- *Business metrics.* Your coach compares data dealing with one or more related performance indicators. Examples of statistical evidence include completed sales, customer complaints, grants secured, meetings held, and accident-free days.

If, for instance, a stated goal was to improve your meeting management skills, obtaining feedback from those who regularly participated would be highly desirable. In their view, are you running more efficient and productive meetings? Can they cite tangible success metrics such as time saved, improved quality control, or speed to market?

Case in Point: Best-Laid Plans

Meena was excited about her promotion to chief procurement officer and eager to make a positive impact. While she had many ideas for improving the department's operational efficiency, she also had some tricky management issues to address. First, she'd been hired over the interim officer, a popular manager who was staying put in the department. Second, she was from the "other side" of a recent corporate merger. Third, the department was a "diversity-free zone" consisting primarily of middle-aged white males. Meena's boss, himself a middle-aged white male, was totally committed to seeing her succeed. He saw her immediate challenges as engaging her team and improving her communication skills. He also recognized that the deck was not stacked in her favor.

After a thorough assessment phase that included an individual behavioral battery and interviewing her direct reports, Meena and I identified two priority action goals involving team building and public speaking. We crafted detailed action plans that her boss reviewed and approved. Then Meena got down to work with specific action steps. These included joining Toastmasters to get public speaking practice and feedback. She began scheduling regular one-on-one and group meetings with her managers, the better to build trust and set clear performance expectations. She worked hard to mend bridges with the person she'd beat out for the position. It was tough going, made none the easier when Meena began digging into operational matters and discovered serious problems. Her confidence in her team and in her ability to meet self-imposed success targets in a few months plummeted.

"Life is what happens to you while you're busy making other plans," John Lennon wrote. Coaching programs are no exception.

To make matters worse, a perfect storm of outside events hit the company, and her department in particular. Wave after wave of regulatory inspections and audits thrust Meena into crisis management mode. Out went her Powerhouse Plan, Toastmasters and all. Instead, for the next four months we focused on her day-to-day performance needs, such as report preparation and presentation, negotiating additional staffing, and fostering interdepartmental cooperation. Her boss, who was even more on the line than Meena, enthusiastically supported the new direction her coaching program had taken.

Meena and her department survived their ordeal by fire. In fact, the battle-zone atmosphere transformed her direct reports into a viable team almost overnight. Petty rivalries and old loyalties vanished.

Meena's anticipation skills proved critical to passing a series of successful evaluations. Finding the time and energy for tactical planning day-in and day-out became our sole coaching goal. Her original Powerhouse Plan sat untouched in our folders.

Under the circumstances, did Meena achieve extraordinary coaching results?

Her boss and the company's general counsel thought so. According to the latter, by clearing all regulatory hurdles, the company saved at least $5 million in outside legal and accounting fees.

Meena and I did eventually revisit her initial plan. It needed major revision because her team-building skills were functioning just fine.

As Dwight Eisenhower said, "Plans are nothing; planning is everything."

EVALUATING A PROGRAM WITHOUT A WRITTEN PLAN

In Chapter Seven, I discussed exceptions to the written action plan rule: brief engagements and retainer-based programs.

Brief Targeted Programs

When you work with a coach for a short period, say, for under ten sessions or less than three months, preparing a full-blown Powerhouse Plan may be overkill. The time required can be disproportionate to the total time you have. If this corresponds to your current situation—or, for that matter, if you find yourself planless for any other reason—you may still be able to use parts of the Powerhouse Plan methodology retrospectively. However, to do so, your goals must be specific and measurable in nature. Ask yourself:

- What were my coaching goals?
- What benefits did I expect?

- Did I achieve these goals? What's the evidence?
- Did I receive the expected benefits? What's the evidence?

Be aware that retrospective responses are subject to hindsight bias, the tendency to backfill or alter information based on current realities. This phenomenon is also known as the "I-knew-it-all-along" effect. In other words, you're at risk of fudging the data, either consciously or unconsciously, to be consistent with how things are now.

Retainer-Based Programs

The overarching goal of many coaching retainers is to maximize your effectiveness on a consultative, as-needed basis. Consequently, there are no specific goals or need for a detailed plan. Does this mean you can't evaluate your program? Absolutely not. However, you do have to take a modified approach. Ask yourself:

- Exactly when did I contact my coach? Why? What was at stake?
- How specifically did my coach have an impact on my performance?
- What did I do that I might not have done otherwise?
- What did I do better than I might otherwise have done?
- What's the evidence?
- What was the value-added of this improvement?
- Based on the above, was coaching a good deal?

Given that executives and managers are operating at warp speed today, they do not always have the answers to these questions at their fingertips. If you're currently in a retainer relationship and haven't kept track of the specifics, don't despair. No doubt your coach has this information and will be delighted to remind you of the excellent value you have been receiving.

TAKING FINAL STOCK

Now that you understand the ins and outs of evaluating your program, you're ready to do it. I designed the program review checklist in Exhibit 9.2 to speed you and your coach on your way.

EXHIBIT 9.2. COACHING PROGRAM REVIEW CHECKLIST.

Comprehensive Evaluation Form	Response Category		
	Yes	No	Not Applicable
Did your coaching program deliver value in terms of:			
1. Tangible results			
On-the-job performance	☐	☐	☐
Business impact	☐	☐	☐
Return on investment	☐	☐	☐
What's the *objective* evidence? (Be specific.)			
2. Intangible results			
Motivation and emotional states	☐	☐	☐
New insights, attitudes, knowledge	☐	☐	☐
What's your *subjective* sense? (Be specific)			
Additional observations:			

Take a deep breath and prepare to be delighted. If your program was grounded in the principles and methods I've shared with you in these pages, you're sure to claim solid success.

If your program is employer funded, very likely your sponsor or manager will receive a summary of your coaching results. Sometimes this is a verbal report, sometime a brief written summary. In either case, it's typically one page. I make a point of sharing the draft version with my clients before sending off the final copy.

Why "Good" Coaching Programs Disappoint

When you make bread from scratch, you can start off with quality ingredients and baking equipment and still wind up with a disappointing loaf. Similarly, coaching programs that look robust at the outset can still deliver anemic results. As a program developer and consultant, I've done numerous postmortems by way of analyzing what went wrong. Not all are avoidable or preventable, but with foresight many are. Here are the most common reasons:

Goal setting

- Goals proved unrealistic to complete in the allotted time
- Goals became irrelevant or too far removed from the client's day-to-day focus

Coach's role

- Inability to hold the client accountable
- Poorly managed trapeze moments (see Chapter Eight for a discussion)

Client's role

- Procrastination or lack of follow-through
- "Acts of God" (for example, health problems or family complications)

How "Perfect" Is Your Coach Now?

Executive coaches thrive on feedback. They develop feedback-rich programs for their clients. They use feedback methods, such as interviews and surveys. They help you squeeze as much actionable information as possible from all possible sources.

The time has come to review your coach and give performance-related feedback—or as some of my clients have been known to say, "It's payback time!" Use the coach evaluation scorecard in Exhibit 9.3 to consider all major evaluation areas. The questions will help you hone in on specific metrics and indicators.

By now, there should be no big surprises. After all, you started by choosing your Perfect Coach, a fully compatible strategic partner. If the two of you have had open communication and a transparent working relationship, consider your evaluation an opportunity to assess value added. Though we seldom think about it, all of the meaningful relationships in our lives, professional and personal, involve value added.

If you have outstanding issues or questions or suggestions for improvement, now's your chance to speak up. You're not acting like a leader if you hold back and instead complain to an associate or human resource manager. In fact, being able to give constructive feedback to others is a core leadership competency. Here's a great opportunity to put this skill to good use.

I said it in Chapter Two and I'll say it again: feedback is the "breakfast of champions."

Final Analysis

"What we call results are beginnings," Ralph Waldo Emerson wrote.

The takeaways from a well-designed, well-executed coaching program yield benefits on an ongoing basis. They raise your game permanently. Consequently, the accrued value of your coaching becomes clear only over time.

Not long ago, a former client of mine, a very talented professional woman, reviewed her coaching experience with the perspective that only time affords. With permission, I share her observations with you.

EXHIBIT 9.3. COACH EVALUATION SCORECARD.

Coach Performance Scorecard	Ranking Key 1 = Excellent 2 = Satisfactory 3 = Unsatisfactory N.A. = Not Applicable			
I. Did your coach . . .	**1**	**2**	**3**	**N.A.**
Perform according to the terms of your agreement? • Professional and trustworthy • Accessible and responsive • Follow through on commitments	☐	☐	☐	☐
Actively help you to achieve your stated goals?	☐	☐	☐	☐
Contribute to your top or bottom lines (or both)? • If so, how and by how much?	☐	☐	☐	☐
Contribute to your general leadership or business effectiveness? • If so, how and by how much?	☐	☐	☐	☐
Help you to manage stress levels or enhance your lifestyle quality? • If so, how and by how much?	☐	☐	☐	☐
Prevent you from doing anything that could have compromised your effectiveness or reputation? That of your department, team, or organization? • What? When?	☐	☐	☐	☐
Otherwise help you to perform better, faster, more efficiently, or more creatively? • If so, how and by how much?	☐	☐	☐	☐
II. General Observations How do you rate your coach overall?	☐	☐	☐	☐
Would you work with this coach again? Why?				
Would you recommend your coach to others? Why?				
III. Additional Comments and Notes				

The bottom-line benefits of coaching are the new strategies that I was able not only to learn but to truly make my own and be comfortable with:

- Look at others and borrow their strategy. (No, it does not mean that you are a phony. "If it works, . . .")

- Give feedback to your team: good, bad, or indifferent.

- Confront the problem when you see it. Sound alarm bells *before* the boat sinks. Don't try to fix it on your own.

- Take 360-degree feedback: "They actually realize I'm good!" Use that!

I entered coaching wanting to learn how to do these things, thinking that I knew what the benefits exactly were. But I did not know what the benefits were until I experienced them. It's like being in a room with a few doors, thinking that once you open a door you will get access to another room just like the one you are in. It will be better because there are two rooms instead of one. But that's not what happens. You open a couple of doors, get to the other side, and realize there are no walls on the other side!

CHAPTER TEN

SENSITIVE AND STICKY COACHING SITUATIONS

Your vision—the ability to look ahead and anticipate possibilities—helped you rise to a position for which leadership coaching is now a reality or viable consideration. You're a pro at "what-if" thinking, able to generate a variety of scenarios and likely outcomes. So when it comes to decisions about executive coaching or your coaching relationship, you may be considering concerns, issues, or extenuating conditions that are relevant to your particular circumstances.

In anticipation of your forward-thinking scenarios (based on years of experience answering these questions by similarly curious and contemplative clients), I'm devoting this chapter to twelve situations that coaching candidates and clients may encounter or contemplate. You will learn practical tips and strategies for resolving the kinds of complex, sensitive, or tricky situations that can occur or evolve over time. Do you want to know how much personal information to share, or whether a coach can follow you from one company to another? How (or when) to fire a coach? The answers to these and other thorny questions follow to help guide your decision making and optimize your coaching experience. Some are quite common; some are thankfully rare. I'll also advise you on ethical issues involving conflict of interest and dual relationships. Case in Point examples from actual coaching engagements will give you a frontline perspective.

Keep in mind, though, that your experience with an executive coach is a relationship, and, like every other relationship, it includes aspects and dynamics unique and known only to the two parties. So even if you think you have all the answers going into coaching, be prepared to engage in dialogue with your coach and to question anything you don't understand.

I've designed this chapter to keep your coaching experience as trouble free as possible. Still, the following scenarios are intended for illustrative and guidance purposes. In real life, situations have their own contexts and shades of gray. Never hesitate to seek advice or get a second opinion.

SCENARIO ONE

I've just been promoted and have been offered the services of an executive coach to help with my transition. Should I accept, or would accepting suggest that I'm not up to the job?

A promotion to a high-level position is a vote of confidence in your abilities, and the offer of an executive coach should be considered strong support for your success. If, for instance, you had purchased an exquisite diamond—even a flawless one—wouldn't you want to have it polished and set in a way that would best display its brilliance? Your company has judged you a gem, and they want everyone inside and outside the corporation to see you shine. Executive coaching is part of the very large investment the company is making in you and should be considered a generous display of respect and high expectations, not an expression of doubt in your capabilities.

It's also important to realize that your company is investing in your potential, not merely rewarding past accomplishments. Company leaders chose you because they believe you can master these new responsibilities better than anyone else they considered for this key promotion, not because they expected you to possess all the needed skills to excel already. If you are moving, say, from a midlevel to a top-tier management position, you will now be operating at a higher "altitude." Even a champion marathoner needs time to adapt if she is to compete at mountain elevations. But it's critical to your effectiveness that you adapt quickly. An executive coach can help you hit your stride without false starts or missteps.

Executive "onboarding" has become a popular coaching application, and with good reason. A decade ago, you might have had the luxury of an extended honeymoon period to acclimate yourself slowly to your new responsibilities, to gradually develop a high-performance management style and work group. But today's workplace is a microcosm of the 24/7, on-demand global economy. The performance pressures and demands of your new title begin *now,* not next quarter or next month. Think of working with a coach as an insurance policy—a form of performance risk management. And it's never too soon to take out an insurance policy. Just as a house fire can occur before a laid-back person pays the first premium on his homeowner's policy, a career-threatening crisis will not necessarily wait for your leisurely adjustment to high-level decision making. You can't insure a house reduced to rubble or a position from which you've been fired.

That's a worst-case scenario, of course. Executive coaching will more often foster great accomplishments than mitigate or prevent disasters. But preparation for both possibilities is vital. Consequently, I strongly urge almost anyone offered an executive coach as part of a promotion package to accept the offer quickly and graciously. You want to start a new job on the strongest possible note because it can be difficult to revisit missed opportunities (or undo missteps) down the road.

There are exceptions to my recommendation. If your organization has a jaundiced view of coaching, similar to the one described in the Emergency Room Myth, you might wish to amend the use of an executive coach. I would suggest either accepting the company's offer but meeting with your coach away from your workplace or arranging for telecoaching services.

Scenario Two

My organization is in a severe budget crunch. How do I make the case for working with a coach now?

When enterprises are in belt-tightening mode, it's imperative to be able to link and communicate the value of coaching to a mission-critical objective or role. To convince those with the yea-or-nay decision to vote yes on the engagement of an executive coach, you must appeal to the decision makers' immediate bottom-line interests. Although you and the company should both realize long-term benefits from working with a coach, it may be difficult to get anyone in your company to see beyond the current crisis. It will be vital, then, for you to match the benefits of a coach to the most vocally expressed needs of your superiors.

Here are some examples of bottom-line objectives that speak to how coaching can make a difference. Keep in mind that any argument you make must promote an economic advantage that will be greater than the expense of engaging an executive coach:

- *Coaching can help you to reduce project or product cycle time.* When a company is in the middle of a financial crunch or crisis, it is more important than ever before to move projects to completion or products out the door as quickly as possible. This is what brings the money in. Unfortunately, slow turnaround may be at the root of the cash-flow problem and is likely to worsen during a financial crisis, when workers are more worried about keeping their jobs than meeting production demands. You could argue that coaching aimed at improving your project management or team-building skills would turn projects around with greater speed and efficiency, and therefore be a profitable investment.

- *Coaching can help you increase revenue, market share, or customer base.* To tackle these kinds of core business activities, a company needs the sustained cooperation and motivation of all its personnel. People need timely information and sustained motivation to deliver against aggressive targets when a company's atmosphere is strained and those in position to motivate you and other corporate leaders are likely suffering stress overload as well. The right coach can help leaders keep strategic focus and optimize execution. He can work with you to keep morale and motivation levels high and promote a winning, rather than a whiny company spirit.

- *Coaching can help you retain key players.* The best employees are the hardest to keep, especially during a fiscal crunch. It's easiest for them to land elsewhere, and they are also the most savvy about the merits of jumping ship before anyone knows it's foundering. But what is the first sign to the outside world that your firm's boat is in trouble? The loss of key players. And what happens when everyone is distracted with exits and coverage gaps? It is more likely to keep foundering.

There's a popular saying: *people don't leave companies, they leave bosses.* Coaching that is geared to helping you retain and maximize your top talent, especially in turbulent or hypercompetitive times, can yield a high return on investment, even when calculated on the basis of retaining a single key member.

- *Coaching helps you do more with less.* At first, this may seem like a contradiction of terms: to spend money hiring a coach when something or someone may have to go. However, during a resource-tightening stretch, competing needs, interests, and office politics can severely challenge objective and effective decision making. Having a coach as an independent sounding board to preview options and troubleshoot problematic developments can help you navigate the stormy seas of increased workload and reduced resources. A coach can also assist you in your efforts to reengage members of a downscaled or reorganized department so they feel integral to the company's successful future rather than the beleaguered survivors.

The key ingredient to any successful argument about engaging a coach is to appeal to its expected return on investment. It is essential that you target your request and cost-benefit analysis to the economic decision maker. Typically this person is not a human resource manager, who holds a staff management position, but someone in a business operations position with profit-and-loss responsibility. The person with budgetary authority is the one you need to persuade.

It will also aid your case to get as many allies as possible behind your request before making your case. You want the decision maker to see the group value of retaining a coach and not consider the expense to be something purely of personal value to you. To counteract this, consider negotiating something of value in return, for example, a one-year commitment to stay.

Two other considerations can be important. If your company has an internal coach program, this might be the route to go since no additional funds are needed. The other possibility is to pay for a coach out of your own funds. If you can afford it and you believe the return on investment is high enough to warrant, private-pay coaching may be a smart decision. Especially consider this option when you are challenged with a high-stakes assignment or responsibility that has the potential to have an impact, positive or negative, on your career.

Scenario Three

I don't have any choice in picking my coach. It's strictly take-it-or-leave-it. What should I do?

First, diplomatically attempt to influence the decision. Directives seemingly cast in stone can sometimes be pried loose with skillful maneuvering. Advise the person at your company who is responsible for assigning coaches of your personal preferences and why. If the company is not contractually bound to a specific external coach or if more than one external or internal coach is available, you may still be able to influence the selection and matching process. If you have a particular coach in mind, promote this person as someone who ideally suits your development needs. For example, perhaps you wish to improve your negotiation skills and the coach you recommend has a national reputation in this area. Avoid discrediting the company's choice. Instead, let the decision maker know why a different coach would better serve the goals of your coaching program. In the case of negotiating prowess, for instance, provide actual applications where your enhanced skills would improve the company's bottom line.

Consider too taking a step back for a moment and regarding the situation differently. After all, the good news is that the company is arranging a coach for you. By now, you're well versed in how to get the most out of coaching. Have you met the company's choice? If not, meet with the coach. It may be that your fears or resentment are unfounded. You may be pleasantly surprised after you've had some contact with him or her. It's possible that your initial concerns had little to do with the specific coach and more to do with lack of input or control. Or perhaps your concerns are coach specific but based on someone else's experience. Don't prejudge what *your* relationship with this coach will be like. Spend some time getting to know the coach before you consider opting out.

The person may not be your Perfect Coach, but you might be able to benefit nevertheless. Maintain a positive attitude. Focus on what you can learn, especially if your coaching program will be brief and its objectives clearly defined, such as interpreting your most recent 360-degree report or preparing your annual development program.

Even if your reluctance proves legitimate, meeting with the coach demonstrates your open-mindedness and bolsters any argument you may make about retaining someone else. In any case, be very wary of flat-out rejecting the company's choice of coach. This could hurt your career, particularly if your organization's culture embraces its coaching program. If your rapport with the assigned coach is less than ideal, manage your expectations and derive as much benefit as you can from the experience. This is certainly not the first, or the last, time you will perform activities that don't meet with your wild enthusiasm. While a subpar experience may color your worldview of coaching, try to keep it from overly shading your future interest in working with a coach.

Scenario Four

What if I'm required to work with a coach as a condition of keeping my job?

This is an extremely serious situation. If you are one step from being dismissed, something has gone badly awry. The simple answer is that if you want to keep your job, work with the coach. But apart from immediate job retention, what value are you likely to derive from mandated coaching?

The key issue here is separating your initial reaction to the directive. You and your supervisor may both feel disappointed, misunderstood, or just plain angry. It is difficult to be enthusiastic about such a high-stakes, emotionally charged issue, and resistance to change, even necessary change, is part of human nature. Before you weigh the value of working with a coach, check and quell any emotions that could harm your assessment. The silver lining in this grave situation is that coaching involves considerable time and expense. Your superiors deem you a valuable asset worthy of the investment. If they didn't, you wouldn't have been given the ultimatum; you'd have been shown the door.

Recall the Myth of Universality: everyone is coachable. A coaching program initiated under duress as a mandatory requirement can still produce a positive outcome, but these are far less than ideal circumstances. Frankly, you may need to make a major attitude adjustment. The key question to ask yourself is: Do you agree with the assessment that led to the coaching offer? At the very least, are you willing to consider the possibility that something about your attitude, people skills, behavior, or performance requires improvement? If yes, then a coaching program may be the solution. But if your motivation is based purely in a desire to retain your job, coaching will likely just defer the inevitable.

In Chapter Two, I noted that for coaching to be successful, you need to possess intrinsic motivation—motivation that comes from within you. Otherwise, extrinsic motivation—in this case, the threat of losing your job—is probably insufficient to support lasting behavioral change. In other words, any change is likely to be superficial and temporary, and you'll probably revert to your old ways when the coaching or probation period is over.

The situation is similar to one in which two people are required to take a driver safety course to keep from losing their motor vehicle licenses. One is aware that her driving habits are inadequate and sees the course as an opportunity to improve her performance behind the wheel. The other sits in the classroom, annoyed, unengaged, her eye on the clock. Present in body but not in spirit, she is unreceptive to changing her attitudes or her behavior.

If you agree to participate in a coaching program, merely going through the motions will be insufficient. You need to regard the program as a beneficial lifeline extended to you by your employer in the hope of mutual advantage. If you are uncertain about the benefits of coaching or your readiness to be coached, suggest an exploratory discussion with one or more coaches to help you allay concerns and make a more informed decision. Consider asking for a trial period. And be sure you understand what changes will constitute acceptable performance levels so that you're clear about your employer's expectations.

You're in the driver's seat (or safety course). Only you can decide how much your job means to you in economic and career terms. Treat the situation as the ultimate wake-up call, and you could acquire the equivalent of vastly improved skills.

Case in Point: Salvage Operation

When I first met Ralph, he seethed with resentment. The chief technology officer for a consumer products company, he was accustomed to giving orders rather than receiving them. But the directive from the company's president was crystal clear: either shape up or ship out. He could change his abusive (and well-documented) management style or accept a severance package.

He regarded me dismissively. There was no doubt to either of us that he viewed me as the enemy. For a quarter-hour he grilled me on my credentials. What did I know about running an information systems operation? What companies had I worked with? Where had I gone to college? What societies did I belong to? How long had I known the president?

Finally, I confronted him with what he had been avoiding: "Can we talk about why you and I are having this meeting?"

"We're meeting because a few *#!$%! bums thought it was easier to complain to HR [human resources] than do their job," he retorted. Then he launched into an expletive-filled tirade about how the president was conspiring to unseat him. "But I have an iron-clad employment contract, so they can all whistle," he said, a smug look on his face. He waved a hand dismissively and turned to his computer monitor. "Nice to meet you."

When I recounted my experience to the president, he shook his head sadly. "I knew this would be a long shot. You were his last lifeline. I won't let him tear this place apart any longer."

Ralph left the company with a substantial buyout and a totally shredded reputation. He could not land another senior executive position in the United States. He worked overseas briefly. The last I heard he was promoting his expertise as a solo consultant.

Alas, not all people or all situations are salvageable. The postscript to this story is that turnover reduced significantly after Ralph's departure. And the president, having learned a painful lesson, prescribed a rigorous selection process for all subsequent senior hiring.

Scenario Five

Should I tell my coach I'm thinking of leaving my current employer? The company is paying for her services.

The range of possible answers to this question is broad. Much depends on the initial discussions and understanding about how confidentiality would work in your program. Being able to think out loud, ponder options, and assess the goodness of fit between your job and your career aspirations and values is central to effective coaching. Any limitations on your ability to do so should be communicated to you at the beginning of the engagement. This is why a written agreement with service terms and conditions is important: you know what information sharing falls properly within your program's scope and privacy domain. If you're uncertain, review your coaching guidelines or ask the coach for a refresher on these points.

Consider also that there's a world of difference between "blue sky" thinking and signing an employment contract with another company. Suppose that you are thinking about jumping ship. What's your motivation? Is it an issue that, if resolved, might firm up your commitment to your current employer? If, for example, you've been passed over for promotion, disappointed with your bonus, or worried that you've grown stale working in the same environment, it makes sense to tell your coach that you're feeling stymied or frustrated. This way the two of you can analyze your situation and options with your current employer. Often your coach's perspective and experience can help clarify job concerns, generate options you had not considered, or get you to look at your situation in a different light. If you're considered valuable enough to merit a coach, then you can be fairly certain that your organization wants to retain and cultivate your productivity and capabilities.

By contrast, if you announce to your coach that you've accepted a position elsewhere but you're awaiting a hefty year-end bonus before advising superiors, you could be skating on thin ice. You could put your coach in an awkward position or create an ethical dilemma for your coach in balancing your interests with your employer's—or not, depending on whether the confidentiality level of your program is complete or limited. For example, in the post-Sarbanes-Oxley workplace, companies may stipulate contractual terms that require a coach to disclose any information that materially compromises their interests. (Based on their professional discipline and principles, some coaches may decline employer-funded engagements with these strings attached.)

For unfettered freedom to review career issues and planning, you may want to consider engaging a separate coach and pay for coaching services yourself. This rules out any third-party rights, restrictions, or conflicts of interest concerning what you can discuss. The benefits can be well worth the investment in terms of long-term career results and satisfaction.

Scenario Six

I'm taking a position at another firm and would like to continue working with my coach. What's the best way to handle this?

This is an issue only when your coaching has been employer funded. Your question and thinking bespeak of a highly valued working relationship. Very likely your coach has become a trusted adviser. Assuming you've already given your current employer notice, go ahead and discuss the possibility with your coach. Moving the professional relationship to a private-pay basis may be possible if neither of you has contractual obligations to the contrary. Together you should discuss how the new arrangement would work, weigh the pros and cons, and define the purpose of coaching. In short, you would be recontracting for services under new conditions and terms.

If you've been recruited by another firm, you may have access to (or be able to negotiate) an executive coach as part of your new benefits package. It is not uncommon for senior executives, technical professionals, and other hot talent to be offered coaching allowances. If you find yourself in this sweet spot, you might consider inquiring if your new company will pay your current coach's services.

If, however, you are leaving to take a position with a competitor, your coach may be contractually prevented from continuing any relationship with you. Her agreement with your soon-to-be-former employer may bar her from working for your new company. Or a coach may have a "quiet period" policy—a time period during which she will not work with a former employer-funded coaching client (for example, sixty days, or three, six, twelve months).

There's another perspective that you should consider. Just as moving on in high school or college involved saying good-bye to a favorite teacher or professor, a job change may be the right time to consolidate your coaching wins and wind down. Working with a different coach might give you access to new perspectives and capabilities. Of course, every situation is different, and much depends on how you and your coach work together.

If you have been paying for coaching yourself, where and for whom you work is irrelevant to your coaching arrangement. An exception is if your private-pay coach also happens to provide services to your new employer. The world is often a smaller place than you think, so this is not as unlikely as it may seem at first.

SCENARIO SEVEN

My employer will pay for only limited coaching. I'd like to continue working with my coach on a private-pay basis. Is this OK?

It depends. Consider wisely the oxymoron, "Make haste slowly."

Clearly, you've realized significant benefits from coaching and your particular coach to want to continue on the basis of personal funds. As a first step, you might want to ask your coach if the option is feasible. Does he work with private-pay clients? Not all external coaches do so. Is he contractually able to make the transition to a private-pay arrangement?

If the answers to these questions are yes, you still need to consider if the idea is prudent and makes sense in the light of the following issues:

- *Could the private-pay arrangement limit the range of permissible discussion topics?* When a coach is under contract to your employer, you are typically free to share and discuss proprietary company information. This may not be possible when a coach is working for you personally. It may be difficult, frustrating, and self-defeating if too many issues you wish to broach are job related but off-limits under the new arrangement.
- *Is there a likelihood that you and your coach will be working together again on an employer-funded basis?* For example, if your company uses coaches on a periodic or cyclical basis to create annual development plans, an awkward and inappropriate dual relationship could be created for the two of you if private-pay and employer-funded services occurred concurrently.

Let's say, for example, that you've been paying your coach out-of-pocket to assess how best to leave the company and, then, before your departure, his services are activated again by your supervisors. Ethically he would not be able accept any assignment that involves working with you. For this reason, many coaches take a cautious, conservative stance and will not work privately with individuals while there's an active contract in place with their employer.

If you and your coach are able to break down any barriers to a switch from corporate- to private-pay sessions, you should perform further due diligence by approaching the person responsible for your organization's coaching program. Currently, many companies have no stated policy and do not want to involve themselves in what employees do on their own time and with their own money. (They do, however, want to protect their trade secrets.) If no policy exists, but the powers that be seem nervous or critical about your proposed arrangement, carefully consider the possible hidden consequences of engaging in what may be perceived as spy practices. Or your supervisors may be thrilled that you want to continue coaching beyond what their budget can handle and may be happy that you want to work with someone they know and respect.

One possible solution is for you and your coach to agree that the switch will be once and one-way only: if you retain him privately, he will not work with you again on an employer-funded basis, at least not while you're at your present company.

At first, the idea of retaining privately a formerly company-paid coach seems simple and sensible—more of a good thing. But as these scenarios illustrate, switching is not necessarily straightforward or desirable. What might have seemed like a good idea can backfire if it is not handled with foresight and sensitivity to the interests of all parties. There is an alternative: retain a different coach. Your current coach may be helpful with this. If the two of you can't see past the hurdles to continuing your coaching relationship, he is in a good position to recommend someone whose coaching reputation and style ideally match your needs.

Case in Point: Sideways Success

Anna, an in-house attorney for a multibillion-dollar business division, was not keen on her future. In fact, she was on the verge of quitting. Born in Pacific

Asia and educated in the United States, she had moved up the corporate ranks quickly. The division CEO considered her his prize protégée. But after facilitating three major acquisitions, she'd grown tired of the constant travel and restructuring activities. In her late thirties, she was reassessing her life and career goals with an eye to carving out more time for herself and her family. The CEO urged her to reconsider. In a last-ditch effort to keep her, he suggested that she take a sabbatical and work with a professional coach to clarify her career goals. Her coaching could be carte blanche—in other words, it could deal with any topic or issue she chose, including departure from the company. Anna passed on the sabbatical offer but opted for coaching.

"I'm burned out, and I don't want to be," Anna told me. "I'm not the type to become a full-time soccer mom. Even my kids tell me this. I'm also not interested in going off and doing the same work I've been doing somewhere else. So what do I do with the rest of my life?"

This was a tall order and not one we could answer in a few sessions. Over time and with the benefit of in-depth discussion, goal setting, and a comprehensive personality assessment, Anna identified entrepreneurial-type activities as those she most enjoyed (and excelled at). These were activities that her current role as corporate counsel allowed only at the margins, not at the core. Realistically, there was no way to reengineer the position to make it her dream job.

Eventually Anna got up the courage to share her dream job description with her boss and mentor, the division CEO. With something tangible to work with, he pulled out all the stops. Although this meant losing her to another division, he was delighted that she'd be staying with the company. It was far better to have a lateral move than an outright loss—a second-best result, he remarked.

Anna joined a technology licensing unit where she became part of a highly skilled and creative team. The challenges and people energized her. She gained considerable control over her work schedule, including flex-time and telecommuting opportunities that were unthinkable in her previous position. She also discovered that she enjoyed teaching and became an adjunct lecturer at a nearby business school.

"Even though I'm an outside-the-box thinker when it comes to business, I'd never have thought of doing something this different on my own," Anna said.

This coaching engagement proved win-win for all concerned: Anna, her employer, and her family.

Scenario Eight

My internal coach just got promoted to a senior position in the human resource department. How can I tell him I no longer feel comfortable working with him?

This can be a difficult, awkward situation. You and your coach are now in a dual relationship—one in which you have work or reporting roles with each other in addition to the coaching relationship. It can become problematic when a conflict of roles and responsibilities occurs.

If you're fortunate, your company will have an ethics policy or conduct code regarding dual relationships that would rule out continuation of coaching. Issues of favoritism, prejudicial evaluation, misuse of power, or the appearance of any of these are addressed proactively. However, in the absence of such a policy and if your relationship with your coach has thus far been trusting and productive, raise the issue directly with him. Avoid making it appear that you are "firing" him and instead suggest that discontinuing the coaching relationship would be the proper action to prevent any appearance of conflict of interest. Couch your discussion in terms of protecting your coach and preserving the gains of your coaching relationship, not on your personal discomfort. Try saying, "I don't want you to feel awkward about wearing two hats" and avoid, "I no longer trust you as my coach now that you have the power to fire me."

Don't be surprised if your internal coach is relieved that you've broached the subject. Chances are that he has had his own thoughts about ending the coaching relationship but was worried that you would be the one to feel rejected.

Scenario Nine

I'm thinking of asking my coach to take on a broader role that would include my team of reports. Is this a good idea?

First, let's be clear that just because coaching is a one-on-one activity does not mean that your coach can't or shouldn't be interacting with other people at your workplace. Your coach may already know members of your team or work group from having interviewed them or having attended meetings or other functions.

When you speak of a broader role, what are you specifically contemplating: facilitating a team meeting, leading a workshop, or getting involved in conflict resolution? It's important that any additional role or involvement remains aligned with your individual coaching program and objectives. Your team members might well welcome your coach's greater involvement as a "group consultant" or "team coach," but this is likely to depend on how they perceive his trustworthiness, not just on his competence or good intentions. Consequently, before proceeding, you should be sure that your coach possesses advanced organizational consulting skills, not just individual coaching capabilities, and is well versed in team dynamics. If your coach does assume a broader role, the chances are that he will need to work along a continuum of individual and group concerns, constantly mindful of his obligations to all parties concerned.

There is no one-size-fits-all answer to this question, since the advantages and disadvantages of enlarging a coach's role need to be weighed on an individual basis. Team-based activities that yield an extremely positive result in one situation could prove disappointing in another context.

As the Chinese proverb says, "Give a man a fish; you have fed him for today. Teach a man to fish; and you have fed him for a lifetime." A preferable option might be to work with your coach to acquire the skills to perform the desired activities yourself. After all, coaching is about *your* learning how to "fish" and being able to fuel your leadership performance for a lifetime rather than being dependent on someone else to fill the role of group fisherman. On the other hand, perhaps circumstances demand action before you personally can acquire the necessary "fishing" prowess. Or the situation is a one-off activity. In these cases, asking your coach to get more involved with your team might be very worthwhile and appropriate.

Just be certain, before proceeding, that you and your coach discuss expected benefits and establish guidelines about information flow and troubleshooting emergent issues.

Scenario Ten

I'm seeing a psychotherapist for personal counseling. Should I tell my coach? If I do tell, will she keep it confidential?

No matter who is paying for your coach or why she was retained, you are under no obligation to reveal intimate or sensitive information about your personal life. This includes health, emotional, religious, and sexual issues, as well as what you eat for breakfast.

This said, expect to provide some background information to your coach about your work-life situation. To be most effective, your coach needs to acquire a sense of who you are and what other roles and responsibilities you have in addition to your professional ones. And over time, you might well share more about your personal world and interests. But you are under no obligation to do so.

Consequently, when it comes to disclosing anything about personal psychotherapy or counseling, the issue is multilayered. First, check your coaching agreement to be sure what information is and is not confidential. Then ask yourself whether disclosure is relevant and to your advantage. It makes no difference whether you're getting employer-funded coaching or you're paying personally.

How will disclosure have a constructive impact on your coaching goals? If you and your therapist are focusing on stress management and work-life integration, sharing this information with your coach may serve a valid purpose. But if you're seeing a psychiatrist for clinical treatment, would this knowledge facilitate or promote your coaching program? If you've determined that an issue does indeed have cross-relevancy, consider these questions:

- Do you have a high-trust relationship with your coach?
- Is your coach likely to view psychotherapy as the positive, self-actualizing service that it is?

For more about the separate roles of personal counselors and career coaches, review the Shrink Myth in Chapter Two. Keep in mind that even if your coach is a trained psychotherapist, the executive coaching relationship is designed specifically for business, workplace, and career-related issues, not to help you improve your personal life. If you're happier at work, you may be happier outside the office as well; however, this would be a secondary or tertiary benefit, not the primary objective.

If you cannot identify a clear and compelling reason of how disclosure will improve your coaching program, then you're always wise to opt for discretion. Observe the dictum: "If in doubt, leave it out."

Case in Point: Déjà Vu All Over Again

Trevor was a likable, articulate marketing manager who had changed employers four times in six years, involving an equal number of relocations. He desperately wanted to make a success of his current position, for both his sake and his family's.

"I guess I don't have a lot of patience," he said by way of explaining his job hopping. "I have all these great ideas to grow the business, but the status quo types who run things just aren't interested. It drives me nuts."

With Trevor's permission, I spoke to several of his former bosses and a number of long-time business colleagues. Many of his colleagues also considered themselves his personal friends. All expressed pleasure that Trevor had decided to seek professional career help. Their feedback was also unanimous: Trevor consistently got in the way of his own success. What he possessed in terms of business knowledge and personal charm he needed to demonstrate in terms of emotional maturity and leadership skills.

"He has an inflated sense of his worth."

"He's great at execution, not at strategy."

"He seems to have an issue with authority."

Though this feedback was humbling, Trevor took it in stride. "At some level I guess I knew I had to be part of the mix," he said.

In fact, Trevor's entire work history revealed a pattern of behavior that had proved counterproductive. In each position he'd held, we were able to identify a cycle that he likened to a marriage: honeymoon, contentment, disenchantment, divorce. Equally telling, in each case he, not anyone else, had forced matters to a breaking point, prompting his decision to leave.

I reminded Trevor that coaching is not psychotherapy. If ingrained or unconscious motivations were driving his behavior and choices, then he should consider personal counseling as a way of preventing his past from continuing to sabotage his present and future.

"Let's put that one in a back pocket for now," was Trevor's response.

In the ensuing months, Trevor focused on enhancing his emotional self-awareness and influencing skills. Then an unexpectedly heated exchange with two senior executives caused him to reconsider.

"Suddenly I just felt furious with them. It was all I could do not to say, 'Either do this or I quit.' I was that close to falling on my sword. Again."

Through a friend's referral, Trevor found a therapist with whom he clicked right away. We wound down his coaching program for the time being. First things first.

The last I heard from Trevor he was still at the same company and had been promoted to senior vice president.

SCENARIO ELEVEN

What if I discover that my coach disclosed something I told her in confidence?

Trust lost is difficult to regain, and confidentiality breaches have the potential of either compromising or permanently destroying a coaching relationship. Fortunately, they are rare. First, avoid the temptation to act rashly or in anger. Take a deep breath, and make sure you have all the facts. Keep in mind that trust works both ways. You don't want to accuse your coach falsely or misrepresent her to others:

- Could the information in question have been known and circulated by someone else? Are you certain you didn't share it with anyone else? Could an e-mail have been forwarded or a fax copy left in a public space?
- Contact your coach, and describe what has transpired. Ask the coach directly if she shared the information in question with anyone else.
- Avoid sitting on your hands and doing nothing. The festering doubt and sense of betrayal will sour the relationship—and, perhaps, no breach occurred.

Things may not always be as they appear. Misunderstandings and oversights can occur. For example, with employer-funded coaching, you might have forgotten or misinterpreted what information your coach may or must provide about your goals, progress, number of sessions, or something else. Remember that coaching privacy and confidentiality may be limited, not all-encompassing.

But what if your coach did in fact breach a legitimate confidence and acknowledges this? How serious was the breach? Did your coach assume something was general knowledge when in fact it wasn't? Was it a slip of the tongue? Sometimes relationships can be repaired and actually improve after candid dialogue and clarification of communication exchange. If you've enjoyed a helpful, trusting partnership with your coach until this incident, don't be too quick to walk away, particularly if the coach is honest and remorseful.

If, however, the breach is indicative of coach incompetence, indifference, or insensitivity, end the relationship. The same applies if you have lost all confidence in the person: the situation is irreparably compromised. If employer provided, whether with an external or internal coach, advise your supervisor, human resource manager, or whoever oversees the organization's coaching program. They will want to know and investigate. In grave cases, if you know that the coach holds a state-issued license or belongs to a professional association with oversight authority, you can consider reporting your experience to that body. Again, such instances are extremely rare. Usually voting with your feet is adequate action. Of course, if you believe the situation warrants, you may consult an attorney to identify any additional options.

SCENARIO TWELVE

When should I consider firing a coach?

Firing a coach is typically an action of last resort. There are two overarching reasons for terminating the relationship for a cause:

- If the coach's conduct has been unethical, such as violating confidentiality or exercising undue pressure on you.

- If the coach fails to deliver the agreed-on services or delivers them in a substandard manner. For example, a pattern of absenteeism, persistent cancellations, or unavailability without explanation might reasonably constitute unacceptable levels of service delivery.

Fortunately, if you selected your Perfect Coach according to the guidelines and criteria laid out in Chapter Three, you're unlikely to find yourself in this unpleasant situation. But if you are, this list identifies major red flag indicators:

- Low or no trust
- No personal rapport
- Major ethical or contractual breach
- Unprofessional conduct
- Methods do not yield desired results
- Applies undue pressure or influence
- Major conflict of interest

As mentioned in Scenario Eleven, if you are terminating due to known ethical misconduct, consider reporting your experience to those with oversight responsibility. If your employer is paying for the coaching, advise your supervisor or coach coordinator. If you are paying personally, you may want to think about informing any professional organizations where the coach is a member. The caveat here is that for practical purposes, you probably cannot do so anonymously, regardless of the assurances you get. Realistically, you will want to weigh the cost-benefit of making a formal complaint as opposed to just moving on. Unless your coach holds a state-issued professional license, the worst that can happen in instances where an investigation finds fault is that the coach has his voluntary association membership discontinued.

Be sure to distinguish between unilateral firing for misconduct or incompetence and discontinuing your coaching program for other reasons. For example, if you find that you have insufficient funds to accomplish goals, little or no rapport with your coach, or diminished commitment to change now, you do have a situation that calls for immediate attention.

Remember the Coaching Readiness Formula from Chapter Two:

Coaching Readiness = Personal Motivation + Time + Funds

If any of these three readiness variables changes significantly, you should discuss the matter directly with your coach. This may be a difficult conversation, but addressing issues honestly and squarely is a hallmark of the mature, responsible person. The same is true if you've come to the conclusion that basic rapport is lacking. You and your coach should still be able to wind down the partnership in an amicable way.

FINAL ANALYSIS

This chapter has given you practical tips and strategies to anticipate and, when necessary, sidestep sensitive coaching situations. But after reading the information in this and previous chapters, you are unlikely to be stymied by any of the problems raised here. The ancient Romans advised, *Praemonitus, praemunitus* (forewarned is forearmed). You've learned that situations that seem straightforward and desirable may be more complex than they originally appear. You've also been reminded of two potentially thorny issues: conflict of interest and dual relationships. These can prove challenging in coaching relationships just as they can be in business relationships in general.

The point bears repeating: if problems do arise, deal with them as quickly and directly as possible. It is better for you, and healthier for your coaching relationship, to discuss concerns, confusion, or resentment immediately so that you can correct the equivalent of a molehill, not a mountain. In fact, these can be unexpected opportunities to deepen the working relationship.

You're now wonderfully equipped not just to achieve exceptional results with a Perfect Coach but to troubleshoot a wide range of possible less-than-perfect situations to boot. You may even be in a position now or in the future to sponsor someone else for business-based coaching. If you are, or if you're just curious about what's happening on the "other side of the street," the next chapter addresses questions that supervisors and collateral sponsors, such as human resource and leadership development professionals, frequently ask about executive coaching services.

CHAPTER ELEVEN

SUPERVISOR AND SPONSOR PLAYBOOK

I'm often contacted by people who are interested in sponsoring coaching for somebody else in their organization or business:

- A board director wants to know how best to raise the subject of coaching with a newly promoted CEO.
- A human resource manager wonders if coaching can help an administrator who's on an express track to derailment.
- An entrepreneur asks if the same coach should work with more than one of her direct reports.

I hear concerns about committing to a long-term investment, concerns about bringing in outside expertise, concerns about whether and when executive coaching can make a difference. For the most part, these are employer-funded situations where the sponsor is a supervisor or boss, or possibly an HR professional. Business advisers such as accountants, attorneys, and management consultants can also figure as strategic partners. One and all, these are people keenly committed to enhancing the performance and success of others. What they need is accurate, relevant information to make smart choices that work for them and their organizations.

I've written this chapter especially for coaching sponsors and the issues they commonly confront or consider. Even if you're interested in executive coaching services for yourself, it's likely that at some point, either now or in the future, you will be in a position to sponsor others for coaching. Also, understanding employer-funded coaching from the sponsor's perspective can be helpful in establishing a winning three-way relationship.

My purpose here is to provide guidance on key ethical considerations and best practices so that as a sponsor, you can make optimal decisions. It bears repeating that my intention is educational, not a statement of official policy or hard-and-fast standards of ethical behavior. The examples are meant to convey the diversity and complexity of today's workplace and business world. They are masked renderings of real-life cases, intended to enhance your awareness and knowledge rather than to be a comprehensive resource on the subject. I've also included practical tips and checklists to highlight key sponsor activities and caveats. Let your thinking be stimulated. You may not always agree with the opinions I express here, or you might think of exceptions. This is fine. Remember General George Patton's words, "If everyone is thinking alike, then someone isn't thinking."

Scenario One

I have someone working for me who, in my opinion, could really benefit from working with the right coach. What's the best way to raise the subject?

There are any number of good ways to raise the topic of coaching. Taking a planned, strategic approach is wise, since you will be prepared to make a strong, persuasive case. This entails creating a context and atmosphere in which the person is most likely to be receptive to the suggestion and to recognize a clear benefit. Of course, it goes without saying that your conversation should occur in a private, one-on-one setting.

Routine scheduled events that can create a natural opening to broach coaching include:

- Annual performance reviews
- Annual or semiannual development planning meetings
- 360-degree feedback review sessions
- Project debriefing and evaluation
- Board meetings

Informal opportunities, such as a casual conversation with the person about promotion or big-picture career goals, can also provide a smooth segue into the subject.

In either case, look for a logical opening to float the idea and test the person's reaction. Some ways to do this might be to ask a question similar to one of these:

"Have you ever had a chance to work with an executive coach on . . . ?"

"What would it be like working with a coach to improve your . . . ?"

Certainly, if you've been pondering how best to raise the topic of coaching, you have already been thinking about how this person could benefit. You will want to be able to convey your rationale and supporting points as specifically as possible. If need be, jot down key points beforehand so you can reference them. Table 11.1 provides guidance on when to call in an executive coach.

TABLE 11.1. WHEN TO CALL IN AN EXECUTIVE COACH.

Situation	Purpose of Coaching
New role	Support success after being promoted
	Facilitate onboarding and assimilation into a new organization
	Aid in the transition from an individual contributor role to a supervisory one
	Transform a technical professional into an effective manager
Current role	Enhance capabilities to deliver extraordinary results
	Provide a confidential sounding board for optimal decision making
	Eliminate any maladaptive behaviors that get in the way of maximum performance
	Create a winning individual development plan
	Prevent job or career derailment
	Troubleshoot interpersonal conflict
Future role	Groom for promotion or expanded responsibilities
	Prepare for a new assignment or project

Approach the topic in an enthusiastic, positive vein, focusing on the person's particular performance or development needs. Would coaching be helpful in adding to existing capabilities? Enhancing promotion prospects? Closing a performance gap? If the goal of coaching addresses a performance gap, cite specific examples that have been subpar. Also be ready to point out how you expect coaching will help the person to improve. If you can provide coaching success stories, either your own or those of others, do so. And don't forget to point out that you and your organization typically provide coaches only to valued employees they are willing to invest in.

Be prepared for questions, especially if the person has never worked with a coach before. If you can't answer fully, promise to get the information and follow through quickly. Listen carefully to any concerns or objections. You can then correct any faulty assumptions or misperceptions. In many instances, you will receive an immediate and highly favorable response. After all, most talented, ambitious people will leap at the chance to upgrade their skills and performance using a one-on-one program. However, if this does not prove to be the case, allow the person time to consider what you've suggested and plan to revisit the matter in the near future. Finally, if the situation warrants, point out any consequences, possible or probable, if the person opts to pass on the offer.

SCENARIO TWO

As the immediate supervisor, what specific things can I do to enhance a person's coaching experience?

Being appropriately involved as a supervisor (or other collateral sponsor) is laudable and can be important to your report's overall coaching goals and success in attaining them. Let me emphasize the term *appropriately involved*. Being either underinvolved or overinvolved can create more problems than are solved.

If you were instrumental in securing a coach for your employee in the first place (and chances are that you were), then you are already familiar with the presenting circumstances surrounding the coaching program. Some coaching programs are initiated as part of an enterprise-wide leadership development program or in conjunction with periodic performance management reviews. Or your supervisee might have a mentor higher up the organizational ladder who got the ball rolling. In these cases, familiarize yourself with the coaching program's objectives, and contribute relevant information and context. If you have not already had a chance to meet your report's coach, which could be the case if coaching is just getting under way, arrange to do so.

One way or the other, you should know what the big-picture coaching objective or objectives are. Furthermore, the coach will want to hear your perspective, thoughts, and analysis of the person's performance and track record to date. She will want to learn about relevant departmental factors such as business imperatives and organizational structure. You should be candid, confident that the coach will exercise discretion in how the information is used.

You should also be apprised of the person's specific coaching goals. If a written action plan is created (and this is the better choice), you might be asked to review and comment on a first draft and sign off on the final version. In this way, everyone—the coaching client, coach, and supervisor—is sure to be operating on the same wavelength. Generally it's wise to have a three-way meeting at this point to confirm roles, responsibilities, time lines, and related matters.

As supervisor, you could also have a direct role as a change partner in your report's action plan. (See Chapter Six for more information about action plans.) For example, you might meet with him on a regular basis to review presentation performance, or you might be responsible for identifying upcoming opportunities to try out new behaviors. (This latter responsibility is extremely important when someone is being groomed for promotion.) How involved you will be and in what capacity depend on the particular action plan in question.

Be judicious in mentioning your report's coaching to others, including the person's peers, coworkers, and external customers or patrons. Casual, off-the-cuff comments can be misinterpreted as either perceived favoritism or negative criticism. Similarly, be cautious about asking others if they see any change in the person. You should coordinate any such activities with the coach first to be sure they are not premature or counterproductive.

Of course, recognize and reinforce positive change when you see it. That is sure to provide your report with motivational fuel for continued work toward coaching goals. Let the coach know as well, since she will also appreciate learning that progress is being made. And remember to communicate to the coach any developments likely to have a significant impact on the coaching program. For example, if restructuring will change the composition of your report's team, you've received a stinging complaint about him from another manager, or professional development budgets are being frozen, advise the coach in a timely fashion so that adjustments can be made as necessary.

If you consistently convey your strong interest, support, and availability and you follow through on any commitments as a change partner, you will contribute greatly to your report's coaching experience.

Case in Point: The Disappearing Dean

The dean was an intense woman with dark, piercing eyes and a no-nonsense air. She and I were reviewing the terms of a coaching contract for Bradley, the associate dean for student affairs and her number two person.

"Do you have any questions?" I asked.

She looked up. "No, everything is spelled out. Now I understand about client confidentiality, so I'll do you one better than what's in this agreement." She paused for emphasis. "I don't want to know *anything* about what goes on behind closed doors. The two of you should meet wherever you want. On campus, off campus, don't tell me a thing. I'll leave you both absolutely alone. Just send me the bill."

While I appreciated the vote of confidence that was implicit in the dean's words, I could not let her retreat so completely from the scene. "Actually, you're going to need to be involved from time to time," I replied. "For one thing, you're in the best position to assess how Bradley's conflict resolution skills develop in the coming months; for another, you'll have to review his action plan when we get to that point."

"Really?" the dean said, her eyebrows rising. "Then I've been mistaken. I thought coaching was like an attorney-client or doctor-patient relationship."

We spent the next quarter-hour going over the three-way nature of employer-sponsored coaching until she fully understood how her participation was important beyond being the funding source.

It's possible for sponsors to go too far in the opposite direction when it comes to respecting coaching privacy. In most situations, disappearing from the program altogether is neither necessary nor desirable.

SCENARIO THREE

I have a great coach and think he could really help someone who reports to me realize much more of her potential. Is this a reasonable idea?

How wonderful that you have a Perfect Coach. But while your motives are well intentioned, if you currently have a relationship with this coach or you're likely to resume the arrangement in the future, what you're proposing is unwise. First, you would be creating a dual relationship—or the potential for one—between you and the coach. Consider for a moment that as your coach, he would be interacting with you as the primary client; however, as coach to your report, he would be interacting with you as the coaching sponsor. Therefore, you and he would have two different relationships. Respective roles and obligations can get blurred. Judgment and objectivity can become compromised all around.

Such a situation increases the risk that a conflict of interest could develop. If, for example, your priorities, needs, or issues were to compete with or oppose those of your report, how could the coach ethically discharge his obligation to each of you? The situation would be untenable and could foster not just disappointment but enduring rancor and disaffection among all parties.

Dual or multiple relationships are certainly not unknown in the workplace, and they are not unethical on their face. But the opportunity for harm or exploitation, either actual or perceived, would exist. This is the principal reason that your idea, though born out of desire to do good, should be dispelled. But there are others as well. For instance, have you considered that your report might not view working with your own coach in a positive light? Privacy and trust are key to a successful coaching partnership. Your report might be worried or suspicious on these counts, yet feel that he could not object without incurring your displeasure.

What if your coach is someone you have not worked with in a long time? What if you're sure that you will not be working with him again? Even under these circumstances, your report is probably still better off working with a different coach, someone who comes free of close association with you.

As you can now tell, what seemed like an excellent idea and a generous sharing on your part should be avoided. When it comes to dual relationships, even the best intentions can have unintended consequences. Enter into them carefully and only when you absolutely must. In this case, preventing a potential conflict of interest from occurring is simple and straightforward: bring another coach on board.

SCENARIO FOUR

I'll be retiring soon as CEO and would like to bequeath my coach to my successor. Is this a good idea?

To what extent your idea has merit depends on a number of factors and considerations. For example, is your successor someone you've been mentoring and grooming internally? If so, does he know your coach already? Does a positive relationship exist between the two of them?

Take a moment to consider what you're proposing from your successor's perspective. Would he readily see a benefit to working with your coach? If the coach has been a trusted adviser and is familiar with the business and its players and culture, having her involved might facilitate a quicker, smoother transition into the leader's position and role. She could prove an asset, a kind of business continuity "insurance policy" as it were, at least on a short-term basis. But if your successor is new to your organization, how might he react to working with someone closely identified with your leadership? Correctly or not, he might have reservations about the coach's objectivity or motivation, or worry about being compared to you. Or he might want to bring his own advisers with him. After all, a new broom sweeps clean.

Another issue concerns whether you will have an ongoing relationship with the organization as a board director, consultant, or owner-shareholder after retiring. If this is the case, your continued association could complicate the development of a new working relationship between your successor and your former coach or create the appearance of a conflict of interest for the coach. Neither would be desirable.

Identifying and working through the advantages and disadvantages of what you're proposing is not something you can do on your own. You will need to raise them with your successor, preferably in terms of a question or an offer, and without exerting undue influence.

Situation-specific variables are critical here. What might prove a sensible course of action in a small-business or nonprofit context, where continuity is important and valued, could backfire in a succession situation calling for innovation and fresh thinking. The personalities of all three parties—you, your successor, and the coach—are also important. The motivation behind your thinking is as well. Are you genuinely seeking to optimize your successor's transition, or are you having a hard time letting go of the reins?

Consider two final points. First, you may have to discount your coach's thoughts on this issue. After all, she's likely to have a strong financial interest in continuing to work with the organization's new chief executive. Second, if your successor is being promoted from within, then it makes sense to connect him now with a different coach who can move up with him.

SCENARIO FIVE

I have someone on my management team who hasn't hit her stride after two years in the job. Is it worthwhile bringing in a coach, or is it too late?

Under most circumstances and certainly when compared against recruitment and replacement costs, rescuing an underperforming manager is worthwhile—if it can be accomplished expeditiously and to lasting effect.

An overarching issue concerns why your manager has not been successful thus far. Is the problem one of ability, motivation, communication, personality—or is it perhaps a lack of organizational resources? Not all performance-related problems are coaching matters. So you first need to determine if executive coaching is the intervention of choice and, if so, how much improvement can be expected over how much time.

Is the manager aware that you are deeply dissatisfied with her performance? It's amazing how many times this seemingly obvious action has not been taken, or the boss's dissatisfaction is conveyed so subtly that the recipient missed or underweighted the import of the message. If you have already put your manager on notice, has she tried, albeit less than successfully, to do better?

As an initial step, you might arrange a consultation with a coach or two to ascertain how coaching would help your manager improve her performance in success-critical areas. Consider including your human resource or organization development specialist in these fact-finding meetings. Then with the information you've obtained, you can begin to estimate whether an investment in coaching is likely to yield the desired results.

Compare an executive coach getting information from a manager's supervisor to a doctor getting information from a patient's relative. Although the information may be relevant and accurate, the doctor still needs to examine the patient directly before rendering an opinion. Therefore, don't be surprised if the coach or coaches you consult ask to meet the manager. There's no substitute for going to the source to determine a person's coaching readiness, as well as her perspective on the situation. Depending on the circumstances, additional assessment or data collection might also be warranted, such as interviewing coworkers or team members, before it's possible to know whether coaching is in fact the proper and preferred intervention.

To repeat, if you've not already done so, you need to have a candid conversation with your manager that identifies both her current performance levels and required success criteria. Raising the subject of coaching at the same time makes sense, though whether you want to do so in terms of a voluntary option or required activity is up to you. If the woman is at serious risk of being demoted or dismissed or not having her contract renewed, this information needs to be conveyed clearly. It also needs to be conveyed to the coach, since agreement on how program information and results will be used in making employment decisions should occur at the beginning as part of the contracting process. (Indeed, some coaches will not accept engagements where a person's continued employment is expressly contingent on his or her coaching outcome.)

Keep in mind that coaching cannot produce the equivalent of a personality transplant or repair interpersonal work relations that have been irreparably damaged. You need to be realistic. If you know in your heart that this manager was a poor fit from the start and nothing short of a new person in the position will do, then bite the bullet. You're trying to avoid the inevitable. Coaching cannot turn this situation around. Similarly, don't fall victim to the Emergency Room Myth described in Chapter One and wait until matters become critical. A coach called in as a "firefighter" may not be able to rescue the endangered party. Especially in situations involving interpersonal conflict and team management problems, calling in a coach early can make all the difference.

Case in Point: Acceleration Needed, Yesterday

The president of a national mortgage company was discussing his senior vice president of sales. "Rick's smart and charming and knows the business. He certainly charmed everyone when we were looking to fill the position last year."

"And now?" I asked.

"He's done a mediocre job so far of directing the sales managers. Granted, there are a number of strong personalities in his department, including several guys who are much older than he is. He's a great salesman himself—he certainly sold us on him—but he needs to step up to the plate and really lead his team. I spelled the message out to him clearly."

"How did he take the news?"

"He admitted that he was feeling more challenged in the job than he'd expected. He pointed out that he'd worked with a coach some years back when he changed jobs and would like to get some help now. I'm all for anything that can get him up to speed. This company has a huge stake in seeing that he's successful."

As it happened, Rick proved to be a highly motivated and capable client and a fast learner to boot. His performance improved so quickly that much to the president's surprise and delight, he earned a decent bonus that year.

SCENARIO SIX

I'm wondering how I can help someone who's hit a career plateau. If I suggest working with an executive coach, I know he'll refuse. Do you have any ideas for a back-door approach?

Any approach to working with a coach, or arranging coaching for someone else, that involves misrepresentation or manipulation is to be avoided. Even with the best of intentions, the end never justifies the means. You run the risk of shattering trust with the person you're trying to help. And once trust is lost, you will find your credibility as a supervisor or sponsor seriously compromised. Moreover, no reputable coach would agree to work with a person under these circumstances. To do so would make him a party to the deception. It would be unethical, plain and simple.

Of course, you need to know why he is so opposed to working with a coach. Perhaps he holds to the Myth of the Individual, limiting himself by thinking that he has to succeed solely on his own. If his objections relate to this or any of the other coaching myths discussed in Chapter One, you're in an excellent position to set him straight. Sometimes education is all that's needed to banish resistance.

Another approach might be to engage the man in joint problem solving around his career and job goals. What is his opinion about why he's been passed over for promotion or high-profile assignments? Ask him how he would go about taking action to get to the next level. A suggestion about coaching might be received more favorably if it comes on the heels of a logical discussion. Your aim here, of course, is to maximize the chances that his own motivation to advance will tilt the scale in favor of the coaching option.

Sometimes when I hear about requests to bring a coach in through a back-door ploy, something else is really going on. A manager or mentor may be avoiding a difficult conversation that he or she doesn't know how to conduct to positive effect. Ironically, if the career-limiting information were conveyed accurately and sympathetically to the person in question, he might deem working with a coach a highly attractive option. In situations like this one, the supervisor or human resource manager might benefit from working with a coach first. Learning to deliver effective performance feedback, especially around sensitive or negative issues, can be a challenge for even the most experienced leaders and administrators.

As a final observation, if there is simply no way to shift this man's receptivity to coaching using appropriate methods, then give it up. His resistance or inflexibility may well be symptomatic of why his career has stalled. Remember the Myth of Universality that says, "Everyone is coachable"? Sadly, people can be their own worst enemies.

Case in Point: Good Intentions, Bad Idea

"Larry definitely wants a coach," the department head told me. She paused, then looked hesitantly at her human resource manager. "But there are just a few things we haven't mentioned yet."

We had been discussing coaching arrangements for one of her senior information technology managers. Suddenly all the positive energy and camaraderie in the office seemed to evaporate, replaced by two people shifting uncomfortably in their seats.

I finally prompted her. "And those would be what?"

"Well," the department head continued, "for starters, he thinks he'll be part of a pilot leadership program, so whoever works with him mustn't use the words *coach* or *coaching*. And he also doesn't know that we think his real issue is his shyness. So whoever works with him would have to help him overcome his shyness without his knowing about it."

"He's very sensitive as well as shy," the human resource manager added earnestly. "We don't want to upset him, which is why we came up with this plan. What do you think?"

What I thought was this: in their desire to help someone they clearly valued and wanted to groom for advancement, these two well-meaning executives had overlooked the matter of bending the truth.

"Is the problem that he's hypersensitive, or is the problem that you're afraid to tell him the truth—that his people skills need upgrading?" I asked.

An hour later, after the real problem of their reluctance was sorted out, the three of us had a straightforward and legitimate course of action in place.

SCENARIO SEVEN

Frankly, I'm nervous about bringing a coach from the outside into the firm because he might learn sensitive information or things that even I don't know about. Can't I insist that he tells me what he finds out?

Engaging an external executive coach is no different from engaging other independent contractors or professional service providers, such as management consultants or corporate trainers. Apply the same practices and methods regarding nondisclosure and confidentiality agreements as you would with the latter. If need be, seek counsel from someone with the appropriate expertise, such as an attorney or procurement agent. However, once you have an agreement in place, you should rest easy regarding the security of your firm's proprietary information, trade secrets, and intellectual property.

Employer-funded coaching involves a three-way professional relationship: you (the sponsor), the coach, and the person being coached (the direct client). Just because primary coaching activities involve the two other parties does not mean that you will be left in the dark. Very likely your perspective and input will help to shape and drive the coaching program from the start. You can reasonably expect, or request, to review and approve program specifics such as goals, progress indicators, and budget expenditures. You will also be kept updated on progress.

If your desire for information goes beyond these aspects, then raise the matter with the coach early on. Together you can settle on appropriate information-sharing guidelines, including what will be shared and when. This is why respective roles and responsibilities should be clarified at the beginning of an engagement and revisited periodically. A zone of privacy is important to coaching success because the coach has to develop a close working relationship with his client in order to be effective. You need to be able to recognize and accept this fact.

Employers generally have rights to other types of information that might surface in the course of a coach's engagement. For example, you would typically be advised of any illegal or unethical activities that came to light. You would also be advised of any situation that posed a serious threat to life or limb. A coach keeps your interests as the coaching sponsor and economic buyer in mind at all times.

So no, you cannot insist on a blow-by-blow account of what is said in actual sessions. Truth be told, many coaching clients talk freely to bosses, friends, family members, and coworkers about what they're doing in their programs. But the choice should be theirs. Go ahead and ask your employee the occasional question about how coaching is proceeding or how he's finding working with a particular coach. In all likelihood, your interest will be appreciated and rewarded with an update. But avoid invasive questions or taking a third-degree approach. Such behavior is inappropriate and could well sabotage the coach's best efforts, to say nothing of your credibility as a sponsor and leader. Remember that the coach wants to optimize the experience and results for you as well as your employee.

This sponsor's caution list describes key situations and actions you should avoid:

- Dual or multiple relationships with the same coach
- Overinvolvement in the coaching client's program
- Underinvolvement in the client's program
- Deceptive practices
- Manipulation
- Undue pressure or influence
- Gossip or inappropriate disclosure to outside parties

Scenario Eight

I think what a manager really needs is personal counseling. Would working with an executive or business coach be a good second-best option?

To determine if coaching is an appropriate intervention in this situation, either as the option of choice or as a second-best option, specific information about the person's presenting issues and behaviors is needed. Of course, this assumes that your concerns are associated with a work-based or work-related performance problem.

In dispatching the "Shrink" Myth in Chapter One, I explained how business coaching differs fundamentally from personal counseling or psychotherapy in terms of scope and objectives. Coaching that is focused on job, management, or career enhancement does not delve deeply into family-of-origin issues or why people are the way they are. Nor does it deal with personal, relationship, or family matters or with clinical mental health issues.

Of course, let's be sure to acknowledge that people's current perceptions, beliefs, values, and capabilities are often influenced by earlier formative events and relationships. After all, nothing comes from nowhere. An executive coach might ask a client, "Why do you think that?" or "How did you come to this belief?" to get a better understanding of the person's underlying thinking and context. But while a coach might dip into a person's past, he does not linger there. Coaching is about present and future performance and possibilities, not about interpreting or making sense of the past.

If, for example, this manager you speak of is going through a difficult life event, such as a divorce or the major illness or death of a family member, an executive coach is no substitute for a personal counselor. This would be the case even if the coach were also a trained psychotherapist or clinical psychologist because executive coaching and individual counseling are two distinct services. Other situations where coaching would be an inappropriate substitute for proper professional intervention include known substance or alcohol abuse, chronic absenteeism, insubordination, and physical intimidation or violence. Instead, consult your employee assistance counselor, human resource manager, or legal counsel for guidance. Just as you wouldn't use a hammer to take care of repairs that require a saw, coaching is the equivalent of a specialized tool: it can be highly effective or the wrong hardware, depending on the circumstances. Here are other cases of when *not* to call an executive coach:

- Clinical conditions such as depression and other mood and anxiety disorders
- Confirmed alcohol or drug abuse or other addictive behaviors such as gambling, overeating, or eating disorders
- Personal, marital, family, or life partner problems
- Physical violence, aggression, or stalking
- Illegal behavior or corporate malfeasance
- Employment layoff or dismissal
- Lawsuits or threats of legal action

The scenarios I've described so far have been straightforward and clearly differentiated. But what if your manager's situation—or your concerns about his job performance—don't fall into any of these categories? What if you're operating on a hunch about what's going on with him and what to do next? After all, you're not a mental health professional.

In fact, performance problems such as a maladaptive interpersonal style or anger management can fall into a big gray zone when it comes to determining which intervention is appropriate and effective. Often, engaging a coach, especially one with advanced psychological training, for a consultation or trial assessment period can be a worthwhile investment. In this way, ambiguous cause-and-effect situations can be clarified, as can the prognosis for effecting desired change through coaching, counseling, or some other approach. Decisions can then be made with greater certainty. If need be, a referral can be made to the proper professional.

As a concluding observation, your concern to get professional help for this manager is commendable. However, keep in mind that executive coaching and psychotherapy are not interchangeable. Neither can substitute for the other. A person with a toothache can't expect to get relief from a chiropractor just because she won't go to a dentist.

Case in Point: Let's Go to the Videotape

The hospital executive director, his clinical practice administrator, and I were seated in a small conference room. Our meeting was exploratory in nature.

The administrator was indignant and more than a little defensive in her tone. "I definitely don't have an anger management problem," she protested. "Maybe I raise my voice from time to time, but that's often the only way to get anyone's attention around here. No one would be making a fuss about this if I were a man."

"That's not the way I see it," the director explained, patient but firm. "Not a week goes by when I don't have someone in my office complaining about your temper. You're running the risk of turning your whole department against you."

"Fine," the administrator snapped, giving the two of us a sample of how she could be under pressure. "Why don't we just put a video camera in my office for a couple of days. Will that satisfy you that everyone's exaggerating about me?"

"You're on," said the director, rising quickly from the chair. "And if the tape shows you blowing up at people, you agree that your behavior has to change?"

The administrator nodded. "Absolutely."

"Then we have a deal," the director said, catching my eye. He wore a look of quiet satisfaction as he strode from the room.

The following week, I received a phone call from the practice administrator herself. "I thought I was ready for my close-up but I wasn't," she said gamely. "Once I saw myself on tape, I was appalled. I told the director he couldn't look because I had erased everything already."

"What did he say?" I asked.

"He wished me well with my coaching."

SCENARIO NINE

Six months strikes me as a very long time to fund anyone's coaching program. If the coach is really good, why should it take so long to get results?

Results is the operative word here. If a person's coaching goals are ambitious and progressive, six months, or even twelve or eighteen months, is not a long time to acquire new perspectives, knowledge, and proficiencies. Remember that changing and improving behavior has multiple phases: learning, practice, competence, and mastery. Two centuries ago, the philosopher Friedrich Nietzsche observed, "He who would learn to fly one day must first learn to stand and walk and run and climb and dance; one cannot fly into flying." Indeed, studies show that the average duration of a coaching program or intervention ranges from roughly six months for middle management to more than one year for senior leadership.

For example, if the objective of coaching is to facilitate the success of a newly hired or promoted executive, it could reasonably take a full year, the equivalent of a complete business or operational cycle, to optimize the transition and benchmark the person's performance. Similarly, if a coach is acting as a sounding board for reviewing real-time issues and tactical execution, say, while a manager is leading a complex project, then the time metrics of the project need to be taken into consideration.

The purpose for executive coaching, the situational context, and desired results should determine the program's duration, not some arbitrary time span. Bake a loaf of bread in the oven at the right temperature for the right time, and you have a perfect result. Bake it for less time, and you get undercooked dough; raise the oven temperature to shorten the cooking time, and you burn the crust.

When it comes to behavioral change, we're all creatures of habit. Even when motivation is high, if we don't have numerous frequent opportunities to practice and integrate new attitudes and behaviors, we're likely to revert to our former selves. This is why change that is superficial has a low probability of becoming permanent. We regress to old patterns of thinking and acting.

In fact, I sometimes draw an analogy between extended coaching programs and orthodontia (dental braces) to make this point:

- The goal of both is improvement.
- Like orthodontia, which involves applying constant pressure to the teeth over months (if not years) to effect desired change, coaching involves incremental, ongoing attitudinal and performance change.
- Remove dental braces prematurely, and the results will be subpar. Discontinue coaching too soon, and the results will be disappointing.
- Once the dental braces come off, a retainer is worn to keep the teeth from reverting to their old positions. Similarly, coaching programs need to include methods and time to habituate the new behaviors and attitudes firmly so the person does not revert to old ways.
- If a dental retainer isn't worn, the results may not be permanent and you won't realize the full benefits of your investment. The same principle applies to coaching.

Of course, you want to be sure that the coach you've engaged is up to the assignment. But coach expertise and seniority do not automatically equate to a briefer program or funding investment. If you're worried that extended coaching will foster overreliance rather than top-flight self-sufficiency, go back to Chapter One for a refresher on debunking the Crutch Myth.

SCENARIO TEN

As a person's immediate supervisor, what should I do if I don't see much improvement or I see her performance drop?

First, how much time has passed? Do not expect to see change immediately. For starters, both the assessment and goal-setting stages can take time. Be patient during this initial period.

One reason that a written action plan is important to coaching programs is that time lines get established. If you've had the opportunity to review her plan, then you should be familiar with the specifics of her learning agenda. You, the coach, and the coaching client should have had a group meeting at this point to confirm when and how progress would be measured and how communication would occur among the three of you. Setting realistic expectations is vital. It's also essential that you don't exert unreasonable pressure or performance demands that could impede rather than support her coaching goals and motivation.

With these caveats, if you still have concerns, consulting the coach first is a wise approach. The two of you can compare perceptions and information and decide on what to do next. The coach can mediate and transform your feedback into valuable grist-for-the-coaching-mill. He might also be able to suggest additional ways in which you can be a change partner in supporting this woman's action plan.

Consider that if you were to speak directly to the woman, she could feel demoralized, alienated, or set up to fail, any of which would be counterproductive and make the coach's task that much more challenging.

Now what if you do actually observe a decline or undesirable change in her behavior or execution? The coach will want to know. But don't overreact. Sometimes when a person is unlearning what she knows and in the early-practice phase with a new approach, a temporary performance dip can occur. As I noted in Scenario Nine, learning takes time, and progress in coaching is not necessarily constant and linear.

If the action plan or program review dates arrive without agreed-to objectives and changes having been accomplished, then it's time to reevaluate the fundamentals:

- Is executive coaching the right intervention?
- Is the individual truly ready for coaching?
- Is the coach the right person for the job?

Refer to the beginning chapters of this book for advice and decision tools on all these points.

Final Analysis

If you're a coaching sponsor, real-world concerns can present many decisions and dilemmas. As I've pointed out, even a sponsor's best intentions need to be examined carefully to ensure that unintended consequences do not result. The fact that you're reading this book is evidence that your mind and heart are in the right places. This coaching sponsor do's and don'ts list summarizes many key points covered in this chapter:

DO be positive, enthusiastic, and supportive.	DON'T be impatient or intrusive.
DO brief a coach on business and operational context, emergent issues, and business success metrics.	DON'T engage in deception or bending the truth, even with the best intentions.
DO honor all commitments made to a coachee and a coach.	DON'T use coaching or engaging a coach as a threat or punishment.
DO be discreet and sensitive in talking about the person's coaching with any third parties.	DON'T use a coach as a stand-in for your own supervisory and mentoring responsibilities.
DO report any significant incidents, business or workplace developments, or events to the coach.	DON'T assume a coach already knows about emergent issues or breaking business developments.
DO consult the coach, when possible, before communicating any negative feedback or news to the coachee.	

BIBLIOGRAPHY

Anderson, M. C. "Executive Briefing: Case Study on the Return on Investment of Executive Coaching." Unpublished paper. Metrix Global LLC, 2001.

Atwater, L. E., and Yammarino, F. J. "Does Self-Other Agreement on Leadership Perceptions Moderate the Validity of Leadership and Performance Predictions?" *Personnel Psychology,* 1992, *45,* 141–164.

Bandura, A. *Social Foundations of Thought and Action: A Social Cognitive Theory.* Upper Saddle River, N.J.: Prentice Hall, 1986.

Bandura, A. "Self-Efficacy Mechanism in Physiological Activation and Health-Promoting Behavior." In J. Madden IV (ed.), *Neurobiology of Learning, Emotion, and Affect.* New York: Raven, 1991.

Banning, K. L. "Now, Coach?" *Across the Board,* 1997, *34,* 28–32.

Bar-On, R. "Emotional Intelligence and Self-Actualization." In J. Ciarrochi, J. Forgas, and J. Mayer (eds.), *Emotional Intelligence in Everyday Life: A Scientific Inquiry.* New York: Psychology Press, 2001.

Battley, S. *Coaching Power: Ten Myths and New Realities.* Stony Brook, N.Y.: Wisemind Publications, 2004a.

Battley, S. *Is Executive Coaching Right for You?* Stony Brook, N.Y.: Wisemind Publications, 2004b.

Bennett, S. "Put It in Writing, Please." *New York Times,* May 9, 2004, p. B9.

Berglas, S. "The Very Real Dangers of Executive Coaching." *Harvard Business Review,* 2002, *6,* 87–92.

Boyatzis, R. E., Goleman, D., and Rhee, K. "Clustering Competence in Emotional Intelligence: Insights from the Emotional Competence Inventory (ECI)." In R. Bar-On and J.D.A. Parker (eds.), *Handbook of Emotional Intelligence: The Theory and Practice of Development, Evaluation, Education, and Application—at Home, at School, and in the Workplace.* San Francisco: Jossey-Bass, 2000.

Brotman, L. E., Liberi, W. P., and Wasylyshyn, K. M. "Executive Coaching: The Need for Standards of Competence." *Consulting Psychology Journal: Practice and Research,* 1998, *50,* 40–46.

Brutus, S., London, M., and Martineau, J. "The Impact of 360-Degree Feedback on Planning for Career Development." *Journal of Management Development,* 1999, *18,* 676–693.

Campbell, D., and Ilgen, D. "Additive Effects of Task Difficulty and Goal Setting on Subsequent Performance." *Journal of Applied Psychology,* 1976, *61,* 319–324.

Carter, C., Ulrich, D., and Goldsmith, M. (eds.). *Best Practices in Leadership Development and Organization Change: How the Best Companies Ensure Meaningful Change and Sustainable Leadership.* San Francisco: Pfeiffer, 2004.

Church, A. H. "Managerial Self-Awareness in High-Performing Individuals in Organizations." *Journal of Applied Psychology,* 1997, *82,* 281–292.

Clarey, C. "In an Epic Wimbledon Final, Williams Prevails." *New York Times,* July 3, 2005, p. 1.

Douglas, C. A., and Morley, W. H. *Executive Coaching: An Annotated Bibliography.* Greensboro, N.C.: Center for Creative Leadership, 2000.

"Drake Beam Morin: Leading Companies Preparing for Boomer Exit by Grooming Talent for Senior Leadership Roles." *PRNewswire,* Nov. 17, 2003.

Dutton, G. "Executive Coaches Call the Plays." *Management Review,* 1997, *86,* 39–43.

Ellis, K. "What's the ROI of ROI?" *Training,* 2005, *42*(1), 17–21.

Ericsson, K. A. *The Road to Excellence: The Acquisition of Expert Performance in the Arts and Sciences, Sports, and Games.* Mahwah, N.J.: Erlbaum, 1996.

"Executive Coaching Process and Administration at Fortune 100 Companies: Fact Brief." *Corporate Leadership Council,* Jan. 2004.

Fisher, A. "Annie Weighs In on Executive Coaching and Untruths on Résumés." *Fortune,* May 13, 2002, p. 189.

Gale, J., Liljenstrand, A., Pardieu, J., and Nebeker, D. "Coaching Survey: An In-Depth Analysis of Coaching Practices: From Background Information to Outcome Evaluation." Unpublished manuscript, California School of Organizational Studies, Alliant International University, 2002.

Goleman, D. *Emotional Intelligence: Why It Can Matter More Than IQ.* New York: Bantam, 1995.

Goleman, D. *Working with Emotional Intelligence.* New York: Bantam, 1998.

Grant, A. M. "Workplace, Executive and Life Coaching: An Annotated Bibliography from the Behavioural Science Literature." Unpublished paper, Coaching Psychology Unit, University of Sydney, Australia, 2003.

Grant, A. M., and Zackon, R. "Executive, Workplace and Life Coaching: Findings from a Large-Scale Survey of International Coach Federation Members." *International Journal of Evidence-Based Coaching and Mentoring*, 2004, 2(2), 1–15.

Hall, D. T., Otazo, K. L., and Hollenbeck, G. P. "Behind Closed Doors: What Really Happens in Executive Coaching." *Organizational Dynamics*, 1999, 27, 39–52.

Kilburg, R. R. "Toward a Conceptual Understanding and Definition of Executive Coaching." *Consulting Psychology Journal: Practice and Research*, 1996, 48, 134–144.

Kilburg, R. R. *Executive Coaching: Developing Managerial Wisdom in a World of Chaos*. Washington, D.C.: American Psychological Association, 2000.

Kirkpatrick, D. L. *Evaluating Training Programs: The Four Levels*. San Francisco: Berrett-Koehler, 1994.

Latham, G. P., and Locke, E. A. "Self-Regulation Through Goal Setting." *Organizational Behavior and Human Decision Processes*, 1991, 50, 212–247.

Locke, E. A., and Latham, G. P. *A Theory of Goal Setting and Task Performance*. Upper Saddle River, N.J.: Prentice Hall, 1990.

Ludeman, K., and Erlandson, E. "Coaching the Alpha Male." *Harvard Business Review*, 2004, 5, 58–67.

Luthans, F., and Peterson, S. J. (2003). "360-Degree Feedback with Systematic Coaching: Empirical Analysis Suggests a Winning Combination." *Human Resource Management*, 2003, 42, 243–256.

Mayer, J. D., and Salovey, P. "The Intelligence of Emotional Intelligence." *Intelligence*, 1993, 17, 433–442.

McCormack, M. H. *What They Don't Teach You at Harvard Business School: Confessions of a Street-Smart Executive*. New York: Bantam, 1986.

McGovern, J., and others. "Maximizing the Impact of Executive Coaching: Behavioral Change, Organizational Outcomes and Return on Investment." *Manchester Review*, 2001, 6, 4–25.

Morgan, H., Harkins, P., and Goldsmith, M. (eds.). *Profiles in Coaching: The 2004 Handbook of Best Practices in Leadership Coaching*. Burlington, Mass.: Linkage Press, 2004.

Olivero, G., Bane, K. D., and Kopelman, R. E. "Executive Coaching as a Transfer of Training Tool: Effects on Productivity in a Public Agency." *Public Personnel Management*, 1997, 26, 461–469.

Richards, L. "Interview with J. K. Rowling." *January Magazine*, posted Oct. 2000 [http://www.januarymagazine.com/profiles/jkrowling.html].

Ruderman, M., Hannum, K., and Leslie, J. "Making the Connection: Leadership Skills and Emotional Intelligence." *Leadership in Action*, 2001, 21, 1–7.

Sala, F., and Dwight, S. "Predicting Executive Performance with Multi-rater Surveys: Whom You Ask Makes a Difference." *Consulting Psychology Journal: Practice and Research,* 2002, *54,* 166–172.

Salovey, P., and Mayer, J. D. "Emotional Intelligence." *Imagination, Cognition, and Personality,* 1990, *9,* 185–211.

Schlender, B. "The Bill and Warren Show." *Fortune,* July 20, 1998, pp. 48–62.

Sherman, S., and Freas, A. "The Wild West of Executive Coaching." *Harvard Business Review,* 2004, *11,* 82–89.

Smither, J., London, M., and Reilly, R. "Does Performance Improve Following Multisource Feedback? A Theoretical Model, Meta-Analysis, and Review of Empirical Findings." *Personnel Psychology,* 2005, *58,* 33–66.

Smither, J., and others. "Can Working with an Executive Coach Improve Multisource Feedback Ratings over Time? A Quasi-Experimental Field Study." *Personnel Psychology,* 2003, *56,* 23–44.

Thach, E. "The Impact of Executive Coaching and 360 Feedback on Leadership Effectiveness." *Leadership and Organization Development Journal,* 2002, *23,* 205–214.

Van de Walle, D., Brown, S., Cron, W., and Slocum, J. "The Influence of Goal Orientation and Self-Regulation Tactics on Sales Performance: A Longitudinal Field Test." *Journal of Applied Psychology,* 1999, *84,* 249–259.

Wasylyshyn, K. M. "Executive Coaching: An Outcome Study." *Consulting Psychology Journal: Practice and Research,* 2003, *55,* 94–106.

Witherspoon, R., and White, R. P. "Executive Coaching: A Continuum of Roles." *Consulting Psychology Journal: Practice and Research,* 1996, *48,* 124–133.

Witherspoon, R., and White, R. P. *Four Essential Ways That Coaching Can Help Executives.* Greensboro, N.C.: Center for Creative Leadership, 1997.

Wooden, J., with Jamison, S. *Wooden: A Lifetime of Observations and Reflections on and off the Court.* New York: Contemporary Books, 1997.

INDEX

239

Benefits: of achieving coaching goals, 26–28, 39; of assessment, 105–106, 116, 124; of coach involvement in action, 148; of coaching action plan, 127–128. *See also* Return on investment (ROI)

Bennett, S., 140

Billable activities, 70–71

Bohr, N., xii

Branson, R., 119

Brief targeted coaching: example of, 87–91; no written plan required for, 128; reviewing results of, 184–185

Brown, R. J., 166–167

Brown, S., 139

Buffett, W., xii, 37

Burnout, coaching to avoid, 29–30, 203–205

Business: documents from, as source of data for assessment, 110; evaluating impact of coaching on, 172, 173, 175; facilitating results related to, 5–6; metrics from, for reviewing Powerhouse Plan–based programs, 182

C

Calloway, W., 159

Campbell, D., 139

Campbell Interest and Skill Inventory, 115

Cancelling coaching sessions, 74, 151

Candidate Coach Evaluation Form, 62

Carter, C., 18

Casey, A., 179

Change: difficulty in handling, 119; necessity of breaking habits for, 164, 230–231; openness to, 28–30, 39

Churchill, W., 82, 96, 128, 168

Cicero, 64, 112, 129

Clients: disappointing results due to role of, 187; information needed

by, for writing agreement, 76; not given voice in coach selection, 196–197; as parties to agreements, 65

Coach candidates: evaluating, 57–61, 62; identifying, 55–57; interviews with, 57–61

Coachability, 14–16, 18, 143

Coaches: background and experience of, 13–14, 18; competencies of, 47–51; internal, 53–54, 67, 195, 205; mentors vs., 11–13, 18; as parties to agreements, 65; role of, 159–161, 187, 205–206

Coaching: defined, 1; engaging in both psychotherapy and, 208–209; focus of, 5–6, 10–11, 18; increasing demand for, xii–xiii; misinformation about, 1–2; psychotherapy or counseling vs., 5–6, 207–208, 227–230; purpose of, ix. *See also* Employer-funded coaching; Private-pay coaching; Retainer-based coaching; Telecoaching

Coaching action plan: basics of, 126–127; benefits of, 127–128; connection between assessment and, 132, 134; goal setting for, 138–142; importance of written, 144–145; Powerhouse Plan vs., 130–131; situations not requiring, 128. *See also* Powerhouse Plan

Coaching agreements. *See* Agreements

Coaching competency, 48–49

"Coaching envy," 3

Coaching goals: clarifying, as prerequisite for coaching, 24–26, 39; determining accomplishment of, 169–170; developed using 360-degree survey feedback, 122; identifying, as coaching model step, 85; identifying benefits of achieving, 26–28, 39; importance of written, 140; location of coaching

ABOUT THE AUTHOR

Susan Battley, Psy.D., Ph.D., is a leadership psychologist, executive coach, and author who has helped hundreds of top decision makers and management teams maximize their performance for bottom-line results. For twenty-four years, she has been advising an international clientele of business CEOs, university presidents, corporate and association directors, entrepreneurs, public officials, and world-class technical professionals and scientists. She has lectured extensively in the United States and abroad on topics pertaining to leadership and strategic organizational change.

Her clients have included JP Morgan Chase, Olympus, Marsh & McLennan Companies, Brookhaven National Laboratory, Jones Apparel Group, Chase Manhattan, Bookspan, and Cendant. She has held appointments as clinical associate professor in the School of Health Technology and Management, Stony Brook University, and as consulting psychologist at the University Counseling Center. She also has experience as a top-level organization ombudsman.

The Clinton White House Office of Science and Technology Policy recognized *Fast Focus on Success,* her radio program on leadership excellence, for its pioneering use of Internet broadcasting. St. George's University honored her as the inaugural visiting professor of its Arts and Sciences College.

Battley is a sought-after media resource on leadership behavior and trends, including CNN, CNBC, National Public Radio, and Bloomberg Television. Her expertise has been cited worldwide in the *New York Times, Wall Street Journal, Chief Executive, Entrepreneur,* United Press International, *Harvard Management Update, Science, CIO\Australia,* and the *Hindustani Times.* Known for her insightful, pragmatic presentations, she speaks regularly to business and professional groups and at in-house corporate events on maximizing leader and organization effectiveness.

The author of two previous books, her articles have appeared in scholarly and business periodicals in the United States and abroad. She holds four advanced degrees, including a doctorate in clinical psychology from Long Island University and a Ph.D. with distinction in economic history from Stony Brook University. She has served on several nonprofit boards and as a nominator to *CFO Magazine*'s Global 100 Leaders.

Battley is the chief executive officer and founder of Battley Performance Consulting.